URBAN HOMELANDS

URBAN

HOMELANDS

Writing the Native City from Oklahoma

Lindsey Claire Smith

University of Nebraska Press / Lincoln

The University of Nebraska Press is part of a land-grant institution with campuses and programs on the past, present, and future homelands of the Pawnee, Ponca, Otoe-Missouria, Omaha, Dakota, Lakota, Kaw, Cheyenne, and Arapaho Peoples, as well as those of the relocated Ho-Chunk, Sac and Fox, and Iowa Peoples.

Library of Congress Cataloging-in-Publication Data
Names: Smith, Lindsey Claire, author.
Title: Urban homelands : writing the native city from Oklahoma / Lindsey Claire Smith.
Description: Lincoln : University of Nebraska Press, [2023] | Includes bibliographical references and index.
Identifiers: LCCN 2022056016
ISBN 9781496215536 (hardback)
ISBN 9781496237279 (epub)
ISBN 9781496237286 (pdf)
Subjects: LCSH: American literature—Indian authors—History and criticism. | American literature—Oklahoma—History and criticism. | City and town life in literature. | Indians in literature. | Oklahoma—In literature. | Indigenous films—United States—History. | Indians in motion pictures. | City and town life in motion pictures. | Oklahoma—In motion pictures. | Indians of North America—Oklahoma—Intellectual life. | BISAC: SOCIAL SCIENCE / Ethnic Studies / American / Native American Studies | SOCIAL SCIENCE / Sociology / Urban | LCGFT: Literary criticism.
Classification: LCC PS153.I52 S63 2023 |
DDC 810.9/8970766—dc23/eng/20230607
LC record available at https://lccn.loc.gov/2022056016

Set in Lyon Text by A. Shahan.

CONTENTS

PHOTOGRAPHS

ACKNOWLEDGMENTS

While writing this book, I experienced some major life events—some joyful (the birth of my daughter!) and some sorrowful (a global pandemic)—which, to say the least, impacted my timeline for completion. Through it all, I have been reminded time and again of how essential and fragile a network of support is to successful research. I have many people to thank for helping me see this project through to its finish line. Most immediately, I want to express my sincere gratitude to the editorial team of University of Nebraska Press, including Matt Bokovoy and Heather Stauffer, for their encouragement (and patience) during the long slog of drafting and revision, as well as Cristina Stanciu and Laura Furlan, who provided helpful comments and guidance on the manuscript even while facing their own personal sorrows and professional challenges due to the COVID-19 pandemic.

Oklahoma State University has been my institutional home for the last sixteen years. I am that rare unicorn who received a job offer back home and never left; OSU has been the perfect place for me to pursue my professional passions. I am grateful for the support of the College of Arts and Sciences and Oklahoma Humanities for supporting this book in the form of university sabbatical, summer, and scholar research grants. The American Studies program at OSU provided additional travel support for a trip to Indian Market, which caused me to miss a day of faculty meetings (no regrets). During summer research, the staff at the Historic New Orleans Collection helped me navigate monuments and walking tours (directing me to ones I could manage in the heat while six months pregnant), which were critical to helping me better understand the way tourism and space connect in the city. Mentors and friends at OSU have cheered me on even when "How's your book coming?" may not have been the question I wanted to hear. Encouragement has come from Ritch Frohock, Carol Moder, Brewster Fitz, William Decker, Katherine Hallemeier, Edward Jones, An Cheng, Sarah Beth Childers, and Janine Joseph. Jeff Menne and the English Department, along with the College of Arts and Sciences, helped me secure an additional award to support the final stages of the production process.

I am a proud product of Tulsa Public Schools, inspired by the many public educators who share my belief that all students here (and everywhere) have a right to a high-quality education. Colleagues and friends in Native American and Indigenous studies at Oklahoma's public institutions, including Amanda Cobb-Greetham, Joshua Nelson, Kimberly Wieser, Rilla Askew, Alyssa Hunziker, Brian Hosmer, and Doug Miller, who are committed to doing their work *in this place*, have my heart. Friends (writers, scholars, and teachers in one form or another) in Native American Literature book club at Whitty Books in Tulsa have helped me keep to a practice of reading for fun, in community. I am indebted to the teachers and staff of Mayo Demonstration School in Tulsa, who have taught my daughter, niece, and nephew during some of the most challenging times for teachers and students of young children. I might have cried during a few Zooms.

My family is deeply rooted in Oklahoma, and many conversations about who we are and why we are here have shaped this book. My mother, Charlene Smith, and mother-in-law, Cathy Newsome, both retired teachers, provided countless hours of childcare during school shutdowns, meetings, and other work obligations. My spouse, Chris Newsome, and our daughter, Lillian, constantly reminded me of the joy and laughter that makes a life, even in hard times. My late father, Dwight Smith, taught high school English for decades in Tulsa and first introduced me to the works of N. Scott Momaday, Joy Harjo, and many others. This book is for him.

I wish to thank the following publications for their support of my work and for allowing me to reproduce portions of Joy Harjo's writing:

Parts of the introduction and chapter 3 appeared as "Talasi through the Lens," in *Settler City Limits: Indigenous Resurgence and Colonial Violence in the Urban Prairie West*, ed. Heather Dorries, Robert Henry, David Hugill, Tyler McCreary, and Julie Tomiak, 251–70 (Winnipeg: University of Manitoba Press, 2019).

"The Flood," from *The Woman Who Fell from the Sky* by Joy Harjo. Copyright © 1994 by Joy Harjo. Used by permission of W. W. Norton & Company, Inc.

"Sleepwalkers," from *A Map to the Next World: Poems and Tales* by Joy Harjo. Copyright © 2000 by Joy Harjo. Used by permission of W. W. Norton & Company, Inc.

"New Orleans," from *She Had Some Horses* by Joy Harjo. Copyright © 1983 by Joy Harjo. Used by permission of W. W. Norton & Company, Inc.

"We Were There When Jazz Was Invented," from *Conflict Resolution for Holy Beings: Poems* by Joy Harjo. Copyright © 2015 by Joy Harjo. Used by permission of W. W. Norton & Company, Inc.

"The Last Song," from *Issue One of Chapbook* by Joy Harjo. Copyright © 1975 by Joy Harjo. Used by permission of Puerto del Sol.

"An American Sunrise," "Washing My Mother's Body," from *An American Sunrise: Poems* by Joy Harjo. Copyright © 2019 by Joy Harjo. Used by permission of W. W. Norton & Company, Inc.

"Santa Fe," from *In Mad Love and War* by Joy Harjo. Copyright © 1990 by Joy Harjo. Used by permission of Wesleyan University Press.

URBAN HOMELANDS

INTRODUCTION

Writing the Native City from Oklahoma

Oklahoma, home of thirty-nine unique Indigenous nations, is a logical place from which to consider the ways that Native Americans experience and express cosmopolitan life. The words *Oklahoma* and *cosmopolitan* do not show up often in the same sentence, however. Why is that? Certainly, Oklahoma's red state politics play a role in keeping this place from being a destination for those, tourists or otherwise, who are seeking to understand or participate in new cultural experiences. And that is a shame, since Oklahoma has produced some of the most influential Native writers and artists, from Will Rogers to N. Scott Momaday, Allan Houser to Anita Fields. These creative giants have had a tremendous impact not only on the local cultural scene but also on the arts across the country and world, exhibiting, performing, and speaking about Indigenous life across eras and geographies while offering the perspective of coming from the former Indian Territory. It is appropriate that the first Native American U.S. poet laureate, Joy Harjo, should come from this place. Contemporary writers from Oklahoma are on the cutting edge of American literature and film, advancing stories of Native life in urban, cosmopolitan environments to new readers and audiences across the world. And yet so far studies of urban Indigenous literature have either insufficiently treated or completely overlooked Oklahoma writers.

Perhaps the omission of Oklahoma from these studies of contemporary urban life lies in this state's uneasy fit with generally accepted histories of adjacent regions. The South notoriously "disappeared" Natives in Andrew Jackson's campaign of Indian Removal; in the West and on the Plains, Native American vanquishment came in the form of being forced to live in reservations. At least until the 2020 *McGirt v. Oklahoma* decision, Oklahoma was not a place where one would find multiple reservations; the typical narrative of Indigenous urbanization as a journey from a rural rez to the big city has not been an effective template, or at least a complete one, for telling the stories of Natives from here. As Indian Territory, this place was actually devised as a "no-place," disconnected (at least as planned) from the sweep of history that would transform North America into the United States. A favorite pastime of Okies is debating what Oklahoma "is." While we ponder whether we are the South, Midwest, or Southwest, the broader United States often reverts to its no-place default. As writer Rilla Askew notes, reflecting on Rand McNally's omission of Oklahoma from its national road atlas in 1994, "Oklahoma's elusiveness in the public mind goes beyond a lack of knowledge: there has long been an almost mystical anonymity to the place."[1] But though the architects of Indian Territory hardly conceived of it as "urban," the convergence of rich and diverse cultures that is such a celebrated feature of modern cities is a bedrock of Oklahoma's history.

Oklahoma is bound to both the South and Southwest and their legacies of conquest and Indigenous survivance. At the same time, mobility, ingenuity, cultural exchange, and creative expression—all part of the experience of urbanization—have been fundamental to people of the tribes that call this place home. Histories of diaspora and urbanization, realities we discuss in contemporary Native studies, have also shaped Native Oklahomans, who have contributed to the economic, political, and cultural development of cities across the country but especially in these regions. While many Oklahomans participated in the Urban Relocation Program of the 1950s and 1960s, an exclusive focus on that program to explain contemporary Native urbanization overlooks the impact of Natives on cities that were not designated relocation sites. Three cities—New Orleans, Tulsa, and Santa Fe—are especially key to uncovering the history of urbanization experienced by Native Americans from Oklahoma. These three cities demonstrate connections that bind Oklahoma to the South and Southwest not only because of their proximity but also because of their importance in histories of geopolitical upheaval and mobility that shaped the establishment of the United States. New Orleans and Santa Fe, colonial headquarters of France and Spain, have been tied to the histories and fortunes of several tribes now based in Oklahoma, and Tulsa has long been considered a cultural capital of sorts for the former Indian Territory. Native American writing from Oklahoma reframes New Orleans, Tulsa, and Santa Fe as spaces that are themselves interconnected as well as deeply indebted to Indigenous peoples, in the past and present, who established and continue to shape these cities. This book, while examining the overlooked histories of Oklahoma Indigenous urbanization relative to these regions, engages literature and film as not just mirrors of experience but as producers of it. Flying in the face of civic landmarks and settler histories that hide and obscure Native origins, on the one hand, and appropriate Native culture for tourist purposes, on the other, this creative reclaiming of Indigenous cities points toward the productive possibilities of recognizing both recovery of untold histories and creative relationships with urban space itself.

It is easy to draw a straight line between the words *urban*, *cosmopolitan*, and *modern* without making clear how these concepts apply to Indian Country or whether we can agree on what these words mean in the first place. I enthusiastically explore the relevance of these words to studies of Indian Country, especially Oklahoma, because of their usefulness in putting to rest settler notions of Native America as inherently backward, provincial, nativist, or homogeneous. I am a daughter of Oklahoma myself, so advancing a new understanding of this place is admittedly close to home. Still, the association of cities with the fashion of the new must be unpacked for its own cultural and historical baggage. In many ways studies of cities touch on well-documented tension between Indigenous and postcolonial studies that results from the two fields' differing approaches to nationhood, history, language, land, and kinship. In their introduction to a special issue of *Interventions* in 2011, Jodi Byrd and Michael Rothberg provide an effective outline of these points of divergence but also create a theoretical meeting place for scholars to find common ground between the "subaltern" and "Indigenous," notably in studies of diaspora, space, and time.

While this project engages most strongly with the field of Indigenous studies, I follow Byrd and Rothberg's lead in identifying the relevance for our field of some concepts that are more often addressed in postcolonial theory. "Urban" America immediately brings to mind postindustrial cities that ushered in the pinnacle of American empire on the world stage, coterminous with the Termination policy of the 1940s to 1960s. While not discounting the importance of this time period for urban Native American literature, I understand *urban* more broadly and spatially. The twentieth century may for good reason be understood as the era when Native Americans urbanized, moving from reservations to cities; however, in their practices of international trade and travel, of structuring dense metropolitan dwellings, and of retaining affiliation with multiple places amid (often harrowing) migration across regions, Native Americans, including those who have come to live in Oklahoma, have long been urban. Urbanity does not rely on our typical timeline of "progress."

In turn, while on one level *cosmopolitan* suggests simply a diversity of peoples and languages found in cities, it also has been a critical concern for postcolonial theorists such as Kwame Appiah and Arjun Appadurai, who consider the relationship between cosmopolitanism and subjectivity in a global context. In her book *Indigenous Cities* (2017), Laura Furlan discusses similarities between networks of globalization that Appadurai describes and the connections that urban Native Americans retain to reservations via stories. She also finds Appiah's "rooted cosmopolitanism" useful for describing the ways people of many tribes in cities are bound both to their homes and cosmopolitan spaces and to others in a meaningful web of relatedness. My own consideration of cosmopolitanism as articulated by these theorists likewise values networks of connection across boundaries of nation, space, and time but applies them differently. In histories and stories of Native Americans from Oklahoma, I do not find the same discreteness of homelands (usually identified as reservations) and cosmopolitan spaces that scholars of Indigenous studies identify in other contexts. I consider ways that Indigenous cosmopolitanism expands beyond flows between reservations and postindustrial cities.

I am intrigued by Appiah's choice of *cosmopolitanism* as a rubric for which to coexist in an increasingly global world. Indigenous peoples have not exactly existed in the idyllic and insulated small hunter-gatherer societies that Appiah suggests are universal to human existence in the premodern world. He prefers *cosmopolitanism* over *globalization* or *multiculturalism* because of its original definition dating to the fourth century BC: "citizen of the cosmos."[2] A cosmopolitan, then, belonged not to a city, not to the earth, but to the universe. This value of relatedness across difference, beyond built environments and "modern" time frames, is useful for understanding encounters across national or cultural difference in histories of Oklahoma as well as the spiritual dimension of those encounters. Appiah notes that cosmopolitanism need not be homogenizing, as people may retain rootedness to multiple places across distances, but he specifies that cosmopolitanism values the choice of free people to do so, with the deplorable conditions of diaspora mostly a thing of the past.[3] This role of choice is perhaps one reason why Indigenous studies scholars bristle at the ways global flows are characterized in postcolonial theory; forced removal and disenfranchisement are inseparable from the experiences of Native Americans still. Nonetheless, in the examples of Muscogee women developing a hospitality industry along trading routes to New Orleans or "settler" tribes becoming involved in the thriving Comanchería economy bound to Santa Fe, one can identify the kind of relatedness across difference that Appiah describes as cosmopolitan, beyond the term's usual associations with the large global cities of today.

Both Appiah and Appadurai stress the importance of art, including media, to cosmopolitanism, and in the case of Appadurai, the possibilities of self-expression that new media affords signals what we may understand as modern. As cosmopolitanism may be unsettled from the limitations of time, so, too, modern subjectivity resists a singular break between tradition and modernity. Appadurai names migration and media—especially electronic media—as definitively modern, impelling the imagination into a global world. More vernacular and experiential than the development of modern economies of nation-states and facilitating connections across boundaries, the forms of experience in this modernity (film and television, for example, or tourism) each have their own genealogies that may not match linear histories.[4] Thus, though uncovering untold histories remains foundational to Indigenous studies (and to this project), a consideration of urbanity beyond (even if bound to) the history of the United States' development as a modern nation-state provides a fuller picture of what modernity might mean for those Native Americans who have long been urbanized. Literature and film, then, and especially new media, are not simply reflections of history; they allow imagination that is powerful, public, and liberatory, even if contested, and they reach ever-growing audiences that call us to reconsider who cosmopolitans are and where they are located.

The work of these theorists aids me in applying and defining key concepts, but a comprehensive body of scholarship on urban American Indians has paved the way for the crucial concerns of Indigenous relationships to place and diverse communities that inform this book. Donald Fixico's foundational *The Urban Indian Experience in America* describes the Urban Relocation Program and discusses its results institutionally and culturally. Fixico's framework for urbanization emphasizes differing roles in response to city life: traditionalist, suburbanite, and middle-class members. He explains that typically while Indians seek to be urbanites, their mindset is Indian, a situation that has led many to crisis.[5] While not discounting the significance of this state of crisis for galvanizing urban Indigenous activism, Susan Lobo argues, in *American Indians and the Urban Experience*, that as new generations of Native Americans inhabit cities, their experiences, including their relationships to urban Indian Country, are varied. In San Francisco she identifies a network of relatedness in cities that is more fluid, situational, negotiable, and diverse than the formalized, federally prescribed boundaries of rural tribes.[6] This network is akin to the phenomenon described by Renya Ramirez in her book *Native Hubs*. Ramirez promotes a concept that Laverne Roberts (Paiute) introduced to her, in which cities are the hub of a wheel, with social networks acting as spokes connecting city Natives to tribal land bases at a distance.[7] Though the contexts for urban Indigenous experiences in Canada are different from those in the United States, Evelyn Peters and Vince Robillard, in their study of First Nations' homeless mobility, present data that shows connections between urban and rural locations in homeless people's movement, rebuffing notions of a sharp rural-urban split.[8] In my focus on Oklahoma writers, I further question demarcations of cities as not-Indigenous and tribal land bases as distant, uncovering ways that past and present Native Americans literally and creatively envision cities as their lands, aside from settler urbanization programs.

In drawing attention to Indigenous histories of New Orleans, Tulsa, and Santa Fe, I am indebted to other scholars who do the work of uncovering Indigenous histories of cities and their connections to their geographical regions, correcting the impression that urban areas are necessarily sites of separation from tribal homelands. Nicholas Blomley's *Unsettling the City* recounts Vancouver as a "settler-city," founded on the imaginary premise of its incorporation on empty land, despite Squamish land rights. He identifies two maneuvers as fundamental to the settler-city: removal of Indigenous people from urban space, which requires imagining them as in the past or in nature; and emplacement of settler society, which makes the city into a white place.[9] Kathi Wilson and Evelyn Peters also emphasize that perceptions of cities as non-Indigenous lands are a spatial ordering of the state.[10] Julie Tomiak presents a similar critique of colonial imaginaries in her study of Ottawa, arguing for "the centrality of asserting collective Indigenous agency and visibility, thereby refuting settler narratives that claim Indigenous peoples, as rights and title holders, do not belong and do not exist in cities."[11] Coll Thrush's *Native Seattle* recovers Indigenous origins of Seattle and investigates ways that city infrastructures, especially "historical" monuments, obscure those origins. Echoing Renalto Rosaldo's exposure of "imperialist nostalgia," or "mourning for what one has destroyed," Thrush explains that cities "indelibly mark their Indian inhabitants in urban ghost stories."[12] These ghost stories appear in monuments to Indigenous people in the very locations in which they have been displaced. Likewise reframing typical notions of urbanization, Nicolas Rosenthal's *Reimagining Indian Country* seeks "to argue from Los Angeles outward."[13] As his title indicates, Rosenthal documents ways that Native Americans have included cities in their definitions of Indian country, valuing mobility and making an important contribution to the growth of the American middle class. Finally, Evelyn Peters and Chris Andersen, in *Indigenous in the City* (2013), remind readers of the history of Indigenous urban sites and settlements, noting that the "creation of Indigenous 'homelands' outside of cities is in itself a colonial invention."[14] These roughly twenty years of scholarship have provided essential language for articulating a diversity of Indigenous experiences in cities, for the most part privileging social histories of mobility within the constraints of settler colonial nation building.

Building on these social histories, I am interested in ways that Indigenous peoples not only make a living but also make a life in America. Along with histories of urban relocation, creative encounters with urban spaces themselves are worthy of further consideration as scholars study contemporary life. For this reason, I bring into dialogue scholars in Indigenous studies with urban theorists such as Henri Lefebvre and his successor Edward Soja for language to conceptualize these encounters. Lefebvre and Soja uncover ways that capitalist commodification of urban space enacts power. Lefebvre, who is largely responsible for socio-theoretical assessments of the urban, draws attention to capitalism's abstraction of urban space simultaneous with fetishism of nature. Lefebvre noticed that France, in capitalist modernity, turns to reconstruction of space for social organization. In the transition from agriculture to industry, agriculture is subordinate to industrial production: "subordinate to its demands, subject to its constraints." Lefebvre explains that the urban is not limited to built environments of cities; instead, through this agricultural subordination, the influence of cities expands to regional, national, and global scales. He states: "This expression, 'urban fabric,' does not narrowly define the built world of cities but all manifestations of the dominance of the city over the country. . . . Of varying density, thickness, and activity, the only regions untouched by it are those that are stagnant or dying, those that are given over to 'nature.'" Lefebvre thereby suggests that the power of the state, centered in cities, exerts its influence broadly, drawing agricultural towns and large metropolises alike into its consumerist influence.[15] Recognizing the ubiquitous influence of the urban for all manner of communities thus supports a necessary recognition of its impact on Indigenous peoples and of Indigenous people's negotiation of this influence. This is an important step in debunking continual association of Native peoples with a preindustrial past.

Lefebvre's remarks on the role of nature in the urban fabric parallels Thrush's discussion of monuments that are erected in areas of Indigenous displacement in North America, though Lefebvre never directly discusses how colonialism figures into the urban fabric. Lefebvre notes that nature is subject to new threats in industrialism, which leads to its fetishism. The transition to capitalist urbanism expands these threats, which ironically leads signs of nature, in the form of open spaces, parks, and gardens, to multiply. For Lefebvre it is the right to the city—over the right to nature (or ideologies of nature)—that is essential, as urban society is a place of encounter among diverse social groups with distinct rights. Anticipating Thrush's later assessment of Seattle's "ghost stories," monuments in

Lefebvre's formulation are objects transformed into ideologies, seats of institutions that colonize space.[16] Lefebvre's discussion of capitalism's fetishizing of the nature that it destroys may shed light on fetishizing of Indigenous peoples in monuments that appear in U.S. cities. As Joni Adamson explains, the western idealization of Indigenous links to "pristine" nature is persistent though inaccurate and veils the impact of environmental racism on communities of color. Considering Lefebvre's comments about ideologies of nature along with urban histories paves the way for understanding the impulse to create parks and monuments that idealize both nature and Indigenous peoples. Lefebvre never examines the literal impact of colonialism, despite his use of the word *colonize* to describe the relationship between nature and the urban fabric.[17] Obviously, there is still much work to do to conceptualize Indigenous experiences in the settler colonial cities of the United States.

Soja makes strides in filling Lefebvre's gaps in his ideas about urban space relative to race and gender. In *Postmodern Geographies* he describes cities as repositories of state power and explains that geography (rendering spatial logic) supersedes history in shaping our understanding of the world. He extends Lefebvre's methodology, naming geographically uneven development as integral to global capitalism and cities as centers of social power through "enclosure, confinement, surveillance, partitioning, social discipline and spatial differentiation." In his case study of contemporary Los Angeles, Soja marks the Watts riots of 1965 as a starting point for the ramifications of inequality that is essential to capitalism. In the shadow of the "governmental and corporate citadel" of downtown Los Angeles, Soja remarks on the stark contrast between the extreme wealth clustered in condominiums, law offices, and corporate headquarters and the hardships of immigrant laborers and the largest concentration of homeless people in the United States. Soja points out the largely unrecognized importance of urban planning to the Los Angeles cityscape, which, though appearing to many as a haphazard amalgamation, is carefully designed in accordance with the labor required to sustain its consumerism. He also names imperialism as a foundational feature of the city: "Securing the Pacific rim has been the manifest destiny of Los Angeles, a theme which defines its sprawling urbanization perhaps more than any other analytical construct. . . . It is not always easy to see the imprint of this imperial history on the material landscape."[18] Like Lefebvre, however, Soja never explores in sufficient detail how this "imperialism" both creates and reproduces urban space, relying instead upon the metaphorical force of the word. Though he details the transformation of Bunker Hill into a center for civic purposes, for example, he neglects to mention the neighborhood's importance to relocatees participating in the Urban Relocation Program. Soja's more recent books *Postmetropolis* (2000), *Seeking Spatial Justice* (2010), and *My Los Angeles* (2014) document a framework for addressing spatial inequality but similarly avoid serious engagement with colonialism or its impact on Indigenous peoples.[19]

Despite this omission, Soja's urging to consider the ways that cities shape social processes, tipping the balance away from a privileging of time over space in urban studies, can help add a new dimension to studies that trace histories of Indigenous peoples in cities. In *Postmetropolis* Soja calls for attention to urban ways of life rather than simply urban development, arguing, "The social-spatial-historical processes that shape our lives do not simply operate *in* and *on* cities, but to a significant degree also emanate *from* cities."[20] He also argues for human lives as intrinsically spatial on many different scales, with the body in complex relation with surroundings, from rooms to the whole earth. In his continuation of these ideas eleven years later, in the article "Beyond Postmetropolis," Soja makes a stronger case for the generative and causal force of cities. Spatial thinking brings to the fore more attention to metropolitan and regional urbanism that structures large-scale cities of today and to ways that communities of the past could be reconsidered as urban. He suggests that notions of agriculture and urbanization as existing on a developmental continuum are false. Instead, many early communities of considerable size were in a mutual relationship with agricultural development and featured tightly organized and relational agglomerations that should be understood to be cities. Finally, as the urban structures regions, changes in, or the disappearance of, clear demarcations between urban and suburban in the present day has brought about concern over the appearance and cultural composition of downtowns and inner cities: "Polycentric regional urbanization has made inner urban cores much more unstable and unpredictable, leading to aggressive city marketing and city branding efforts, shifting public investment, policy, and planning from an emphasis on basic social needs to a hypercompetitive entrepreneurialism, desperately using public resources to attract new private investment and tourist traffic."[21] The writers of my study confront just this push for city branding and tourism, which can simultaneously fetishize and disappear Indigenous peoples even as those peoples are integral to the arts and cultural communities that shape urban life.

Through dialogue between urban and Indigenous studies, one can recognize the ideologies of power—and conquest—that mark urban spaces where Indigenous peoples reside, but also important are ways in which these residents participate in the production of the city as oeuvre, to use Lefebvre's term. Lefebvre's later writings, namely *The Production of Space* (1974), move beyond theorizing space itself to investigate the processes and practices that create it. Lefebvre emphasizes social relations in the city as "a production and reproduction of human beings by human beings, rather than a production of objects." Lefebvre's recognition of human agency—and resistance—in urban space is important for recognizing American Indians' active role in creating urban cultures despite their disenfranchisement. Further, Lefebvre points toward art as evidence of the city's value to its residents, even when bureaucracy reigns supreme. He explains that the appearance of art reflects a city's use value—not just exchange value—because of the importance of its unique history to its citizens. A city's value above and beyond exchange makes it an oeuvre and holds the promise of a "transformed and renewed right to urban life."[22] Indigenous art, including writing and filmmaking, can thus be understood to be an enactment of a right to the city, an expression of the value of the urban community to its Indigenous people. Of course, as American cities are on Indigenous lands, this right has never been relinquished! Nevertheless, in the face of the urban ghost stories that Thrush describes, Lefebvre's critical language is useful for describing Indigenous artistic and cultural resistance to the spatial dimensions of settler erasure. Native writers from Oklahoma not only uncover their histories but also assert their rights to the cultural life of cities.

To conceptualize the spatial dimensions of Native experience in cities, including creative responses to objects-turned-ideologies, I draw on the work of Dean Rader, Mishuana Goeman, and Furlan. Rader, in *Engaged Resistance* (2011), interrogates public art that captures colonial symbolic discourse about Indigenous peoples. Though not specifically centered on urban locations, Rader's study links romantic stereotypes of Indians rendered in car lots to the "high art" of government grounds in Oklahoma City, Tulsa, and Santa Fe to reveal how such images reinforce problematic purposes of tourism. He argues that the "aesthetic activism" of visual and literary artists in these locations defends Native identities from these purposes.[23] Goeman, in *Mark My Words* (2013), uses Lefebvre's theories of space as a springboard for her discussion of (re)mapping, or spatial decolonization, in which Indigenous women unsettle settler space through literature. Goeman names colonial spatialities—specifically maps, surveys, field reports, and such—as critical to the erasure of Native mobility and the general acceptance of a dichotomy of urban-reservation Native.[24] In *Indigenous Cities* (2017) Furlan seeks to re-narrativize U.S. history by unsettling ideas of Natives as rooted peoples and arguing instead for recognition of off-reservation Indigenous peoples, in the aftermath of Relocation, as cosmopolitans who create new diasporic communities to reclaim the space of cities.[25] My work follows these texts in arguing for the power and relevance of Native American literature beyond the reservation novel and extends the conversation to new understandings of where urban spaces can be found—in both space and time—and how they have structured the identities and cultures of Indigenous peoples of the former Indian Territory.

While a thorough historiography of New Orleans, Tulsa, and Santa Fe is not possible in one book, much less a book that is devoted to analysis of literature and film, a journey, albeit brief, into the role of now-Oklahomans in the Indigenous histories of these cities is necessary for understanding how the writers of my study tell the stories of their characters, their selves, and their communities. Chapter 1, "Beyond Monuments: Tracing Indigenous Histories in New Orleans, Tulsa, and Santa Fe," provides an overview of Indigenous histories of these three cities, highlighting spatial ideologies across these urban landscapes that render false narratives (or "Indian ghost stories") of Indian absence. This chapter clarifies how and why Oklahoma factors into both the developments of the settler empire in the South and Southwest and the agency of Indigenous peoples in trade, labor, travel, and cultural expression. For this discussion I am indebted to the work of many historians, especially David Bernstein, Kathleen DuVal, Pekka Hämäläinen, Christopher Haveman, and Claudio Saunt, who challenge assumptions of Native defeatism in the story of the expansion of the

United States. Bringing together histories of the Creek Confederacy with the Texas Revolution and of Cherokee "settlers" with the Comanchería within a book about urban-based jazz poetry and experimental film is certainly unconventional. A broader understanding of the forces at play in the establishment of Oklahoma and the participation of Native people in the development of modern cities in this area is necessary, however, when other frameworks of urban Indigenous studies do not neatly apply.

The chapters that follow present close readings of fiction, poetry, song, and film within these historical and spatial contexts, bringing to the fore ways in which the urban experiences of Oklahoma Natives offer a unique and more complete picture of urban Indigenous arts and scholarship. The second chapter, "'Where It All Started': Native American Literatures and the City of New Orleans," is a study of ways that LeAnne Howe, Joy Harjo, and Sterlin Harjo evoke images of New Orleans as their creative inspiration. By referencing jazz, song, and historical figures such as Sieur de Bienville and Hernando de Soto, these writers recover New Orleans as an important touchstone in the histories of Native peoples. But beyond this history, the city is very much a muse for present assertions of Indigenous sovereignty in an intercultural world. Through stories these writers claim New Orleans as an Indigenous urban place.

The third chapter, "Finding Tallasi: Native Tulsa in Literature and Film," against the backdrop of narratives and symbols of Indian disappearance that appear in several locations of former allotments so crucial to the founding and incorporation of the city, I discuss the visual artistry of Elisa Harkins; the recent work of Joy Harjo, including her memoirs and jazz musical in progress; films and television series by Sterlin Harjo; and other web series and podcasts to argue for a unique Oklahoma urban Native experience. In my reading Tulsa is unlike other cities discussed in urban Indigenous studies because of its position as an Indian town, both in its founding and in the present, and because of its relationship to the histories of both Indian Territory (the result of Indian Removal) and the state of Oklahoma. These circumstances highlight the ways that Tulsa can be understood as both Indigenous urban diaspora and urban homeland. Tulsa's Indigenous literature and film depicts both a reckoning with the alienation that Removal and statehood caused and a reconciliation with this history in the creative realm.

Finally, the fourth chapter, "'The City Different': Writing Oklahoma in Santa Fe," provides a critical approach to the thriving Native cultural scene in the city, which is so influenced by the artistic accomplishments of Indigenous Oklahomans. Institutions such as Dorothy Dunn's "Studio School" at the Santa Fe Indian School and the Institute for American Indian Arts, along with an array of galleries and museums, have fostered the careers of many Oklahoma Native artists, with complicated relationships to the marketing and commodification of Indigenous images and products. Though Santa Fe prides its history as a trading center and epicenter of Native American and southwestern arts, a disconnect arises between the city's marketing of itself and its problematic relationship to the conquest of Native America. This chapter investigates Santa Fe as a microcosm of sorts for the problems and possibilities of such "Indigenous" cities. I argue that writers including Lynn Riggs, Joy Harjo, and Sterlin Harjo achieve a delicate balance: as they thrive within international creative communities, their work also reflects—and often rebuffs—the expectations of the market. These writers attract readers and viewers to such spaces of difference but also challenge us to reconsider our consumption of the empty symbols that market "Indianness."

My emphasis on bringing Native urban histories relative to Oklahoma into conversation with critique of ideologies of Indigenous absence in these cities stands at the crossroads of nationalism and cosmopolitanism in Native American studies. While I believe a nationalist approach may limit recognition of urban and multi-tribal peoples who cross all manner of cultural borders in cities, the distinctive histories of Natives from Oklahoma (especially eastern Oklahoma) do not reflect a distancing from tribal affiliations that has been discussed as a feature of Indigenous diasporic writing. Instead, and perhaps because of the absence of reservation experiences in these tribal histories, Oklahoma's urban Native writing presents a persistent bond with homelands both in and beyond Oklahoma, as if to document and reclaim lands that may not be immediately recognizable to others as Indian Country. This creative and critical positioning, to bring Oklahoma into the conversation about Indigenous modernity and the arts, is the ultimate aim of this book.

1

BEYOND MONUMENTS

Tracing Indigenous Histories in New Orleans, Tulsa, and Santa Fe

New Orleans, Tulsa, and Santa Fe are regional urban centers, distinguished in arts and culture as well as influential in the economic and political history of the United States. New Orleans and Santa Fe were tremendously valuable assets for France and Spain, and the jockeying for power and influence between those countries impacted Indian Territory, the "no-man's-land," as it were, between the South and Southwest. In addition to being critical to European plans for this continent, both cities are significant—though not widely acknowledged—in histories of urban Native Americans. Important for tribes with ancestral homelands nearby as well as for those migrating to these areas for trade and new opportunities, New Orleans and Santa Fe are remarkable for the ways Native Americans have shaped them. Between these cities, Indian Territory was imagined as a place purposely outside of conceptions of "progress." Yet as tribes—original peoples of the area as well as nations forcibly relocated there—made their life in Indian Territory, they engaged in complex negotiations with power brokers, Indigenous and otherwise, who insured their participation in trade, travel, and military alliance. Native Americans founded and transformed the city of Tulsa into its place as a cultural capital of Indian Territory (later Oklahoma), and Tulsa is linked to New Orleans and Santa Fe in stories of urban Native Americans who navigated the transformation of these regions into the United

States, always-already identifying homelands in multiple places, often at a distance from their places of ancestry.

Though England, Spain, and France are recognized as the major players in controlling networks of trade and settlement in the Trans-Mississippi West before the ascendancy of the United States, Indigenous peoples also exerted considerable power and influence over the use of land and resources in these areas, not as hamstrung by the boundaries of Indian Territory as the new Americans would hope. Osages and Comanches dominated much of the commerce on the southern plains in the eighteenth and nineteenth centuries, making use of their expertise to intimidate European and American leaders who sometimes faltered beyond their command from cities like New Orleans. Southern emigrant tribes adapted to new environments and developed strong alliances in the complex political ecosystem that developed at the confluence of East and West, especially as the Comanche empire kept competing imperial powers at bay. Drawing attention to the historical relationship of Indigenous peoples of now-Oklahoma to a host of cultural, political, and regional influences supports a clearer understanding of Indigenous urbanization in this part of the world and makes the pairing of the words *Oklahoma* and *cosmopolitan* not such a stretch.

Native Homelands in New Orleans

New Orleans is a city strongly associated with cultural mixture; its history as a center of the Atlantic slave trade and its attraction of immigrants from across the globe have driven its multifaceted arts and music scene as well as its attractiveness to tourists. The city is so prominent in the histories of southern Indians, yet Native legacies in New Orleans remain mostly invisible. Though Indigenous images appear on some monuments and in performances such as Mardi Gras Indian parades, problematic histories of dispossession are obscured in these nods to Nativism. However, New Orleans is a site of historical and creative inspiration for Native Americans, especially writers, who emphasize Indigenous roots of Mardi Gras and jazz in New Orleans and highlight connections to communities in Oklahoma. New Orleans is a homeland that is integral to a broader understanding of urban Indigenous studies and is a muse for present assertions of sovereignty in an intercultural world.

Choctaw and Muscogee peoples in Oklahoma share ties to New Orleans through histories of trade, refuge, removal, and war, as do Louisiana coastal tribes, including Houma, Pointe-au-Chien, and bands of Biloxi-Chitimacha. According to Daniel Usner, during the eighteenth century "the villages of Chaouacha, Bayogoula, Houma, Acolapissa, Chitimacha, and Tunica—the names of once larger tribes—were all situated within a hundred-mile radius of New Orleans and participated heavily in the evolving colonial economy." Usner goes on to document the in-migration of communities near Mobile (the capital of Louisiana at that time)—Apalaches, Biloxis, Chahtos, Mobilians, Pascagoulas, and Taensas.[1] The century saw competing advances into the area from the English, French, and Spanish, which depended upon the participation or resistance of Indigenous nations to these advances. Robbie Ethridge emphasizes coalescence relative to this geography, noting that many of the Mississippian tribes of the South were groups joined together in new social formations; by the early eighteenth century, she explains, "a new South was emerging," distinguished by large Indian nations and enslaved Africans as well as new ecological circumstances.[2] She notes that both Jean-Baptiste Le Moyne de Bienville (who would be known as the "Father of New Orleans") and his older brother, Pierre Le Moyne d'Iberville, visited this area at the turn of the eighteenth century, finding that tribes were moving in response to disease or threats from outsiders, finding protection with the French, fleeing the aggression of the English, or joining up with other tribes along the Mississippi River.[3] This early Indigenous history of New Orleans reveals ways that Native peoples affiliated, moved, and reformed their communities among diverse Native and non-Native groups.

Economic sovereignty as well as this demographic density supports recovery of New Orleans as a site of Indigenous urbanization. An exchange economy was fundamental to the region until the late eighteenth century, with Native peoples both inside and outside of New Orleans driving trade. Though some histories of Indian participation in southern plantation economies emphasize Natives' eventual dependence on colonists for their livelihoods, Usner points out that colonists were initially just as dependent upon the Indian market, neglecting agricultural endeavors in favor of acquiring food in the form of crops, meats, and prepared dishes from Native Americans.[4] Ned Sublette likewise describes the desperation of French colonists in Louisiana in the aftermath of the Seven Years' War, who, without support from France in the early eighteenth century, had to "go native or starve."[5] They disbanded several times to live with Natives, who helped them survive. A pattern of dependence on Indigenous trade was established here that would be echoed in the Osage and Comanchería economy of the West (including Indian Territory) in the coming decades.

Though the exchange economy gave way to colonial production of cash crops, Native Americans in Louisiana continued to adapt trading activities to new realities and were visible, though increasingly marginalized, in the city. With the United States' independence from Great Britain and its 1803 purchase of Louisiana from France, Native peoples in the area faced a greater influx of settlers to New Orleans and remained active in the city's growing economy and society. In the nineteenth century, Indians were fixtures in the street life of New Orleans, especially at the French Market and other neighborhood markets along historic trading routes.[6] According to Usner, "Indians became increasingly marginal people on the rapidly changing urban scene, but they continued to integrate the New Orleans marketplace into their own annual cycle of social and economic activities. Through this evolving relationship with the city, American Indians distinctively influenced the culture and landscape of New Orleans."[7] Natives' prominence in the marketplace drove reciprocal encounters with the tapestry of nationalities in New Orleans, marking the cosmopolitan culture of the city through jazz, sport, and even voodoo.[8]

Among the tribes who lived and traded in New Orleans, Choctaw people were especially significant both in negotiations with colonial strategists and in entrepreneurial endeavors in the city. After the seventeenth century, when a distinct Choctaw entity began to develop from previous varied bands, groups of Choctaws nonetheless at times found themselves on competing sides of conflicts between the British, Spanish, French, and Americans. However, most Choctaws developed strong trading relationships with France in the Mississippi Valley largely at the direction of Jean-Baptiste Le Moyne de Bienville. They allied with Spain in its 1763 acquisition of New Orleans after France's defeat in the Seven Years' War.[9] Spain ceded Louisiana back to France in 1800, officially transferring control three years later, in 1803, and France then immediately turned the area over to the United States the same year through the Louisiana Purchase. From that time on, Choctaws remained on the side of the Americans, fighting with Andrew Jackson against the Creeks at the Battle of Horseshoe Bend in 1814 and against the British at the Battle of New Orleans a year later. With the victory of the Americans, Choctaws were thus subject to America's designs to relocate southern Indians west to Indian Territory (now Oklahoma) through the Treaty of Doak's Stand in 1820 and the Treaty of Dancing Rabbit Creek in 1830.[10] Some Choctaws resisted removal and maintained communities that became recognized as the Mississippi Band of Choctaw Indians and the Jena (Louisiana) Band of Choctaw Indians. The Choctaw Nation came to have jurisdiction over roughly eleven thousand square miles in the southeastern part of the state of Oklahoma.[11]

Choctaw women were formidable players in trade with various colonial entities that were constantly jockeying for power in the Mississippi Valley and in New Orleans even after the signing of treaties that decimated the Choctaws' land base in the South. James Carson notes that Choctaw women sold produce and crafts and began growing cotton for the creation and sale of cloth, while men concentrated on raising livestock. Choctaws continued their active trade on the Natchez Trace, and the high number of women producing goods and selling in city markets, including both the LeBreton Market and the French Market, impressed visitors to New Orleans.[12] According to Jerah Johnson, these women persisted, though smaller in number, into the early twentieth century.[13] Johnson explains that the Choctaw women "vanished" at that time because of intermarriage with those of African ancestry and their absorption into the classification of free people of color, who were concentrated in the Faubourg-Treme neighborhood. What if we understood Choctaw women as adaptive rather than disappearing? Ethridge contends that Choctaws were able to adapt aspects of the European market to their own culture and does not interpret a failure to assimilate as lack of success.[14] The Choctaws' introduction of gumbo filé to the culinary world is just one example—and appropriate symbol—of their worth.[15] The contribution of Choctaws to the culture of New Orleans continues to inspire their descendants.

Like Choctaws, Muscogees sought to protect their sovereignty in their southeastern homelands through trade and alliances amid a flurry of colonial incursions that placed a high value on control of New Orleans. Trade and travel are part of Muscogee narratives, which resonate beyond but are relevant to interactions with intercolonial rivals in the South. Angela Pulley Hudson describes Tie Snake or Horned Serpent stories that warn

Muscogees of the dangers of traveling and, in particular, consuming taboo food while traveling. These stories, she explains, locate the snake within rumbling waters, which are common features of Muscogee landscapes: "These themes reflect the natural world of Creek country, where frequent river crossings were a dangerous fact of life. But they also incorporate southeastern Indigenous beliefs regarding the separation of basic categories like earth and water, as well as a concern with bodies of water as portals to the chaotic underworld." Reflecting this strong association with water, Muscogees encountered traders near the Chattahoochee River along the Lower Path, which connected Augusta, Georgia, to New Orleans; and along the Upper Path, which extended north of Augusta into northern Mississippi, leading to other nations such as Cherokees, Chickasaws, and Choctaws. Muscogees often encountered strangers, including European traders and enslaved people of African descent, along these paths. The growing presence of African Americans in the South was tied to these paths, which allowed some people of African descent a degree of comfort with Native cultures, including Indigenous languages. The paths facilitated the activities of the Creek Confederacy but would also come to be critical to the American campaign to decimate Creek authority in the region. After the Louisiana Purchase in 1803, Jefferson set his sights on New Orleans as key to the growth of the cotton trade in the South, which energized his campaign for a new Federal Road into the city.[16]

Understanding Muscogees as a confederacy rather than a singular tribe is crucial to understanding the complexity that pervades their history of contacts with Europeans in the South and their relationship to New Orleans. Muscogee people were organized into Upper and Lower Towns, with separate political bodies that were not always consistent in their agreements with outsiders. Further, Muscogee towns were designated as either white or red, corresponding to associations with peace or warfare, respectively; clans in the towns were also white or red.[17] Similar to the Choctaws, Muscogees benefited from trade with Europeans as they had from trade with other tribes; they provided deerskins and food first to the Spanish in exchange for manufactured goods, especially weaponry. The British, however, became their closest European allies, and Muscogees provided horses and even enslaved Choctaws and Gulf tribal members to the Carolina colony in exchange for guns and other manufactured goods.

Ethridge points out that at the turn of the nineteenth century, the lives of Muscogee people were interwoven with those of other nations and races, with the borders of Muscogee country far from impermeable as their leaders continually negotiated their economic position on a generally level basis among European rivals. As was the case with Choctaw women, Muscogee women had a key position in this frontier exchange economy, selling clothes and baskets as well as produce, meats, and baked goods to whites and African Americans.[18] Ethridge argues that Muscogee women were largely responsible for the tribe's growing reputation for hospitality, which expanded into lodging and entertainment for travelers.

The growing presence of non-Indians in Muscogee homelands caused more conflict within the Confederacy, however. Muscogees, mostly based in the Upper Towns, who opposed the expanding cultural influence of the Americans and were inspired by Tecumseh's pan-Indian resistance movement, were known as "Red Sticks." Kevin Kokomoor cautions against understanding this Red Stick insurgency as simply born of nostalgia for a long-ago era. Red Sticks, he contends, were committed to unity as well as nationhood, and while some were stridently and consistently anti-European, he points toward the Muscogee-European prophet Hillis Haujo (or "Crazy-Brave Medicine") as an example of a Red Stick leader driven chiefly by spirituality.[19] At Burnt Corn Creek, American soldiers attacked Red Sticks on their way back from obtaining munitions from the Spanish in Florida.[20] The Red Sticks retaliated against the Americans and their Muscogee allies at Fort Mims and, in their convincing victory, outraged the American public. Thus, the Red Stick War quickly became a U.S. war against the Muscogees.[21]

This war was an opportunity for Andrew Jackson to build support for his broader campaign for Indian dispossession in the Southeast, which would shape the formation of Indian Territory and later Oklahoma statehood. In 1814, with the assistance of some Cherokees, Choctaws, and Muscogees, Jackson led his soldiers to Horseshoe Bend, the last battle of the Creek War, where the Red Sticks suffered their most devastating casualties. With the Treaty of Fort Jackson, signed in 1814, Jackson stripped Muscogees of over twenty million acres (more than half of their homelands), shattering the Creek Confederacy. Though a few prominent "friendly" Creek families were permitted to retain small tracts in Alabama, today comprising the reservation of the Poarch Creek Band of Creek Indians, Jackson's actions were universally punitive.[22] The Muscogees who had allied with Jackson were devastated; they had been under the impression that their assistance would aid their desire to hold onto their ancestral lands.[23] Toward the end of 1814, Jackson learned of a British plan to attack New Orleans, and he mobilized troops. Jackson had long seen New Orleans, a prime engine of the American economy, as important to his plan to destroy the Muscogees. Part of a movement to expand and improve roads, Jackson directed the opening of a road from Tennessee to New Orleans that came to be known as "Jackson's Military Road."[24] Facing a superior British force, Jackson and his soldiers secured New Orleans in January 1815. This British defeat, as Claudio Saunt suggests, must have further weakened Muscogee hopes for a turnaround.[25] With the British out of the way and Native landholdings diminishing, the subsequent decades ushered in Jackson's architecture of Indian dispossession in the East.

The shifting balance of colonial power from Britain to Jackson's America complemented an eventual alignment of Muscogee leadership with the U.S. Confederacy, which would have implications for the Muscogee Nation in Indian Territory. As the British left the South in 1815, they left a fortified warehouse at Prospect Bluff, along the Apalachicola River in Florida. Muscogees and Africans escaping enslavement began traveling there en masse to join Red Sticks and Seminoles. U.S. Indian agent and slave trader Benjamin Hawkins began to offer bounties to deputized Muscogees for hunting down runaway slaves, with the ultimate goal of destroying the fort. Muscogee leaders, notably William McIntosh, signaled an acceptance of chattel slavery, making capturing and returning runaway slaves a priority. Kokomoor concludes, "Not only was the Creek leadership continuing to reassert control over its remaining territory, it was supporting the larger idea of the South in the process."[26] Muscogee removal was mandated in the Treaty of Indian Springs of 1825, which, negotiated by William McIntosh and signed by six Lower Town leaders, was not widely accepted across the Creek Confederacy and was in violation of a law passed by the National Council forbidding any chief from agreeing to cede Muscogee land.[27] McIntosh was executed for his violation the same year.

In the lead-up to the Indian Removal Act of 1830, which gave Andrew Jackson the authority to grant lands west of the Mississippi River to tribes in exchange for their lands in the Southeast, Muscogee country transformed to cotton country, accompanied by an influx of African-descended people. The land sessions of the Creek War's end brought American boosterism, documented in promotional advertisements and travel guides, for new white settlements invigorated by booming commercial markets tied to cotton and other commodities.[28] Most Muscogees ceded their lands with the Treaty of Cusseta in 1832. However, the Second Creek War in 1836 demonstrated that some who remained, mostly Upper Creeks, were committed to retaining their homelands. This resolve was evident in increased ceremonial activities, an uptick in the purchase of guns and ammunition, and incidents of violence against whites.[29] Ultimately, these resisters were also removed to Indian Territory, transported through New Orleans. Over the course of a decade, approximately twenty-three thousand Muscogee people were relocated across the Mississippi River.[30] The trauma and transformation of this upheaval would be shared in the stories of generations.

As histories of Choctaws and Muscogees reveal, New Orleans has served as a center of trade and transition for Native peoples of the South, particularly those who would move to Indian Territory. Natives are critical also to the rich cultural scene of the city. Congo Square rivals gumbo as the example that best captures this heritage. Those familiar with this hallowed site associate it with the persistence of African musical traditions in North America and the evolution of jazz. Enslaved Africans gathered at Congo Square during French rule, which permitted Sunday to be non-workdays. Their descendants continued celebrations there, using African instruments to perform traditional songs and dances. The square was located close to an Indian portage route that ran through the French Quarter. In the French period, it served as a public market; this market precedes its celebratory function.

Native Americans feasted near Congo Square, considering the area to be holy ground.[31] Into the nineteenth century, Natives and free people of color played the Indian sport *raquettes* on the grounds.[32] The site was a place for cultural exchange, with Native American and African influences marking the dances and music making that were a precursor to Mardi Gras Indian traditions and second line jazz. These feasts, games, and performances point toward the social and spatial ways that humans experience city life beyond urban development, an example of what Edward Soja describes as the social-spatial-historical processes emanating from cities. The contributions of Native Americans to the cosmopolitan culture of the city are remembered in the writings of their descendants in Oklahoma.

Mardi Gras Indian traditions still recognize Native Americans in the social scene of New Orleans, though whether Native Americans are honored or appropriated in these traditions is a matter of disagreement. The literature on Mardi Gras Indians mostly focuses on the performances as statements of survival and subversion, linked to organizing for civil rights within a restrictive, racist southern society. In an interview with Rachel Breunlin, Ronald Lewis, who founded the House of Dance & Feathers, explains that Native Americans are being honored through performance that creates a new space for African American protest: "Coming out of slavery, 'You're not going to give us a place in society, we'll create our own.' In masking, they paid respect and homage to the Native American for using their identity and making a social statement that despite the odds, you're still not going to stop." Noting that the return of Mardi Gras Indian performances was a powerful statement after Hurricane Katrina, Breunlin explains that "in taking to the streets on Mardi Gras day, they symbolically reclaimed their neighborhood."[33] Like Breunlin, Cynthia Becker assesses Mardi Gras Indian performance as cultural mediation that challenges white southern racial constructs. She ultimately concludes that "Black Indians, who pointedly omit depictions of the military defeat of Native Americans in their beaded patches, sometimes walk a fine line between self-empowerment and the reinforcement of Native American stereotypes."[34]

Some scholars are not at all convinced that Mardi Gras Indian masking is so empowering. In a compelling response to the aftermath of Katrina from an Indigenous studies standpoint, C. Richard King links the performances with "a long history of appropriation, misrecognition, and symbolic power." He observes that American Indians were all but erased from reports of the crises that Hurricanes Katrina and Rita created, even as "the media has displayed an abiding fascination with the Mardi Gras Indians."[35] King names tourism as a factor that distorts histories of racism—and colonialism—in the city and asserts that an enduring Black-white paradigm in journalistic and scholarly responses to Katrina and Rita also fuel this misinformation. Mardi Gras Indians are essential to a story of the city's uniqueness, its exotic flavor outside of a typical American framework. Yet as history shows, New Orleans was a key notch on Andrew Jackson's belt, the linchpin of his conquest of the South and eventual rise to the American presidency on a platform of Indian dispossession. As Mardi Gras Indians have received more exposure, they have become more emblematic, it seems, of a city's—and a nation's—capacity to turn away from its history.

Despite their presence at the iconic Congo Square and depiction as resisters in masking traditions, Native Americans receive a disorienting treatment in civic monuments around New Orleans, which likewise exposes the limitations of built structures for interpreting urban life. A few plaques and historical markers make mention of Indigenous legacies, with some sites entirely unmarked. This phenomenon exemplifies what Coll Thrush calls urban Indian "ghost stories." In Thrush's analysis of place stories in Seattle, "stories of ghosts and totem poles and dispossessed chieftains cast Indians only as passive victims of, rather than participants in, the urban story."[36] Along with their inclination to avoid untold truths about urban Native Americans, these markers reflect associations between urban areas and exclusively built environments. Ari Kelman, like Soja, writes of postmodern geographers' tendencies to focus on built rather than natural environments in cities such as New Orleans since urban spaces are understood to be abstract products of discourse. Kelman urges reconsideration of material forces—namely, urban nature in the form of the Mississippi River.[37] Since Native Americans are so associated with nature, they are "disappeared" in urban environments.

Public commemoration of conquest in cities also represents Natives passively. Perhaps the strongest emblem of the way in which Native Americans are present yet passive in New Orleans cultural markers appears in the monument to Bienville in the French Quarter north of Conti Street. There, in a small park called Bienville Place, the statue contains three figures: Jean-Baptiste Le Moyne de Bienville (credited as the founder of New Orleans), Father Athanase Douay (the French monk who accompanied Bienville), and an unnamed Native American (presumably the guide who led Bienville to the site). Bienville is at the highest height, looking regal, with Douay standing with a Bible below him and the Native American in a feathered headdress sitting cross-legged and holding a pipe. This ghost story, as it were, tells a familiar yet problematic tale of Indigenous dispossession. First, the positioning of the figures reifies the supremacy of the colonist as "founder" of the area. Though Bienville was responsible for commissioning the design of the French Quarter and naming the city, his supremacy in the New Orleans origin story overlooks the importance of Native peoples to the economy and military history of the area. Second, the generic Indian figure in the monument, seated in a pitiable stance of defeat, wears little clothing except for a feathered address. The statue reflects an imagining of a Plains Indian rather than local dress. This "historical" marker places yet displaces Indian nations in the French Quarter, telling a quintessentially American origin story that drowns out the contributions of Choctaws, Muscogees, and local Louisiana tribes to New Orleans history and culture. In this narrative Natives are affixed in the (invented) past, without participation in the lively urban scene adjacent to the square.

Though New Orleans origin stories in official monuments incorporate a semblance of Native participation, they leave out foundational parts of the city's story. Next to Café du Monde, a stop on every tourist's itinerary, a monument commemorates the importance of the Mississippi River to the city's founding. It reads: "New Orleans—First sighted as Indian Portage to Lake Ponchartrain and Gulf in 1699 by Bienville and Iberville. Founded by Bienville in 1718: Named by him in honor of Duke of Orleans, Regent of France. Called the Crescent City because of location in bend of the Mississippi." Like the statue at Bienville Place, the plaque includes but overshadows the importance of Native American trading to the city's founding; the colonizers' "sighting" of the portage is the originary moment. Yet the portage was key to the development of commerce and culture in the city before 1699, even though there is scant recognition of the portage route in city markers aside from the mention here. Though as Freddi Evans explains, Native American dwellings, as well as early French settlements, have been documented along the portage and in the French Quarter, historical markers with city sanction have not been placed there.[38] That said, in the years since Katrina, New Orleans has begun to market this road as a desirable touring site, highlighting its former LeBreton Market and its recent energetic Caribbean and reggae scene.

Not far from the Bayou Road portage route, Congo Square remains in a corner of Louis Armstrong Park adjacent to the French Quarter. Though the grounds are not expertly maintained, a marker nevertheless alerts visitors to the historic significance of this location. The sign reads:

1. Monument to Bienville, New Orleans. Photo by the author.

> Congo Square is in the "vicinity" of a spot which Houmas [*sic*] Indians used before the arrival of the French for celebrating their annual corn harvest and was considered sacred ground. The gathering of enslaved African vendors in Congo Square originated as early as the late 1740s during Louisiana's French colonial period and continued during the Spanish colonial era as one of the city's public markets. By 1803 Congo Square had become famous for the gathering of enslaved Africans who drummed, danced, sang and traded on Sunday afternoons. By 1819 these gatherings numbered as many as 500 to 600 people. Among the most famous dances were the Bamboula, the Calinda and the Congo. These African cultural expressions gradually developed into Mardi Gras Indian traditions, the Second Line and eventually New Orleans jazz and rhythm and blues.

Like the other monuments that mention Native Americans in New Orleans, this sign assigns Houma Indians to a pre-European age. While of course Native Americans were the majority population at that time, their absence from the descriptions in the marker of activities in the square in the years since, including connections to Mardi Gras Indians, still relegates Indigenous Louisianans to the past.

Other placeholders likewise recognize yet obscure Native Americans in the cityscape. At the French Market, a historical marker provides context for the adjacent retail center and farmers market. Its inscription reads:

> Native Americans traded here from ancient times when waterways were the highways of America. The market on the banks of the river linked the Mississippi Valley with the Gulf Coast by way of the Esplanade Ridge to Bayou St. John and through Lake Pontchartrain to the Gulf of Mexico. After the arrival of the French the market on the levee grew to include the products of the world as New Orleans grew around it. In 1791, the Spanish city government established a city market and built the first market hall, a butchers' market at St. Ann Street and the river. Over two centuries, many buildings have been built, and some have been lost to fire, hurricane and the changing economy. The market became known as the French Market with the arrival of the Anglo-Americans who named old things in the old city French, but other cultures contrib-

2. (*top*) Armstrong Park, New Orleans. Photo by the author.

3. Congo Square, New Orleans. Photo by the author.

> uted to the market. Africans, Spanish, Haitians, Italians, Germans, Irish, Jews, Dalmations [*sic*], Greeks, Syrians, Lebanese, Filipinos, Chinese, other Asians, Latin Americans, and many more. Colonial New Orleans was Caribbean Creole, enriched by the Acadian agricultural community giving the city and market the cuisine, the music and the style which make them unique. Changes in the technology for the production and distribution of food in this century changed the market, but as the cycle of change continues, the joy and vitality of the traditional market regain prominence.

Keywords in this passage, like the statue at Bienville Place or the marker at Congo Square, support a typical frontier narrative of New Orleans history. Native Americans traded only in "ancient" times. The arrival of colonial entities brought global influence to the market as well as building construction. The market received its name from Anglo-Americans, who, in ascribing "French" influence to it, overshadowed the long list of nationalities active in commerce at the site. Absent from this list are Native Americans, such as Choctaw women, who were so instrumental in supporting the local economy.

Tulsa: Indian Town

As New Orleans is for Louisiana, Tulsa, the heart of what was once Indian Territory, is an arts and culture capital of Oklahoma. This standing is in no small part due to the thriving Native American arts scene in the city. But unlike New Orleans, Tulsa does not make lists of top tourist destinations. However, its cultural institutions, like the Crescent City's, are inextricably linked to histories of Native American commerce, politics, and arts as well as the dispossession of Native lands. Because of Tulsa's geographical importance in Indian Country, one of two large urban areas in a state that is home to thirty-nine federally recognized tribal nations, its relevance to studies of urban Indigenous experiences should be obvious. Urban Indigenous studies in the United States have primarily addressed the circumstances of the Urban Relocation Program, and Tulsa, though it was a relocation city beginning in the late 1950s, was not one of the prominent sites for the program. As Donald Fixico details, many Oklahoma Indians did participate in the relocation program but joined Natives from across

4. French Market entry, New Orleans. Photo by the author.

the country in cities such as Los Angeles, Chicago, and San Francisco, led by the promise of widely available factory work, housing, and other bigger opportunities than could be found close to home.[39] Still, Tulsa was and remains an Indigenous city from its founding as a Muscogee town, and its history and culture lie at the crossroads of East and West. This position as a bridge between areas and eras of American expansion and Indigenous mobility makes Tulsa an interesting subject for studies of diaspora and cosmopolitanism.

Assessments of Indian Territory as a no-man's-land, without a distinct historical or regional identity, may proceed from its position outside of historiographies that emphasize European—British, French, and Spanish—settlement. That does not mean that this area was disconnected from modernity and its accompanying realities, in terms of both European commitments to their colonies and Indigenous participation in new markets, alliances, and cultural shifts. Scholars have challenged long-accepted myths about "the West" as a space defined by European power and Native American submission and, in these reconsiderations of history, have recovered connections between Indigenous mobility and urbanization in now-Oklahoma. Brandi Denison cautions against exceptionalism, asserting: "The American West . . . remains a contested site of multiple histories, narrative, memories, and identities, and, most important, the product of an ongoing process of cultural memory."[40] Further, scholars such as Pekka Hämäläinen, Kathleen DuVal, and Juliana Barr emphasize the importance of Indigenous power in these histories. Hämäläinen, in *The Comanche Empire* (2008), calls the Comanchería a hegemonic and imperial power that continually blocked European ambition on the southern plains. DuVal, in *The Native Ground* (2006), joins histories of the Southeast and Southwest, uncovering centuries of Indian domination in the Arkansas Valley. Barr, in *Peace Came in the Form of a Woman* (2007), reframes the colonial history of eighteenth-century Texas as "a story of Indian dominance" based on kinship rather than European constructions of state and racial difference.[41] These checks on notions of this area as empty space help clarify Oklahoma's role.

While Tulsa's incorporation as a city proceeded from relocation of southeastern tribes, people of many Indigenous nations were living and trading there well before the U.S. government deemed it a catch-all for nations pushed out of their lands elsewhere. Northeastern Oklahoma was an area of diverse Indigenous encounters that may be assessed as historically urban. Jean-Baptiste Bénard, Sieur de la Harpe was commissioned by New Orleans–based general Jean-Baptiste Le Moyne de Bienville to establish a trading post among the Caddo tribe along the Red River, currently the southern border of the state of Oklahoma.[42] Having done so, La Harpe endeavored to travel north to secure additional alliances, making first French contact with Indigenous peoples in now-Oklahoma. There in 1719, he found an area inhabited by six or seven thousand Tawakoni people, a group that would become part of the Wichita tribe, along with traders and travelers of other tribes, such as the Chickasaw, who were curious about what this French expedition was up to. The post La Harpe wrote of in his diary consisted of villages near the Arkansas River several miles south of present-day Tulsa, which were regularly vacated in winter for bison hunting. This Wichita area was adjacent to the Osage Nation to the north. This network of Wichitas eventually moved south toward the Red River, becoming more active in trade with the French and connecting with other groups of Wichitas that eventually became headquartered in the western Oklahoma town of Anadarko as the Wichita and Affiliated Tribes.

Before the establishment of Indian Territory in 1834 on the heels of the forced removal of southeastern tribes, Osages, Quapaws, Comanches, and Caddos were ascendant in the south-central part of the continent, with France and Spain eager to make inroads and agreements with them to shore up their colonial projects, commanded from New Orleans and Santa Fe, respectively. DuVal points out the diversity of the Arkansas Valley, now western Arkansas and eastern Oklahoma, where Europeans and several Indigenous societies followed ambitions to control trade and influence in the region.[43] Though France determined that the entire area from roughly the Mississippi River in the East to just east of Santa Fe in the West was "La Louisiane," DuVal notes that this map was continually disputed by the English and Spanish and irrelevant to Native Americans. While France saw the middle of North America as a last chance for its colony's success, Osages were growing more powerful. By the end of the eighteenth century, pressure from Osages would expel Caddoan peoples, including those who would eventually reorganize as Wichitas, in part because of the Osages' carefully cultivated relationship with French traders. After the Louisiana Purchase in 1803, the United States brought different expectations to Indian-white relations, with the goal of teaching Native Americans to live like whites. Spain contested the United States' understanding of its new borders, still hoping for influence in the area. According to DuVal, in 1805 the governor of New Mexico sent Spanish troops throughout "contested

Louisiana," hinting at upcoming war with the United States as a reason for the Natives there to seek friendship with Spain.

Along with Osages, Comanches were dominant in the central South; the might of Comanches continually thwarted the plans of European colonists, especially the Spanish, to subdue Native Americans and control the West. Hämäläinen's study of the Comanchería reveals just how tied the fortunes of would-be colonizers were to the actions of the assertive Comanches: "For a century, roughly from 1750 to 1850, the Comanches were the dominant people in the southwest, and they manipulated and exploited the colonial outposts in New Mexico, Texas, Louisiana, and northern Mexico to increase their safety, prosperity, and power." Comanches often pitted European interests against one another and grew in power and influence "from their ability to extract political and material benefits from urban-based societies in New Mexico, Texas, and the Great Plains."[44] Because of the Comanchería, Texas and Spain fell short of their aims to build wealth in their northern territories, and France, though buoyed by its alliance with the Osages, was blocked from extending Louisiana's reach into the commercial landscape farther west. This growing commercial network contributed to the Comanches' ascendance, as they established and expanded fairs first in the pueblos and later east, where a thriving market in bison hides and other animal products, as well as captives, drove commerce.

Increasingly, trade with Comanches was essential for economic survival, especially for Governor Cachupin of New Mexico, who feared that alienating Comanches meant defeat to "French New Orleans."[45] In 1762, as the French were surrendering Louisiana, including its claims in eastern Texas, to Spain with the Treaty of Fontainebleau, Spain was also negotiating a peace with Comanches, which would seem to suggest a tipped balance of power toward Spain. Yet Comanche expansion continued eastward into now-Oklahoma and Texas, with accelerating raids on Spanish settlements in Texas becoming part of a network of raiding and trading between East and West. Juliana Barr documents ways that Frenchmen in Texas, strongly bound to the market economy emanating from New Orleans, had adapted to gendered Caddo marriage customs in order to negotiate diplomatic and economic advantages, deferring to Indian dominance there as a strategy to compete with the Spaniards.[46] It would seem that the Spaniards would now see their influence expand in Texas due to their deference to the

Comanches, and yet the result was the opposite: Comanches came to dominate the entirety of the Texas plains. As in the East, after the Louisiana Purchase of 1803, the Spanish were further weakened, seeing their empire collapse by 1821.[47]

In the first part of the nineteenth century, while the United States was enacting its plan for Indian Removal and national expansion, the Comanchería was likewise expanding and opening new avenues for trade that would involve many Indigenous nations in ways that the United States did not anticipate. With U.S. victories over European colonial campaigns, the clamor among settlers for safe occupation of Native lands in the East increased, and during James Monroe's presidency, from 1817 to 1825, the tenor of solutions to the "Indian problem" became more aggressive. As Andrew Jackson waged war, Monroe's policy transitioned from voluntary to forced removal, culminating, during Jackson's presidency, in the Indian Removal Act of 1830. The steady arrival of emigrant tribes to the Arkansas Valley and southern plains, coterminous with growing U.S. participation in trade and travel there, disrupted the geopolitical landscape. Establishing Indian Territory in 1834 was for the United States, according to David Bernstein, not only key to its national expansion but also a calculated effort for the young country to prove itself among more established European empires. Indian Territory would be a space for acculturation, the United States expected, but also a sign that it acknowledged human rights by creating a safe territory for the people it vanquished. Bernstein's study of mapmaking challenges the idea that Indian Territory was a bounded space, however. Indian Territory, he argues, "allowed the American public to construct a commemorative Indian past while they waited for Indians to become extinct."[48] In reality, even as the removal era was among the United States' most notorious genocidal campaigns, emigrant tribes participated in new markets, negotiated new alliances, and did what they had to do to rebuild in the West. While still culturally connected to the East, they became major players in trade and travel, including along trails that connected New Orleans with the western trading hub of Santa Fe.

The activities of eastern tribes in the newly established territory would figure in to the end of European power on the southern plains in ways not widely acknowledged. Though this upheaval contributed eventually to the ability of the United States to transform the Southwest into states, it is crucial not to gloss over the ways that the presence of these arriving Native Americans largely determined the future of the state of Oklahoma and its present political and cultural realities. It was not long after voluntary removals began that President Jackson acknowledged that all was not going according to plan in Indian Country. The Osage Nation viewed incoming Cherokees as invaders to their home in the Arkansas Valley and reacted with years of raiding. Cherokees cultivated alliances with other emigrant eastern tribes, such as the Choctaw, and Osage foes, such as the Quapaws. They retaliated, culminating in the Battle of Claremore Mound in 1817. Brian DeLay, in *War of a Thousand Deserts* (2008), notes that Jackson's campaign for Texas was orchestrated to provide more space for Native emigration as well as better management of conflicts between eastern and western tribes; the volatile situation was being publicized in the *Cherokee Phoenix* as a reason for Cherokees remaining in the East to hold strong against removal.[49] DuVal puts the number of arriving Cherokees at approximately five thousand, explaining that "these trans-Mississippi expansionists . . . drew a metaphorical border between themselves as 'civilized' and the Osages as 'savage,'" allowing them to "make the Arkansas Valley their own native ground."[50] Eastern tribes now became invested in the Comanche-driven international marketplace just as the United States was also cultivating trading relationships with Comanches and seeking to increase its influence farther westward toward New Mexico. With American trading interests compromised by the violence and raiding between the Comanchería and Indian Territory, an agreement was reached with the Treaty of Camp Holmes in 1835; it was negotiated between the United States and eastern and western tribes to keep the peace as many more Native peoples would arrive in succeeding decades.

Emigrant Indians created economies in this territory that capitalized on its landscape and entrepreneurial possibilities, much as they had in the East, hard as the United States pushed to acculturate them. With the agricultural possibilities much different from the farming that had shaped their cultures, they experimented with bison hunting and livestock trade, becoming middlemen between the Comanchería in the West, where material goods, including guns, and commodities such as corn and tobacco were in high demand, and the Arkansas and Missouri Territories in the

East, which sought animal products and horses.[51] Drawn into this thriving economic orbit as well was Mexico, via Texas, a base from which eastern Comanches supplied the Choctaws with horses and cattle that were becoming increasingly important to their livelihoods in Indian Territory.[52] Parallel to the Indian roads and routes that were integral to the economies of the East, trading routes developed that were becoming much more heavily traversed. Three well-established routes crossing Indian Territory connected the Comanchería, with thriving markets in the city of Santa Fe and northern and eastern New Mexico, with the urban centers of St. Louis and New Orleans.[53]

While European and Anglo-American explorers are often heralded as pioneers of U.S. trade along routes such as the Santa Fe Trail, Comanches, eastern tribes, and Indigenous travelers from quite a distance gathered for enormous trade fairs along the border of the Comanchería and Indian Territory, suggestive of an urban, international trading environment. Indigenous intermediaries were key to Euro-settler mapmaking as well as the expansion of commercial markets between East and West. Removed Indians, growing in number, introduced slaves into this trading market, supporting their establishment of southern-style plantation economies in Indian Territory that mirrored the previous homesteads of slaveholding elites. The Comanchería also became increasingly multiethnic, drawing to it those of many groups, including eastern tribes and enslaved African Americans, because of its economic opportunities. The success of Indigenous entrepreneurship on the southern plains and the retreat of competing European empires convinced the United States of the great potential and feasibility of further expansion westward, ironically leading to the Comanchería's defeat as well. Because of the power of Indigenous trade, both Texas and New Mexico became steadily distanced from Spain and later Mexico, and the relentless market for bison and livestock ecologically depleted the eastern Comanchería, weakening Indigenous control of the market and emboldening U.S. traders and military leaders to achieve their goal of transforming the West into colonized states, set in ink with the Treaty of Guadalupe Hidalgo in 1841.

Just as Indian Territory was at the center of a confluence and upheaval of imperial and Indigenous power that would shape the West in the modern era, it also was a staging ground for the violence of the U.S. Civil War, which left its southern imprint on the experiences, including urbanization, of Native peoples within it. In contrast to the founding of Oklahoma City to the West, ushered in by "Boomers" who clamored for settler rights to Indigenous lands, Tulsa's incorporation and early history was Muscogee led. Between Removal and the Reconstruction era of U.S. history, the Muscogee Nation in Indian Territory would come to incorporate Native Americans who were seeking refuge from conflicts with western tribes as well as African Americans, some enslaved and some on the path to freedom. When faced with rebuilding their community to the west, the Muscogees would maintain their Mississippian roots in the organization of tribal towns and other cultural practices. They would also signify their southeastern orientation in their imposition of racial hierarchies that were typical of the South's plantation economy.

The founders of the city of Tulsa were Muscogees who endured the United States' genocidal campaign of Indigenous dispossession in the South but retained their organization of Muscogee civic and ceremonial life as they situated what remained of their community in Indian Territory. Tulsa derives its name from the Muscogee name "Tallasi," an important tribal town in Muscogee homelands of the South. Located in Alabama, Tallasi (now Tallassee) was a stop on Hernando de Soto's expedition to the Southeast from 1539 to 1542, the same journey that led to the Spanish explorer's death in the Mississippi River.[54] Tallassee, birthplace of Chief Osceola, was a council center among Upper Towns along the Tallapoosa River, where Red Sticks resided. Towns of the Creek Confederacy shifted in importance according to their leadership and size, with newer *taliwas*, or "daughter" towns, forming when mother towns became less manageable due to growth or when, especially after the encroachment of non-Indian settlement, the economies of mother towns were no longer sustaining their people. Tallassee's daughter town Loachapoka, established along a tributary of the Tallapoosa River, became an influential Muscogee community in its own right, and it was there that the first Tulsans held their last council before removal to Indian Territory.

The Tulsa metropolitan area of today is within three tribal jurisdictions—Cherokee, Osage, and Muscogee—and the Muscogee Nation represents several communities from the Southeast that arrived in Indian Territory at different times and with different political leanings, generally but not exclusively corresponding to their affiliations with Upper or Lower Towns. Those from Loachapoka who were the first to form a town at the site of present-day Tulsa were some of the later arrivals, having remained staunchly opposed to removal. Associated with Lower Towns, McIntosh's family and followers, including enslaved African Americans, eventually settled in Indian Territory in the Three Forks area at the convergence of the Arkansas, Neosho, and Verdigris Rivers. Divisions within the Muscogee Nation over the role of enslaved citizens with African ancestry had become starker in the lead-up to removal, as Muscogee leaders were seeking to operate within the racist framework of southern states. To survive, they were desperately "elevating themselves at the expense of their black neighbors."[55] At the same time, traditionalists were protesting the presence of non-Muscogees in their communities, both African Americans and white missionaries who were preaching to them, in some cases advocating for removal.[56] These racial fault lines fractured intermarried families and contributed to conflicts with Muscogees with African ancestry that still endure.

Removal to Indian Territory had been devastating, with human, political, economic, and emotional consequences that are difficult to approximate in the hindsight of history. Sickness was a constant companion during the journey, and Muscogees already in Indian Territory remarked upon the weak appearance of the later arrivals to Fort Gibson. Of those imprisoned because of their role in the Second Creek War, nearly 15 percent died along the way.[57] The others, leaving from the five camps and transported by private contractors hired by the United States, likewise were subjected to a lack of provisions, exhaustion and sickness, bad roads, exposure to harsh weather, and dangerous crossings across rivers and rough terrain. A generally agreed upon estimate of the human toll is that half of Muscogees making the journey never reached the West.[58] Those who survived, including Afro-Muscogees, were uncertain of their future among their past enemies, the McIntosh, in Indian Territory or among those of other tribal communities, especially Osage and Cherokee, who were also adjusting to life in what would become northeastern Oklahoma. Though Muscogees who made the journey lost so many possessions, unable to transport many valuables in the first place and subjected to looting by white speculators and opportunists along the way, they retained their ceremonial life, carrying with them remnants of fires from their homelands that would be paramount to starting over. The keeping of this fire is fundamental to the story of Tulsa's founding.

Though the Loachapoka town site was destroyed in the Second Creek War, its importance as a place of council and its relationship to its mother town, Tallasi, is evident in the founding of a new town site in Indian Territory. Histories of early Tulsa by Angie Debo, Danney Goble, and David Proctor discuss the care with which Muscogees, led by Achee Yahola, founded Locvpokv near the banks of the Arkansas River (now just south of downtown Tulsa) and started a fire from the cinders they carried during their removal journey. The fire marked this location, now known as Council Oak Park, as an important site for ceremonial and civic life. In keeping with the layout of towns in their southeastern homelands, Creeks in this new community came to Locvpokv (or "Looker Poker") for gatherings while establishing sites for home and trade nearby. These site names were versions of Tallasi ("New Tulsa," "Tulsa Cedar River," "Old Tulsa," "Big Tulsa"), and eventually the area was called "Tulsey Town."[59] Finally, the name was recorded as "Tulsa" when the first post office was established in 1879.[60]

The divisions in Muscogee society in the South endured in Indian Territory; the affiliations that bound families to Upper or Lower Creeks impacted alliances with either the Union or Confederacy in the years before and after the Civil War. Poorer emigrant Muscogees remained concentrated near the confluence of the Arkansas, Neosho, and Verdigris Rivers in Indian Territory, while descendants of William McIntosh constructed southern-style plantations supported with slave labor in areas farther from tribal towns. The wealthy Muscogees conducted business with white slaveholders in Arkansas and Texas and also built wealth in trade fairs in the Comanchería.[61] Their growing facility with western trade led business in eastern Oklahoma to rival the trading hub of New Orleans. Commodities such as corn, potatoes, and rice found markets in nearby burgeoning cities, including Van Buren, Arkansas; Muscogee trade in rice was especially preferred by nearby whites to exported rice from the Crescent City. The potential for more support in the form of commodities and labor drew the attention of Union and Confederate officials to Indian Territory.[62] Mirroring laws in slaveholding southern states, the southeastern tribes with plantation cultures—Muscogee, Chickasaw, Choctaw, and Cherokee—passed slave codes that restricted the freedoms of African Americans living in Indian Territory, though these tribes retained communal landholdings beyond the plantations of individuals. Beginning in 1861, with most of the tribes, including the McIntosh, now in Indian Territory allying with the Confederacy, the Loachapokas ("Loyal Indians"), including Afro-Muscogees, sought refuge in Kansas out of a desire to remain neutral.[63] After the war ended, the Loachapokas returned to Indian Territory in 1866 and remade their community despite the tumult that their opposition to the Confederacy had caused.

In the latter years of the nineteenth century, though McIntosh and Loachapokas had a long history of opposition, they began to share the area of Tulsey town, with families becoming intermingled and with members of the Perryman family, descended from the McIntosh, becoming the most important civic leaders in early Tulsa. Lewis Perryman had established a trading post in 1846 at Thirty-Third and Rockford Avenue (now Zinc Park), and members of the Perryman family, who had lived in the Big Spring area northwest of Loachapoka, moved to Tulsa, in part to escape an epidemic of cholera.[64] As kin of the McIntosh, allies of the Confederacy who adopted the slave-based economy of southern planters, the Perrymans (though switching alliance to the Union in 1862) had amassed wealth through slave labor. The 1866 Reconstruction treaty with the United States mandated that the Muscogee Nation grant citizenship to those they had enslaved, and African Americans worked, lived, and intermarried with the family and other descendants of the McIntosh faction. Lewis had sixteen children in all, with three of his sons—George, Josiah, and Legus—becoming strong leaders of the nation. George Perryman, who signed Tulsa's first charter, married Rachel, a Lochboga, and their home on their cattle ranch at Thirty-Eighth and Trenton (now in midtown Tulsa) was the site of the first post office, where Josiah was postmaster. The Perryman Cemetery at Thirty-First and Utica Avenue is today a visible reminder of the family's residence in this area. Legus practiced law and served as chief of the Muscogee Nation, following in the footsteps of his grandfather, Benjamin Perryman. George and Rachel had many descendants, including Mose Perryman, whose homestead remains in southern Tulsa near the Arkansas River. The Perrymans rapidly expanded the cattle trade in the area, which also attracted the interest of whites, who began moving to the area as well.

Despite the prominence of the Perrymans in the city of Tulsa, Muscogee families found themselves increasingly marginalized amid the growing presence of settlers, owing to the success of the cattle industry, allotment mandated by the Dawes Commission, and the coming of the railroad to Tulsa all occurring in the 1880s. Those with African ancestry, who, in contrast to trends in the post-Reconstruction South (including the nearby Cherokee Nation), had been enjoying greater political power, access to education, and the incorporation of Freedmen towns, were now subject to regressive racial categorization with the imposition of the Dawes Allotment Act in 1887. The act, carried out by officials of the Dawes Commission in the 1890s, along with breaking up the tribes' landholding rights in favor of individual land ownership, also paved the way for a Jim Crow system that would be foundational to Oklahoma statehood in 1907.[65] Once Muscogee lands were allotted to individual families instead of being held communally, the Perrymans, a large extended family, still retained many acres. However, land remaining after allotment to Native families in Indian Territory began to be occupied by more and more non-Natives. In addition, many Muscogee families during the latter decades of the century became intermarried with whites, some of whom were opportunists who married Muscogee women to gain access to their allotments. With the Curtis Act of 1898, tribes in Indian Territory became subject to federal law, tribal courts lost their authority, and towns could be incorporated and platted by anyone.[66] Non-Natives flooded into the area as the legal framework for statehood was quickly falling into place.

Though Indian Territory was supposed to remain the domain of Native Americans, the commodification of natural resources such as coal, lead, zinc, and especially oil fueled the clamor for the territory to become a state.[67] Two oil fields were integral to the growth of Tulsa and its role in statehood. In 1901 oil was discovered in Red Fork on the allotment of the Muscogee wife of J.C.W. Bland, and soon after, the Tulsa town site was platted, entirely within the Muscogee Nation.[68] The opening of the Glenn Pool oil field in 1905, a large, underground lake of oil just ten miles south of the Bland site on the allotment of Muscogee citizen Ida Glenn (an ancestor of Joy Harjo), further accelerated the influx of settlers seeking profit on this land. Between 1900 and 1907 the population of Tulsa increased by 425 percent.[69] Tulsa became known as the "oil capital of the world," a reputation that has waned since the 1980s yet is foundational to the establishment of the state of Oklahoma in 1907. The imposition of Jim Crow laws in Oklahoma, begun in the 1890s and accelerating in the lead-up to 1907, was a cornerstone of the new state, as the first law it passed, Senate Bill One (commonly called "the Coach Law") imposed segregation of African Americans in trains and streetcars.

With the incorporation of non-Indian town sites and the establishment of a state, this area grew into a diverse, metropolitan community. Oklahoma may not be immediately recognizable to most as "Indian Country" since tribal jurisdiction elsewhere in the United States typically applies in reservations or rancherías at a distance from cities. In Oklahoma, however, cities remain on land within tribal jurisdictions. Though statehood had a devastating impact on tribes in Indian Territory, the Muscogee Nation and other tribes, especially Cherokee and Osage Nations, are nonetheless deeply involved in providing services for their citizens as well as pursuing business and cultural opportunities in Tulsa that contribute mightily to the city's and state's economy.

The Tulsa landscape, still marked by the fading glory of its heyday as the oil capital of the world, contains reminders of its origin as Tallasi and the former allotments that are the grounds for civic landmarks. These landmarks include Council Oak Tree; Josiah Perryman's post office; the Perryman Ranch, an event center still managed by Mose Perryman's descendants; the former City Hall building, built on the site of Rachel Perryman's later home; the Tullahassee Creek Indian Cemetery, final resting place of the family of the Confederate soldier Thomas Adams; Swan Lake, site of the city's first amusement park, built on the former allotment of Annie Hodge; Woodward Park, a serene location of manicured gardens in the historic district of oil mansions; and Owen Park, the first public park in the city. Woodward and Owen Parks contain monuments, similar to monuments found in New Orleans, that simultaneously acknowledge and obscure the reality of Indigenous rights to Tulsa. As Coll Thrush and Dean Rader have discussed, urban monuments depicting Native peoples are texts themselves, with messages that convey settler colonial imaginings of Indian disappearance. These signifiers are, for Thrush, ghost stories that cast Indians as passive victims of, rather than participants in, stories of urban life. Rader notes that public art with tourist purposes, often fitting an "Indian action figure" mold, captures colonial symbolic discourse about Native peoples.[70] Monuments in Tulsa follow these examples, with the caveat that in Tulsa tribal jurisdiction remains in force in these locations simultaneous with legacies of dispossession.

Woodward Park, home of the Tulsa Rose Garden, is located on the former allotment, formerly known as "Perryman's Pasture," of Hellen Woodward. Since her mother was a full-blood member of the Loachapoka community, at age fourteen Hellen received an allotment of 160 acres from the Five Civilized Tribes Indian Commission. Her white father and guardian, Herbert Woodward, sold the allotment in 1909 without Hellen's consent to the city of Tulsa, as she was a minor who was required by law to have a guardian manage her financial affairs. She lost a battle to regain her land in a 1929 court decision that set a precedent for the city's condemning land outside of the city limits for public purposes. In 1946 Hellen sold another piece of her allotment for the development of Utica Square, now Tulsa's toniest shopping center.[71] Most Tulsans have no idea that the setting of their engagement or high school yearbook photos is land transferred to the city through questionable tactics. There is a nod to this Native American presence (or absence), however, in the park. A large sculpture, *Appeal to the Great Spirit*, part of Cyrus Dallin's *The Epic of the Indian* series, faces the closest traffic light, depicting a Plains Indian on horseback with arms outstretched in prayer and braids resting on his shoulders. An Italian model posed for the project.[72]

Owen Park, just west of the city's central business district downtown, was also formed from allotments. The park's namesake, white businessman Chauncey Owen, sold the land belonging to his Muscogee wife to the city in 1909, the same year that Hellen Woodward's allotment was sold. Several monuments in Owen Park point toward differing narratives about how the story of Tulsa's origin is told. The Indian Nations Monument at the northeast corner of the park was erected by the Daughters of the American Revolution in 1935 to acknowledge the cession of Osage land mandated by the Council Grove Treaty of 1825. As a result of the treaty, the Osage Nation ceded its lands in now Missouri, Arkansas, and Oklahoma, moving to a reservation in Kansas, and provided safe passage for travelers on the Santa Fe Trail, a commercial highway between Independence, Missouri, and Santa Fe. A second key outcome for the United States was

5. *An Appeal to the Great Spirit*, Woodward Park, Tulsa. Photo by the author.

that this cession would provide land in Indian Territory for Muscogee and Cherokee citizens who were being forced to relocate from the Southeast under various treaty agreements beginning in the 1820s and heightened with the passage of the Indian Removal Act of 1830. Owen Park sits at the intersection, in history and geography, of these overlapping tribal jurisdictions. The monument's inscription reads: "On June 2, 1825, the Osage

Nation, under treaty with the United States, granted certain lands to the Government for the use and benefit of the Cherokee and Creek tribes who were being removed from the Southern States. This monument is to commemorate that treaty and to mark that spot where lands of the three great nations joined."

At first glance this monument is a tribute to these three nations. This language, however, glosses over the conflict that this agreement caused between Osage people and Cherokees especially, since later, under the Drum Creek Treaty of 1868, the Osage Nation would return to the area that had been transferred to Cherokees, leaving both nations with smaller landholdings. Further, nowhere acknowledged in this language is the reality of the primary role of the United States in these large-scale and devastating land cessions. Did these three nations passively trade these lands with the idea that they would one day have a picnic in a park together? Not to be left out, in 1950 the Tulsa Association of Pioneers installed a monument with the inscription "in honor of the charter members of the association living in Tulsa, Indian Territory and vicinity for thirty years from 1881 to 1921 and other pioneer families." In 1976 the board and batten home of Reverend Sylvester Morris, a Methodist missionary to tribes in Indian Territory, was relocated to the park and restored as "Tulsa's Oldest Surviving House." The space of Owen Park, then, has become a script for telling stories about passive Indian dispossession and, apparently, passive pioneering. It is telling that these monuments are also located in parks, bringing together Thrush's Indian ghost stories with Lefebvre's critique of monuments as ideologies that colonize space and fetishize the nature they destroy. Despite the acknowledgment through these monuments of the site as a repository of Tulsa history, these historical markers in fact reveal little about the history of this land.

Of late, attention to the ways Tulsa attends to—and disappears—its history has focused on the Greenwood District because of the centennial of the 1921 Tulsa Race Massacre. In the early twentieth century, Greenwood became a thriving African American community with national notoriety because of historical circumstances unique to Oklahoma. The state's African American population was comprised of both descendants of relocated southeastern tribes and settlers attracted by the call of boosters, led by Kansas native Edwin McCabe, who promised cheap land and freedom

6. *Indian Memorial*, Owen Park, Tulsa. Photo by the author.

from racial discrimination, even campaigning for the establishment of an all-Black state.[73] As whites clamoring for statehood poured into the state and the institution of segregation solidified long-standing racial divisions, Oklahoma's African Americans, who had been actively participating in the varied industries of the state's economy, such as cattle and oil, now found themselves walled off from white markets. Segregation created a need for an insular, African American–serving economy, which in Tulsa became concentrated in the Greenwood District, or "Black Wall Street."

Tulsa's Black Wall Street attracted the attention of African American celebrities and political leaders from across the country, notably Booker T. Washington, because of its Black wealth and its representation of the entrepreneurial spirit that seemed to promise racial progress. Its location also contributed to its growth, as Black business leaders such as Sam and Lucy Mackey bought homes that had passed into African American hands through purchases from the Cherokee Nation, which shares with Muscogee Nation a jurisdictional boundary that bisects Greenwood. According to scholar and writer Hannibal Johnson, the neighborhood became a hub of Kansas City jazz, with musicians such as Earl Bostic and Jimmy Rushing, Charlie Parker and Charlie Christian, honing their craft in the nightclubs there: "Nowhere were the hypnotic rhythms of African American life in Oklahoma expressed more poignantly. . . . guitar licks and saxophone wails filled the streets. Pulsating rhythms wafted through the air from open windows and doorways. . . . Electric and eclectic—that was Greenwood."[74] Similar to jazz performance birthed at Congo Square, Greenwood was a space of cultural coalescence and creativity galvanized by its location in an Indigenous city.

African Americans across the country were not the only ones noticing this remarkable Black business district, complete with jazz clubs, a movie theater, grocery store, and emerging professional class of attorneys, doctors, and real estate brokers. More and more prominent members of Tulsa's white community were accelerating Ku Klux Klan activity at the same time that African Americans, motivated by their service in World War I, were rejecting white supremacy outright. In 1921, corresponding to an unprecedented national uptick in lynching, Tulsa was becoming a terrifying place, with scant law enforcement. Rumors of an alleged assault on a white girl, Sarah Page, by a shoe shiner, Dick Rowland, sparked violence. Though Sarah Page retreated from her accusation of assault, it was too late. With a sensationalized account of the incident published in the *Tulsa Tribune* on 31 May 1921, a lynch mob began assembling. Ultimately, approximately fifteen thousand armed whites amassed and directed their ire at Greenwood, killing African Americans in the streets, setting their

7. Greenwood Avenue, Tulsa. Photo by the author.

homes and businesses ablaze. A generally accepted estimate of the number of African Americans murdered is three hundred, though a concerted effort to hide documentation of the massacre by local media at the time makes that count unreliable.[75]

Black Tulsans were determined to rebuild and had success, though the Urban Renewal Programs and construction of a major interstate in the neighborhood in the 1950s and 1960s stunted Greenwood's rejuvenation. At present, the result of efforts by the 2021 Centennial Commission, nonprofits, philanthropic organizations, and local politicians and activists, a multitude of new development projects commemorate 1921 with the intent to foster economic prosperity in North Tulsa. Along with this flurry of activity, however, comes concern about how the story of this neighborhood will be told and who will benefit from its telling. Adjacent to the redevelopment of Black Wall Street, the Tulsa Arts District is big money. As is the case in many cities, local leaders are banking on the renovation of abandoned warehouses, construction of new galleries and museums, and the appearance of yoga studios, breweries, and coffee shops to lure new hip residents to downtown. The Tulsa Artist Fellowship is creating an arts colony in the entertainment district. These investments demonstrate what Soja describes in his more recent works as typical of the ways cities now structure regions that extend far from the urban core, leading to downtown instability and the use of public funds not for social needs but for tourism and private investment.

As construction projects abound downtown, some businesses within the Greenwood District are branding themselves as being within the Tulsa Artist District instead, which is visible evidence, in the view of local activists, that gentrification is threatening the preservation of Tulsa's Black history. As part of the Vision 2025 economic development package approved by voters in 2003, plaques to commemorate businesses lost in the massacre were funded and installed throughout Greenwood. But in 2019 a local advocate for Greenwood, Orisabiyi (Kristi) Williams, noticed that several of the commemorative plaques were missing from the neighborhood. Upon reaching out to the city of Tulsa, Williams learned that the Ross Group, a construction firm spearheading the downtown's redevelopment, had removed and was storing the plaques during construction. Combined with the Tulsa Arts District branding, Williams concludes that these projects have "usurped three blocks of Greenwood." Commenting on the Ross Group's actions, she asks, "This is sacred land, historic sacred land . . . and this is what we do with it?"[76]

This sentiment, that Greenwood is "sacred land," is repeated often among those with an interest in seeing Black Wall Street return to its success as a mecca of Black prosperity while also honoring those who were lost to and those who survived Tulsa's most harrowing night of racial terror. In Tulsa the words *sacred land* resonate strongly with Indigenous peoples, especially Osage, Cherokee, and Muscogee, who share the experience of being racially profiled, terrorized, and disenfranchised in the city they built alongside African Americans. As institutions now embark on a long-overdue reckoning with their complicity in America's racist past, drafting land acknowledgments, developing diversity plans, and marketing solidarity, Indigenous land acknowledgments are au courant. On Greenwood Avenue, however, rattling off a one-dimensional reminder at the start of a conference or business meeting that "we are on Muscogee land," without acknowledging the promise and pain of Black Wall Street, feels offensive.

The act of commemoration, whether in the material form of a park monument or in the practice of land acknowledgment time and time again becomes a kind of ideology subject to forms of erasure that accompany urban development. Though greater attention to the original peoples of the land on which we reside is a positive step, short statements (not unlike monuments) from institutions that are in many ways disappearing those peoples through gentrification and a failure to commit to true changes are simply symbolic. In the case of Black Wall Street, commemoration and acknowledgment expose already existing tensions between Natives and African Americans. Afro-Muscogees and other descendants of the Freedmen, who were instrumental in the prosperity of Greenwood, have been repeatedly disenfranchised from their rights as tribal citizens. At the same time, conversations about Black Wall Street as African American land conflict with understandings of Tulsa as Indian Country and under tribal jurisdiction. The need for healing in this community is palpable, and though the creative arts sometimes carry the trappings of tourism and investment, they are also the means for many Indigenous and African American Tulsans to claim their rights to the city.

The "City Different" . . . and a Missing Foot

Like New Orleans and Tulsa, Santa Fe is an artistic hub. As Louisiana's history encapsulates the colonial histories in the South and East that undergird Native stories in Oklahoma and Oklahoma's history informs creative expressions of traumatic migration and resettlement, New Mexico's history exposes pressures and realities that have shaped the stories of Indigenous creatives in the latter part of the nineteenth century and beyond, as America formed as a capitalist nation-state spanning the continent. New Mexico, and in turn Santa Fe, departs from typical frameworks of urban Indigeneity in several ways that necessitate new approaches to diverse urban Indigenous experiences. Myla Carpio, in her study of Indigenous Albuquerque, asserts that early scholarly contributions to this area identified a post–World War II timeline of Indian urbanization to the neglect of longer urban histories, which in turn limited these contributions to the problems Native Americans have had adjusting to modern American cities.[77] Other historians emphasize the distinct relations between Spanish colonizers and Natives, particularly the drive of religious conversion, that contribute to New Mexico's difference from other western states. They point out the significance of Pueblo communities, early New Mexican cities, that complicated typical approaches to frontier "settlement." In providing an overview of Santa Fe's development as a significant urban homeland for many Oklahomans, I highlight connections not only between New Mexico and Oklahoma but also between Santa Fe and New Orleans, noting the regional dynamics of colonial occupation, Indigenous resistance, and urban creativity that distinguish the writing of urban Natives from Oklahoma.

As it had in the East, France eagerly pursued expansion of its empire in the land that would become New Mexico, but Spanish influence is fundamental to understanding the unique meeting of cultures of this area. The figure of Juan de Oñate looms large in accounts of the colonization of New Mexico, including the establishment of Santa Fe, with his status for some as "founder of New Mexico" continually contested. Following Spanish rule, Mexico held power from 1822 to 1846, when the United States cemented its authority over the area with the Treaty of Guadalupe Hidalgo. Adam Hodge, Ned Blackhawk, and James Brooks have asserted the primacy of violence in these periods—especially in the form of slavery and captivity that both Indigenous and European peoples participated in—that have marked the conquest of the Southwest, challenging one-directional, triumphalist fantasies of European strength. Oñate's accomplishments for the Spanish Empire, according to Joseph Sanchez, Robert Spude, and Art Gomez, changed the course of New Mexican history, especially the significance of Santa Fe, forever, and an onslaught of rituals of violence, cloaked under the guise of "progress," defined these actions. Under Oñate's governorship, the Camino Real de Tierra Adentro, which up to that point followed several existing trails, was further defined and shaped into a major thoroughfare for travel and commerce between Mexico City and points north. Oñate named Santa Fe as an outpost in 1605 and paved the way for its establishment as the terminus of the trail and the capital of New Mexico in 1610.[78] Though soon after Oñate resigned the governorship, his aggressive actions are generally noted as primary to New Mexico's growth into a viable colony for Spain.

Following Oñate's governorship, the Santa Fe province was key to the accelerating Spanish campaign to missionize Pueblo peoples; it was also a site of Indigenous resistance in the form of the Pueblo Revolt of 1680. Santa Fe was the only Spanish town in the area at this time, the residence of nearly fifteen hundred settlers in haciendas and ranches, and more settlers were invading the larger valley and encroaching on Pueblo communities.[79] Under the governorship of Pedro de Peralta, the Spanish population became concentrated in Santa Fe, and Pueblo peoples were pressured to live in fewer and larger towns. The colony required tribute and forced labor from Indigenous citizens under the *encomienda* system, and Pueblo forms of worship were banned, with missionaries desecrating sacred objects and torturing and executing medicine people. Popé, a medicine man of the Ohkay Owingeh Pueblo (then called the San Juan Pueblo) who had been imprisoned in 1675, led an army of Pueblos of many different tribes against the colonists in August 1680. The Pueblos successfully drove the Spanish and other non-Pueblos out of Santa Fe, killing several hundred (including twenty-one priests) and destroying Catholic symbols and structures.[80] For the following twelve years, the Pueblos were free of Spanish rule, and though it was a brief period of independence in the colonial era, this disruption of Spanish designs on northern New Mexico made a lasting impact. Spain had never lost a province to Indigenous people before, and the viability of Pueblo sovereignty in the face of European colonial might was evident. Though Pueblo peoples had developed strong ties to some settlers through intermarriage, the success of the Pueblo Revolt sent a powerful message.[81]

Spain's campaign to retake Santa Fe laid the groundwork for later colonial incursions into New Mexico, culminating in New Mexico's establishment as a U.S. state. In 1692 Diego de Vargas, who had been appointed governor of New Mexico, began a concerted effort to control Santa Fe with the aid of hundreds of settlers based in El Paso, Texas. Indigenous inhabitants of Santa Fe resisted strongly, though weakened by prolonged drought, and Vargas enacted an aggressive assault on the town, executing many of the resisters and declaring victory for Spain by the following year.[82] In the ensuing decades, the competition between Spain and France for influence in the "New World" affected northern New Mexico as it did Louisiana. Interest in the promise of Santa Fe for trade and colonial strategizing increased, with the French becoming bolder in their actions to connect northern New Mexico to their settlements in Louisiana, regardless of Spanish resistance or fears of travel across the southern plains (including Indian Territory).

In 1739 the Mallet brothers reached Santa Fe and Taos, proving the feasibility of European travel between the two regions and piquing French enthusiasm for trade in the area. Additional French trading parties, which were not well received by Spanish officials, visited in the next few years, but as the French and Indian War accelerated, French-Spanish relations changed in the face of conflict with Britain. Defeated, in 1763, France transferred ownership of Louisiana to Spain, though French traders continued to explore new (to them) routes between East and West. Notable figures were Pierre (Pedro) Vial, who identified trails from Texas to Santa Fe and Santa Fe to St. Louis, and Francisco Fragoso, who followed a route between Santa Fe and New Orleans via Texas. These trails, along with Indigenous trade routes supporting the Comanchería's exchange economy, were small steps leading to the major transformation in trade that occurred in the nineteenth century.

As was the case in Louisiana, the growth of the United States became a significant factor in changing relationships between France and Spain and in Santa Fe's role in trade, migration, and travel between Louisiana and New Mexico that crossed Indian Territory. These growing links across regions not only expanded commerce, however: they also introduced smallpox. Adam Hodge traces the smallpox strain(s) that proliferated in the Southwest to New Orleans and subsequently Mexico City.[83] The spread of disease surely factored in to a realignment of imperial influence. On the heels of a period of drought, the powerful Comanches were newly pressured and more vulnerable in the 1780s, with demand for horses and bison products ever-expanding among other tribes, New Mexicans, Texans, and Anglo-

American traders.[84] To Spain's surprise, France signed over Louisiana to the United States with the Louisiana Purchase in 1803 and heightened Spanish anxieties about defining the western border of the United States; more and more Anglo-American settlers were making their way to New Mexico under the impression that Santa Fe was within U.S. boundaries. Mexican revolutionaries saw their cause gain ground, culminating in Mexican independence in 1821. A roughly twenty-five-year period of Mexican governance of Santa Fe followed, in which Mexico recognized Pueblo property rights, driven by the promise of Tresgarantias (three guarantees): religion, union, and independence. The Santa Fe Plaza became a site for commemorating and dramatizing the relationships between Pueblos, settlers, and conquerors, with pageantry tied to political pronouncements.

As European influence receded, both Mexico and the United States rapidly expanded trade and travel into Santa Fe, which accelerated the transformation of Indian Territory away from the no-man's-land it had been perceived to be and strengthened U.S. resolve to make New Mexico its own state. In 1821 William Becknell headed a party of traders and their merchandise along the trail between the Missouri Valley and Santa Fe, opening the door to new waves of traffic and notoriety for what became known as the Santa Fe Trail.[85] With James Polk's ascendancy to the U.S. presidency on a Jacksonian platform in 1845, Americans were emboldened in their interests to head west and seek new wealth through land and resources. Rebuffed in his offer to purchase lands in the Southwest from Mexico, Polk began a military campaign to invade areas that had been understood to be within Mexican boundaries, marking the beginning of the Mexican-American War in 1846. An Army of the West, under Stephen Kearny, was dispatched to occupy New Mexico that year and claimed victory without a shot fired. As others had done, Kearny stood at the Plaza and promised a bright future under his leadership, in which property and religion would be respected.[86] New Mexicans were understandably skeptical. Phillip B. Gonzales documents ways that in the lead-up to annexation, Nuevomexicanos, or Hispanos, were increasingly aware of their place in the coming racial hierarchy—below Euroamerican settlers and above Native Americans and African Americans—under the imperial order of the United States.[87] Gonzales argues that Nuevomexicano elites sought to leverage a role in the political order even as they found the growing commercialization and Americanization of northern New Mexico distasteful. In 1848, with the signing of the Treaty of the Guadalupe Hidalgo ending the Mexican-American War, most of the Southwest—large areas of Arizona, California, Colorado, Kansas, Nevada, New Mexico, Texas, Utah, Wyoming, and Indian Territory—became the United States.

Santa Fe boomed in population and evolved culturally. The capital Santa Fe became army headquarters, with Taos continuing as an important commercial center. New modes of communication, transit, and military investment brought more Americans to New Mexico with the might of the United States backing them. In the Red River War of 1874, tribes of the southern plains—mainly Cheyenne, Comanche, and Kiowa—who were labeled as "hostiles" were defeated and forced to submit fully to reservations, opening eastern New Mexico and the Texas Panhandle to settler occupation.[88] Pueblos found American rule to be no less considerate of their status as nations, in keeping with similar patterns in the South. The Butterfield Overland Mail route was, by 1858, connecting St. Louis to San Francisco, with a network of outposts that led through southeastern Oklahoma and across Texas and New Mexico. With the coming of the railroad in 1878, waves of homesteaders came across Oklahoma and Texas, bringing "strong views on prohibition, a fundamentalist religion, and a tradition of populist dissent."[89] African Americans also sought a new life in New Mexico at this time, yet they were met with competition from Mexican laborers for jobs as well as segregationist and exclusionary laws that southern newcomers imposed. James Brooks's *Captives and Cousins* (2002) details how the slavery system, or captive exchange, of the Southwest borderlands was kin embedded, different from the chattel slavery of the American South. But with the growing power of Anglo-Americans in the area in the mid-nineteenth century, similar racist laws were passed, including laws excluding free African Americans from the territory and forbidding interracial marriage with white women. By statehood in 1912, New Mexico was shaping up to be culturally connected to the rest of the nation, deeply impacted by similar events and attitudes that shaped the histories of Louisiana and Oklahoma.

Santa Fe was now fully accessible and marketable as a destination to Americans interested in the state of New Mexico, now promoted as a "Land of Enchantment." Carpio draws a distinction between urban histories of

New Mexico and Indigenous life elsewhere. Urban Indian life has thus far been studied mainly as a contemporary phenomenon of gathering people of many tribes together to form new communities in places where Native people have long been (presumably) vanquished. Yet in the history of Santa Fe, it is people not Indigenous to the area who have found themselves wrestling with their own identities as newcomers and continually cobbling together new communities in the face of strong Indigenous resistance. The mix of cultures in New Mexico has prompted references to it as "the tricultural state," a nod to its Indigenous, Spanish, and Anglo cultures (notably leaving out African Americans) that glosses over the contested histories that formed relationships among those cultures. The most poignant example of this conflicting perception of New Mexican history concerns the recognition of Oñate as founder of New Mexico, a man admired especially by those with Spanish ancestry.[90] Pueblo people, of course, view Oñate as a symbol of Spanish colonization, and many still perform dances and ceremonies that honor the warriors of the Pueblo Revolt. In 1998, when New Mexico commemorated its four hundredth anniversary, a statue of Oñate was erected north of Española, not far from the Ohkay Owingeh Pueblo, the ancestral home of Popé. An unknown person cut off the statue's foot, symbolizing a rejection of his position in settler collective memory. In 2020, in the wake of worldwide protests of the killing of George Floyd, the Oñate statue was removed and placed in storage.

As in New Orleans and Tulsa, Indigenous cultures have become central to the marketing of New Mexico as a tourist destination, following hundreds of years of colonization of Indigenous lands and communities. In Santa Fe the early twentieth century saw intentional campaigns and regulations to construct buildings in Spanish colonial and pueblo design (however loosely interpreted), while Indian material culture was being commodified and sold, often dictated in its aesthetics by non-Indian civic and railroad boosters.[91] The railroad was instrumental in fostering the growing artist colonies in Santa Fe and Taos, which were comprised mostly of individuals from back East who were attracted to the inexpensive cost of living, stunning landscape, and a perceived "authentic" Old West of Hispanic and Indian influences that appeared to be rapidly fading. Journalist Charles Lummis, who traveled the American Southwest advocating for historic preservation and critiquing U.S. Indian policy, coined the phrase "See America First," which the Santa Fe Railroad adopted to promote (somewhat ironically) further settlement in the area. With the construction of the Route 66 highway in 1926 (later realigned and paved as a Works Progress Administration project in the 1930s), New Mexico was on the path of hundreds of thousands of migrants making their way to California from Dust Bowl communities, notably Oklahoma. These travelers left their cultural imprint along the way, strengthening cultural ties between New Mexico and the southern plains. Some never made it to their final destination and instead chose to make a new life in New Mexico and other southwestern states.

As New Mexico was newly on the radar as a destination, the promotional campaigns of boosters and the realities of the impact of settler colonialism were intertwined, if not fully acknowledged, in Santa Fe and Taos. Most writers who headed west enjoyed the patronage of Mabel Dodge Luhan, a social networker and literary salon host who wrote to her friends in the East of the opportunities out west. Mary Austin, D. H. Lawrence, and Willa Cather all headed to New Mexico, where they found inspiration for their literary representations of the Southwest as key to the soul of America. Like Lummis, writers and artists, whose residency in northern New Mexico drew them near to Pueblos, became sympathetic to the struggles of Indigenous New Mexicans in the face of U.S. assimilationist policies and the rapid growth of the settler population. They used their creative expression and privilege among the literary and artistic intelligentsia to protest policies of the Bureau of Indian Affairs, not fully aware of their own blind spots regarding Indigenous experiences. In 1922 the New Mexico Association on Indian Arts (now the SWAIA) was founded, which hosted the annual Santa Fe Indian Market to preserve Indigenous arts and crafts, a market that to this day brings in millions of tourist dollars to the local economy.

The Santa Fe Indian School (SFIS) also contributed to this growing arts focus in the city and spurred the careers of many Native American artists and writers from Oklahoma, from Allan Houser to Joy Harjo. Founded in 1890 as a relatively typical Indian boarding school, SFIS followed the example of the Carlisle Indian School in Pennsylvania, with the goal of assimilating Pueblo children into non-Native society. But on the heels of reforms backed in the 1930s by John Collier, the school developed a strong focus on the preservation of Indian arts and crafts, coinciding with the broader commercial promotion of arts and writer colonies. It was a

8. Indian Market, Santa Fe. Photo by the author.

particular kind of art that was emphasized: so-called traditional Indian painting taught by the non-Indian teacher Dorothy Dunn. Dunn emphasized to students the importance of the commercial success of their work within the non-Indian marketplace and urged her charges to represent images of Indian life that would appear untainted by western influence. The conventions of this style were themselves invented, but nevertheless this method proved successful for painters known as the Kiowa Five (Six) of Oklahoma and the San Ildefonso School, though some students, such as Allan Houser, bristled at the rigidity of the form.

SFIS was closed and merged with the Albuquerque Indian School in 1962 to make way for the Institute for American Indian Arts (IAIA), a move that was not supported by some Pueblo leaders who wished to maintain a vocational school in Santa Fe.[92] IAIA's cofounders were George Boyce, longtime BIA school administrator, and Lloyd Kiva New, a Cherokee fashion designer from Fairland, Oklahoma. While the IAIA is now a tribal college with a flourishing arts and creative writing program, it began as a project of the Eisenhower and Kennedy administrations that was aligned with the goals of termination in the 1950s and 1960s. As Joy Gritton reveals in her history of the IAIA, "The institute's curriculum stressed those aspects of art education that administrators felt would ease the transition to an assimilated lifestyle and insure commercial success in the non-Indian art market." Further, George Boyce, the school's director, Gritton notes, "paid close attention to the students' physical environment and ordered nonstandard BIA furnishings and foods for the institute's living quarters in order that students cultivate needs and tastes that would later translate into their adoption of American consumerist habits."[93] This philosophy of education coincided with the establishment of Santa Fe Indian Market in 1922 in order to promote craft production as a means for Indians to find employment, achieve a greater sense of self-esteem, and enact cultural preservation of traditional items, the meaning of *traditional*, of course, resonating with non-Native ideas of Indian authenticity. IAIA is now a major force in cultivating and supporting Native aesthetics on a world stage, having hosted Houser as a faculty member for thirteen years and counting among its ranks others with Oklahoma ties, such as Tommy Orange (Cheyenne Arapaho), Eddie Chuculate (Creek), Richard Ray Whitman (Yuchi-Muscogee), Brandon Hobson (Cherokee), Anita Fields (Osage-Muscogee), and Jennifer Foerster (Muscogee).

Much like Congo Square in New Orleans or the Tulsa Arts and Greenwood Districts in Tulsa, Santa Fe's Plaza District is littered with images and monuments that capitalize on its mythic associations with Native Americans while at the same time reinforcing a one-sided telling of its problematic history. A primitivist aesthetic, informed by tourist expectations, has long cast a shadow over Santa Fe's arts and literary scene while also stirring critique and responsive work from Native artists, writers, and intellectuals. Dean Rader's *Engaged Resistance* (2011) explains that Santa Fe's statues and sculptures are "part and parcel of the argument Santa Fe makes about itself."[94] He identifies a stereotypical action figure image of Natives—as warrior, savage, and prototype of (bare-chested) physical beauty—in these sculptures that stirs non-Indian nostalgia, the "absent presence" that Carpio also describes. Leah Dilworth's *Imagining Indians in the Southwest* (1996) calls the Southwest an "American Orient," with Native Americans "central to these imaginings."[95] Sylvia Rodriguez describes the process of mystification as foundational to the Taos–Santa Fe art colony, "a cultural process which perpetuates the social order by suffusing it with a shared sense of awesome, transcendent meaning."[96] Chris Wilson argues that mythmaking is fundamental to Santa Fe's culture in both positive and negative ways; while the myth is made up, it has also "fostered one of the most active art and myth-making centers in the United States."[97] He points toward pageants as exemplifying this duality. The tourist image of romantic adobe villages has been continually on display through stylized performances designed for entertainment over cultural preservation. Molly Mullin, in her study of influential Bryn Mawr women in *Culture in the Marketplace* (2001), makes clear that while white women such as Mary Austin were in some ways championing more appreciation of Native culture during their residence in Santa Fe, their interest in Indians was intertwined with enthusiasm for anthropology, shopping, and real estate and did not lead to more enlightened thinking regarding race and culture.[98] All of these studies of the contradictions and possibilities of Santa Fe art tourism demonstrate the larger history of American colonialism, wherein "exploration," trade, and national expansion endure in commercial and cultural enterprises.

It would be a mistake to assume that the relationships between tourists, dealers, and patrons is entirely one-directional, however. Much of the critique of Santa Fe's idea of itself focuses on representation, but it is important also to recognize the social order and interactions that occur through artistic patronage and commerce. Based on fieldwork in Santa Fe, Deirdre Evans-Pritchard concludes that Native artists affiliated with Indian Market generally want to be recognized as artists, not cultural representatives, though some will "respond to tourists' needs for cultural significance by telling them just what they want to hear."[99] Karl Hoerig points out that Indigenous peoples' participation in exchanges with tourists is not necessarily a loss of agency: "Not only do cultural performances in touristic settings have meaning and authenticity for those who perform them, but engaging in the business of tourism is also real and authentic

9. Palace of the Governors, Santa Fe Plaza. Photo by the author.

experience for indigenous people." With social forces at work that are similar to the context of masking traditions in New Orleans, Native performers may engage tourism with purposes that are not always apparent to non-Indian visitors. Evans-Pritchard notes that some Pueblo dances are a form of clowning and burlesque. These performative talk-backs "serve to reaffirm community values" for tourists who, in their search for an "authentic" Indian experience, display sometimes inappropriate behavior.[100] Jill Sweet also emphasizes that burlesque is important for meaning making when Pueblo dancers are confronted with tourists; these expressions are "a means to incorporate those others and to define themselves in contrast to those others."[101] Whether selling products in chamber of commerce–sanctioned venues or providing seasonal entertainment for tourists on holiday, Indigenous creatives, including many from Oklahoma, respond to and reframe the myth of Santa Fe in ways that are significant for their communities.

Histories and ideologies of New Orleans, Tulsa, and Santa Fe share critical threads that inform urban literature by Native American Oklahomans. First, Indigenous peoples, including ancestors of those now in Oklahoma, were foundational to the early histories of these cities and major contributors to their economic, cultural, and political activities, at the same time that they were connected to the homelands of their ancestors, though these homelands are often framed as inherently rural. Second, in circumstances such as relations between interconnected Muscogee towns or the large-scale international trade of the Comanchería, we can expand notions of "the urban" beyond its important but limiting associations with the built environment and the contemporary era. Third, these histories make clear the connections across regions and spaces—in this case, the South and West—that have informed the experiences of Native Americans, giving relevance to studies of the Native diaspora that are not only contemporary flows of Indigenous peoples from rural locations to postindustrial cities. While still recognizable as nations, albeit at times reorganizing and reforming, and often without the privilege of choice in these patterns of migration, Native Americans in Oklahoma have long participated in cosmopolitanism and the situations of change and crises that characterize modernity. Finally, Native Americans are essential to the histories of arts and culture in these cities, in hospitality markets and trade, crafting of material goods, participation in ceremonies, and presence in places that would eventually become destinations for tourists even as settlers glossed over their presence. In the chapters that follow, I highlight ways that Native American writers reclaim these spaces.

2

WHERE IT ALL STARTED

Native American Literatures and the City of New Orleans

For challenging usual paradigms of Native American urbanization, New Orleans, Louisiana (NOLA), is a useful staging ground. Indigenes' experiences in a "modern" (understood to be urban) world are oft-repeated subjects of inquiry and interpretation across disciplines. But as Henri Lefebvre suggests, "modernism" is less useful as a framework for critique than engagement with "modernity." Scholarly occupation with modernism (and Natives' relative fit with or access to it) reveals more about illusive "triumphalist images and projections of self" than about Natives' engagement with modernity. Modernity suggests reflection: "We contact it in a series of texts and documents which bear the mark of their era and yet go beyond the provocation of fashion and simulation of novelty. . . . We owe the concept of modernity to the contributions of people who have tried to explore these crises and confusions."[1] Native American writers' representations of New Orleans do not offer images of the city simply in service to a modern aesthetic (an aesthetic that, of course, is imbued with all sorts of colonial implications). Instead, New Orleans is a place for deeper reflection on tribes' foundational yet largely untold historical, economic, and cultural legacies in the area. For LeAnne Howe, Joy Harjo, and Sterlin Harjo, New Orleans also informs narratives of dynamic Native life in Oklahoma. This chapter presents analysis of writing and film by these writers to reveal the historical and cultural bonds between New Orleans and Indian Territory (now-Oklahoma) that speak both to the American campaign to disappear Indigenous nations and the participation of Native peoples, including Choctaw and Muscogee, in the growth of cosmopolitan cities from their earliest days.

"Choctalking" on NOLA

I have traced ways that Native Americans have shaped New Orleans and have figured into the city's role in the region, nation, and world at the same time that the city's markers and performances of its history de-emphasize these contributions. In the face of this contradiction, Choctaw writer LeAnne Howe makes her community visible, articulating a history that is not recognized in settler histories and creating her own markers of important Choctaw sites, even when those sites are geographically distant from Choctaw homelands in Oklahoma. Connecting New Orleans and later Choctaw homelands, Howe shows ways that urban life may structure Indigenous lives and contribute broadly to a spatial understanding of human relationships to their surroundings. In addition, Howe's impulse to create with this knowledge is an enactment of a right to the city and its cultural life. In her explanation of "creating kin," Howe expresses cosmopolitanism as relatedness across difference and upends linear time in favor of this relatedness across the cosmos.

In the prologue to her 2013 collection of essays, *Choctalking on Other Realities*, Howe explains the process of creation as holistic and collective, naming it "tribalography." She explains: "My obligation is that I must learn more about my ancestors and myself in order to create. Then I must render all our collective experiences into a meaningful form. I call this process 'tribalography.' Whether it is fiction, poetry, a play, or history, American Indian writers and storytellers create tribalography to inform ourselves and the non-Indian world about who we are." Howe's accomplishments as a writer and filmmaker who gives voice to the experiences of Choctaw people are well recognized. I want to emphasize the diverse geographies that she draws into Choctaw—and American—worldviews. Howe explains that her writerly inspiration arose from her "hung[er] for urban stories about Southeastern Indians," and thus, though New Orleans for the most part renders Choctaws invisible, Howe's tribalography foregrounds Choctaw storytelling, especially accounts of women's power in the city's origin.[2]

Howe creates a reformed American origin story in her essay "The Story of America: A Tribalography." She begins the piece with the statement, "America is a tribal creation story, a tribalography." She goes on, "It is with absolute certainty that I tell you now—our stories also created the immigrants who landed on our shores." She asserts that the ability of immigrants to identify themselves as Americans arose from tribal stories about how to unify amid difference, to create connections, and to make consensus. She calls this a lesson in "creating kin" and a story that thus created America, including Natives and non-Natives. Howe describes this origin story as a useful framework for revisiting histories that so often relegate Natives to the margins. One such history, that of the deerskin trade, is critical to the formation of New Orleans. As Howe explains: "When all the tribes in the Southeast began to hunt deer to near extinction in the eighteenth century, a relationship evolved between Indian hunter, deer, and foreigner. . . . This does not mean that all sides are equal, but rather all sides have agency and are networking." Evidence of this agency is present in the untold stories of Choctaw women that reference both oral literature and written historical documents.[3]

Howe's tribalography has made a strong impact on Native American studies, as it provides a subversive language for acknowledging yet recasting settler colonial dominance in Choctaw—and American—history and culture. Dean Rader's foreword to the *Choctalking* volume calls tribalography "the most significant theory of American Indigenous writing to emerge in the last 20 years—maybe ever."[4] Joseph Bauerkemper likewise praises Howe's model: "Tribalography critiques settler colonialism without being circumscribed by it. . . . Tribalography imagines and remembers otherwise, moving beyond mere critique to underscore and to creatively fuel the ongoing transformations constitutive of the process of decolonization."[5] Jodi Byrd places Howe's tribalography alongside Jean O'Brien's and Philip Deloria's critiques of U.S. mythmaking, asserting, "The notion of tribalography becomes not just a method, but a powerful theoretical tool in reading counter against the stories the United States likes to tell about itself and others."[6] Byrd emphasizes that tribalography is centered in Chickasaw and Choctaw cultures but has global relevance, as she finds Howe's concept useful for navigating the persistence of colonial culture in social media networks. Thus, tribalography is a way for Howe to describe her creative process at the same time that it has an ontological dimension for theorists and scholars like her.

Howe's contribution to urban Indigenous studies is evident in tribalography, especially her rendering of New Orleans. Howe's characters are cosmopolitan, with powers of negotiation, or creating kin, across generations, geographies, and Choctaw and non-Choctaw populations. Dean Rader has argued that Howe's intervention into literary discourse successfully bridges tension in the field of Native American studies between nationalist and cosmopolitan impulses. In addition, Howe's writings mostly circumvent discourse of urban relocation, since the Choctaw story of New Orleans is the city's origin story, not a development of the contemporary era. As a result, similar to Edward Soja's argument about the causal and regional force of cities, a divide between rural and urban homelands is inaccurate. Alternatively, Howe presents a fluid relationship between the city, mounds and towns in the Southeast, and Choctaw towns in Oklahoma. In *Earthworks Rising* (2022) Chadwick Allen notes that Howe is determined to show in her writing ways that Choctaws return continually to southeastern homelands, physically, intellectually, and imaginatively.[7] Though she draws on historical accounts to tell the history of Choctaw New Orleans, Howe demonstrates creative encounters with the geography of the city itself. In a spatial dimension of tribalography, she refigures monuments of colonial erasure and foregrounds Choctaw participation in the production of urban space.

In *Shell Shaker* (2001), Howe's first novel, generations of Choctaw women in the eighteenth and twentieth centuries must enact strong leadership within their communities to thwart the treacherous actions of corrupt male authority figures. These women are expert negotiators and strategists, and they are linked to the legacies of French individuals who are credited with the founding of New Orleans. The icon of female power in the eighteenth-century portion of the novel is Shakbatina, a shell shaker who sacrifices herself for her people. She has an important role as a storyteller; she begins the novel with a recounting of the story of the *Inholahta*, the Choctaw peacemakers. She also cultivates healing plants and salt to drive a successful trading enterprise along the river.[8] In the modern-day passages of the novel, a trio of sisters must channel the spirit of Shakbatina to save the tribe from a Choctaw casino magnate with mob ties; of particular interest to this study is Adair, a woman who has had a successful career as a broker in New Orleans. Shakbatina and Adair may be understood to be arbiters who create kin in their respective times, taking action to save their worlds.

In a nod to *Moby Dick*'s Ishmael, Howe introduces her heroine Shakbatina as a consummate storyteller. Shakbatina begins her creation story by naming herself in Choctaw words, translated to English as "Call me Shakbatina, a Shell Shaker." She is also an authority figure because, as is appropriate for a Choctaw citizen of a matrilineal society, she documents her descent from Grandmother, the first Choctaw Shell Shaker. She then describes the origin of *Inholahta* people, whose actions are inspired by Grandmother's loyalty and leadership in the wake of the death of her husband, Tuscalusa. Tuscalusa, leader of Mississippian people and an accomplished stickball player, led the resistance to Hernando de Soto at the Battle of Mabila, where he died, in 1540. Reforming typical historical accounts of Tuscalusa's actions, Shakbatina names Grandmother as a collaborator in setting a trap for de Soto. She explains: "Unbeknownst to de Soto, the man standing before him was only a shell. All that Grandfather had been, his essence, was held inside of Grandmother for safekeeping. It was part of their sacred plan."[9] From the tribe's earliest contacts with colonizers, therefore, women, as Shakbatina recounts, were keepers of authority, in this case literally embodying leadership.

Over the course of the novel, Shakbatina is inspired by peacemaking in addition to strong examples of female leadership and diplomacy. Even after her death, from the spiritual realm, Shakbatina urges on her daughter Anoleta's own role as a Choctaw diplomat when Anoleta's husband, Red Shoes, becomes corrupt under the influence of European colonizers. In their last encounter, Shakbatina tells her first born: "Ask our friend, Jean Baptiste Bienville, to fight Red Shoes and the *Inkilish okla*. Bienville hates them as much as we do."[10] Thus, Shakbatina displays the alliance between Choctaws and Bienville that facilitated the Frenchman's success in New Orleans. Nitakechi, Shakbatina's brother, adopted Bienville into his clan, and though his love was apparently unrequited, Bienville was infatuated with Shakbatina. A speaker of the Choctaw language, Bienville recognized the tribe's authority and even enjoyed being treated as Shakbatina's pet. Shakbatina plans to watch over the Choctaws from Nanih Waiya, the "Mother Mound"; her memory, as well as the aid of Houma people (Choctaw relations), galvanizes preparation for war. In this way Howe retells the area's origin story, providing a counternarrative in the form of a strong Choctaw woman to the defeated Indian figure present in the monument, or ghost story, of Bienville Place.

Shakbatina's sway endures with the novel's shift to a twentieth-century setting, and though most scholars focus on Auda, Auda's sister Adair is at least as significant in Howe's rendering of Choctaw leadership and of spatial tribalography. Adair has earned the trust of her clients: "Her clients trust her to manipulate profits for them based on tax advantages. Marriages. Divorces. Retirement. She either talks them into investing a wad of money into the S&P 500, or cautions them against being too greedy." Her business acumen is a result of her credentials as holder of an MBA degree from Southern Methodist University, coupled with her heritage as a Choctaw woman. Howe writes of Adair: "Because Wall Street is very superstitious, people believe she had the ability to predict the future. They assumed it was her Native upbringing. In this case, they were right." Presumably, many of Adair's admirers are non-Indians who are influenced by stereotypes that ascribe to Natives stereotypical shamanistic tendencies. But Adair is also savvy enough to know how to capitalize on these assumptions: "If people wanted to think she was prophetic, that she has Indian spiritual powers, so be it. Just as long as she didn't become like so many others on Wall Street. Predatory."[11]

Against the backdrop of important diplomatic and trading roles for Choctaw women, Adair's accomplishments are more historically accurate then stereotypical. Just as Grandmother and Shakbatina were able to do in interactions with colonizers and their allies, Adair capably assesses situations of conflict and opportunity and espouses competent leadership. She values this connection: "Adair tells herself she's following a tradition established by her ancestors. After all, Indians were the first commodity traders of the New World. She does much the same by providing a communications network that brings people together who want to exchange one thing for another: pork bellies, cotton futures, computer company shares, technology stocks, or U.S. treasuries. Maybe she's her ancestors' toehold in New Orleans, the one to re-establish a Choctaw power base."[12] Inspired by her ancestors, Adair is uniquely equipped to steward those who trust her through threatening financial situations, evidenced in her protection of clients from the actions of Michael Milken and Ivan Boesky. More important, she emphasizes her goal of bringing people together, or creating kin.

Not only does Adair represent the historical significance of Choctaw businesswomen in New Orleans, but she also reclaims the city spatially in her encounters with its unique geography. As her ancestors did, Adair is receptive to the messages, which appear in sunlight, of the Choctaw spiritual figure Hashtali. Light bathes the city in the morning, as Adair receives Hashtali's messages from her eleventh-floor office window. Though Adair asserts the importance of Choctaws to the city's history, she is acutely aware that this Choctaw role has been erased. Nevertheless, in her mapping out of the city, she demonstrates an alternative spatial experience, especially marked by Choctaws' relationship to the Mississippi River. She explains:

> Across the city is the ancient river, the Mississippi. Being at the earth's edge is where Adair feels most alive. She can't imagine living anywhere else but New Orleans, where so much Choctaw history occurred. Yet there remains no trace of her people. Amazingly, nothing. The town was laid out in the elbow of the river, an outpost of the Old World, in 1718. She imagines how the shifting power struggles influenced its birth. First there were the Indians who pushed flat boats down the river to trade, then came the French with the sailing corvettes, followed by the Spanish, whose ships sank when they tried to penetrate the mouth of the Mississippi. Waves of immigrants from all over the world would come later.[13]

Echoing Howe's articulation of the story of America, Adair narrates a creation story of New Orleans from a Choctaw perspective that creates the immigrants that landed on its shores. Further, she privileges the material or natural world—the river, the sunlight—over an exclusive relationship to built structures. Though these impulses proceed from Choctaw beliefs, they also resonate with a privileging of space over time in the work of urban geographers like Ari Kelman and Edward Soja.

An especially important component to Adair's spatial story of New Orleans is her description of the home of the Sieur de Bienville, renowned as the founder of New Orleans and an efficacious trader (much like Adair). Adair's interest in the area is fueled by her historical research; a local librarian has told her that Bienville "had the finest house in the French Quarter." Locating his former residence on the map by naming the streets and other buildings that would have surrounded it, Adair mentally reconstructs the residence, imagining it in materials appropriate for its architectural context: slack lime whitewashing on its exterior, wainscoting inside, and linen-enclosed window frames. Its most important function is to receive and entertain Choctaws. Adair explains: "Bienville built the large house to entertain Choctaws. That much is acknowledged, even by white historians. It was a calculated move on his part; by hosting Choctaws for several weeks every March, the French governor was insuring the safety of his colony."[14] Adair thus imaginatively constructs a historical site in the French Quarter, where Choctaw histories have been erased.

This portrait of Bienville's residence is an opportunity for Adair to tell an alternative history of commerce in New Orleans, which is akin to Howe's alternative origin story of the deerskin trade in "The Story of America." Adair explains:

> In 1700, Choctaw commodity traders could hand off a portion of their shares of French goods to other tribes eager to get in on the action. Their trading partners would swap the goods, and the system reproduced itself all over the Lower Mississippi Valley. French goods were low risk, high liquidity. If the Choctaws got mixed up in a war, they could rely on their trading partners for support. Just like England and America do today. Market sense, that's what her people had long before there was a Wall Street with its "low risk, high liquidity" jargon. *Mabilia*, Mobile, was the trade jargon of her people. It's Choctaw for slick. . . . she wonders why historians, including her sister, focused on Indian warfare, instead of Indian commerce.[15]

Adair thus emphasizes Bienville's leadership not as a heroic "discoverer" akin to Christopher Columbus but as a partner with Choctaws who were active agents in trade and diplomacy, with their own market savvy. In effect, according to this history, Choctaws invented Wall Street. In light of Choctaws' participation in the economies of both the Southeast and the Comanchería farther west, this conclusion is no stretch.

Because of Choctaws' removal from their homelands in the Southeast to Indian Territory, elders in the contemporary settings of *Shell Shaker* mostly reside in the Choctaw Nation of southeastern Oklahoma, where both history and space are linked to those previous homelands. There Adair and her sisters find themselves, like their ancestors, working together to secure the future of their tribe, when a corrupt chief, Redford MacAlester, is killed. In the Oklahoma setting, Howe creates parallels to the settings of the South, including homelands along the Mississippi River as well as the Bienville residence in New Orleans. Like the old Choctaw towns, the elders of the community reside in cottages that Auda designed to replicate the spacing of dwellings in Choctaw old towns. An Okie version of Bienville, Dixon Durant, a French-Choctaw, is noted as the founder of Durant, where the Choctaw Nation of Oklahoma is headquartered. Nowatima, a survivor of Removal whose relationship with Dixon Durant resulted in a daughter, builds a large home that serves generations, including Adair's mother, Susan. The home, like Bienville's New Orleans residence, is described as "stately" and reveals traces of Choctaw-French history as well as its importance as a community center. Filled with toys of neighborhood children, it also contains a library that is a de facto family museum: "A French musket that once belonged to a famous Choctaw warrior rested on the fireplace mantle, and two ancient Choctaw burden baskets sat on a side table. The family's most precious possessions, however, were stored in a small trunk in a corner of the room: a tiny black and white porcupine sash, and some turtle shells. Both were said to have belonged to a powerful ancestor, a shell shaker."[16] Tribalography, as in the New Orleans section, pervades Choctaw characters' experiences with space as well their understanding of history in the novel. And while it should be obvious to all that Natives were founders of Oklahoma (if not by choice), it is nonetheless imperative to articulate this Choctaw role in the origin story of Oklahoma. Moreover, the relationship between Choctaw homelands in both the Mississippi River Valley and Oklahoma is presented as reciprocal and foundational to telling Choctaw and American stories.

While the novel's settings move from east to west as its time period moves from past to present, a nod to the future leads the characters east again. By the end of the novel, Adair and her sisters have reconnected with other kin, including Uncle Isaac Billy, who is rekindling a relationship with Delores Love, a funeral worker and modern bone picker. Back in southeastern Oklahoma in her golden years, Delores has been dreaming of Isaac. Her vision evokes the legacy of Shakbatina and her other shell shaking maternal ancestors. She explains the dream to Isaac: "It is a long time ago. We are ourselves but different. You are a monthly visitor to my town and we marry. I become pregnant, then I die. Somehow, I watch as you place a blue necklace of glass beads around my neck so I'll remember. Then I am dancing beside you in a dress made of *fichik hika*, shooting stars—you know, the little stars who sacrifice themselves when they fly to the ground to unite earth and sky."[17] Isaac reveals that he has been having the same dream, and he announces to Delores that he is convinced of her role as *Imataha Chitto*, the reuniter of Choctaw tribes in Oklahoma and Mississippi. A moving representation of the spatial dimensions of Choctaw spirituality emerges, which also brings to mind Appiah's discussion of cosmopolitanism as a relatedness that extends to the cosmos.[18] Delores's embodiment of this Choctaw figure is a critical aspect of her engagement with the physical spaces of both Oklahoma and Mississippi.

Howe creates a symbol of these tactile encounters with Choctaw spaces in the form of a lump of ever-expanding bread dough that Delores transports from Durant to the Nanih Waiya mound in Mississippi. In Choctaw oral history, this mound, or Mother Mound, located at the headwaters of the Pearl River, represents the Choctaw homeland.[19] As Delores reflects on the events of her life, the trauma of boarding school, and memories of her family, she kneads the dough, gathering with her sister and other women in the Billy home. Suddenly in her kneading she is transported to a vision of the birth of the Nanih Waiya mound, a sacred event that unites Choctaw ancestors. Significantly, Delores describes the mound as "like an emerald city," noting the importance of such mound sites as urban centers.[20] Back in the Billy kitchen, the bread dough has now become Mississippi mud, which Delores interprets as a sign that Redford McAlester must be buried in soil near the mound in Mississippi. The mound will become a space for a reunion of kin through this burial, but as Allen cautions, a careful understanding of earthworks reveals that mounds can also be containers for "spirits of the difficult dead" (like Redford), not simply gravesites to lay humans to rest.[21] With the mud in tow, the women and an intergenerational group of Choctaws embark on the concluding journey of the novel, stealing McAlester's coffin and transporting it to Nanih Waiya.

Delores's leadership creates an emotional reunion of eastern and western Choctaws as well as a literal melding of soil that has formed in both Mississippi and Oklahoma geographies. At the mound Delores finds the earth to be "soft and open from recent rains, like the pores of skin," an inviting image for Choctaws gathering there in spirit and in person. After discussing with a distant Mississippi cousin, Earl Billy, a plan to deposit McAlester's body in the mound and cover it with the mud hauled from Oklahoma, Delores meets the eastern Choctaw women who have come from Alabama, Louisiana, and Texas. Delores understands the mound to be "truly a sacred place," anchored in the legacies of Choctaw navigation and trading along the Pearl River, a significant source of swamp habitat throughout Mississippi and Louisiana that empties into the Gulf of Mexico.[22] Imagining the view of the river from the perspective of two blue herons who land at Nanih Waiya Creek, Delores unites a community of Choctaw relations who will contain McAlester's spirit; in Allen's reading, this act promotes healing.[23] As Patrice Hollrah notes, this ending solidifies the novel's emphasis on the Choctaw philosophy of "life everlasting."[24] Bathed in light, Choctaw women in this scene, like those before them, represent the leadership of their community in a bond across the Gulf Coast and Oklahoma that will endure. Kirstin Squint calls this moment a counter-removal, referring to her interview with Howe to emphasize the connections between not only the soil of both geographies but also the Choctaw place names that preserve these connections to the Gulf in Oklahoma.[25] This marking of Choctaw places underscores the broader Indigenous historical and cultural context of New Orleans and its reach to present-day Choctaw communities in the Gulf region and in Oklahoma.

While highlighting connections between Choctaw communities across these geographies and making those connections visible in her rendering of New Orleans, Howe does not shy away from addressing the additional connections—and tensions—between Choctaws and other disenfranchised groups, especially African Americans. Parade and masking traditions of New Orleans draw scrutiny about lines between honor and appropriation that can appear blurred when symbols of Native American culture are employed during Carnival, even in the shadow of monuments and other civic displays that render Native Americans invisible. Having countered this invisibility in *Shell Shaker*, Howe, in a story from her 2005 collection of prose and poetry, *Evidence of Red*, more directly considers the place that

Choctaw history holds in a larger story of people of color in New Orleans (and more broadly, the settler colonial foundations of the United States).

Howe begins her story "The Chaos of Angels" by presenting the concept of chaos from a Choctaw perspective. Called "Huksuba," chaos is the reaction to a collision of Upper and Lower Worlds that form Choctaw cosmology. Jodi Byrd explains that Howe's presentation of Huksuba as a frame for the actions of the story suggests not only the destructive realities of chaos but its creative, generative potential. Placing the story's lesson at the beginning of the narrative, Howe writes: "*Huksuba*, or chaos, occurs when Indians and non-Indians bang their heads together in search of cross-cultural understanding. The sound is often a dull thud, and the lesson leaves us all with a bad headache."[26] This opening certainly does not portend resolution to the conflicts between Indian and non-Indians, but it does provide a tone of humility that is necessary for crossing the kind of cultural divides that are rendered in the story.

In a hotel courtyard in New Orleans, the narrator, reflecting the importance of water to Choctaw understandings of the universe, goes for a swim in the night, where she encounters a Black woman. Occurring in February, an important time of year for the Carnival celebrations that culminate in Mardi Gras, this encounter between the two women becomes a representation of the linked histories of peoples of New Orleans and brings the narrator to reflect on her own relationships to her history and culture. At first the narrator ignores the woman's attempts at attention getting. When turtles disguised as doormen enter the courtyard, the narrator explains, "They've come to remind her that the conquering hordes only thought the Choctaw camps were abandoned and the dogs were mute, and the stains on their hands, red-colored and blue, were sweet scent." The Black woman leaves, laughing, to which the narrator responds, "The joke is on her."[27] At this point the narrator seems satisfied with the lesson *she* has taught the woman about the centrality of Choctaws to the history and geography of the area, yet the story does not end here. According to Squint, of the most important lessons of "The Chaos of Angels" is the narrator's reconsideration of Choctaw-French colonial alliance.[28]

On a flight to Dallas from New Orleans, after consuming a strong red drink that a Haitian flight attendant delivers, the narrator experiences a dream that prompts her to reflect on her own grasp of the relationships between Choctaws, French colonizers, and the cultures of New Orleans and beyond. Bienville, the narrator explains, is still visible on the streets of New Orleans, shaped by his relationships with Choctaws. According to a story the narrator's grandmother has shared with her, Choctaws, after Bienville rudely suggested a trade of beads for land while he was a guest at their feast, traded the Frenchman Bayougoula swampland, believing the land would be useless to him. But as the narrator ponders this story, she understands that "the joke was on us"; the Choctaws have been forever shaped by their relationship to Bienville as well. In her dream Bienville appears with a saxophone, delivering a soliloquy about a woman who gazes upon a pair of coupling lovers dressed in white. The narrator is startled awake and finds a frog-faced man dressed as a cowboy, complete with a belt buckle that reads "Bull." The frog asks the narrator if she is practicing safe sex and explains that his intrusive question is linked to her own thoughts about sex, water, and power, coincidentally all concepts that pervaded the narrator's experience at the hotel pool. Based on the frog-man's preoccupation with cats and "'Old World' sexual culture," the narrator concludes that he is Bienville in disguise. Bienville-as-frog asserts, "Reality is a rubber band you can pull in any direction," and after scolding the narrator for her behavior at the swimming pool, he begins playing Stephen Foster's "Beautiful Dreamer."[29] Because the lyrics to the song evoke images that associate women with death, it is a fitting end to the discussion with the frog, who emblematizes the patriarchal and divisive legacy of colonialism.

Initially rattled by the "chaos" of her mind that has spurred the frog dream, the narrator then recalls dream memories that privilege Choctaw creation signified in images of birth from Nanih Waiya. In these memories the narrator is led to a better appreciation for shared kinship across cultures that is, importantly, personified in women at the end of the story. Displacing the frog as the narrator's airline seat mate, the woman from the hotel responds to the narrator's call for help, asking her: "Haven't you forgotten that the French took some of your relatives to Haiti where they made a new home there? How could you forget that we are sisters? Maybe the joke's on you, after all?" The woman then leads the narrator to the front row of the first-class section, where Grandmother indicates that she is "finishing the joke." "We all must work hand in hand," she urges. "Never forget we are all alive! All people, all animals, all living things; and what you do here affects all of us everywhere. What we do affects you, too." The three women, hands held, watch *Star Wars* together, with the narrator concluding, "In the tribal ethos, being isolated from one's relatives is the worst horror we can imagine, so we hold each other tight in the scary parts and wonder what will happen next."[30] Like the ending of *Shell Shaker*, this conclusion is a fitting rendering of Howe's tribalography, in which kinship subverts settler colonial erasure of Choctaws and their kin. The dream elements of the story, offering a window into the narrator-writer's mind, also foreground the subversive realm of creativity, productive even in chaos. And more directly than in her first novel, this conclusion unites relations across artificial divisions of race and across geographies outside of the United States.

The reference to *Star Wars*, as well as the encounters with Grandmother and Bienville, hint at an additional layer to creating kinship—movement across space and time—that Howe develops more fully in relation to land, community, and diplomacy in her novel *Miko Kings* (2007). Howe comments on the novel in "Embodied Tribalography," the concluding essay of her collection *Choctalking on Other Realities*. As the essay's title suggests, tribalography is deepened through embodiment, "a reciprocal embodiment between people and land." In composing *Miko Kings*, Howe determined that Natives' "physical movements emplotted the land with . . . attributes of survival" and that important connections across time enjoin ballgames and earthworks in Native North America. Noting that ballgames' lack of time limits, counterclockwise movement, and pitching in the center (similar to the Choctaw ceremonial center pole) mimic Choctaw relationships to water and wind, Howe also points toward the proximity of ballfields to earthworks sites to argue that the unrecognized origin of baseball is the land itself. Further, Howe recounts Choctaw oral tradition, which traces ballgames to animals and birds, as evidence of the link between embodiment and ball playing. These stories describe physical transformation to acquire wings, rather than the use of sticks or bats, as the key tool for successful play. The most important lesson, rather than competition, is peaceful cooperation, or "fictive kin" with those who are not members of the group but are teammates. Fictive kin is a component of Choctaw diplomacy in which a Fani Mingo/Minko, an outside advocate, facilitates relationships with other tribes and foreigners.[31]

Howe's research on embodiment through ballgames extends her study of chaos, or Huksuba, as a productive, spatial meeting of worlds. Whereas Huksuba results from worlds colliding, however, ballgames are correlated to worlds overlapping. Howe turns to anthropologist F. Kent Reilly, who draws a parallel between the religious significance of the meeting of Choctaw Upper, Middle, and Lower Worlds and the rich biodiversity of overlapping environmental zones, or ecotones. Ecotones, as environmental as well as time zones, provide a framework for Howe's attention to the significance of ball playing among Oklahoma tribal members today. Again referring to Choctaw stories about ball playing in Oklahoma, she provides examples of embodiment that traverse time and space: gathering snakeroot (a practice going back centuries in the Southeast) to raise money for entrance fees and using body movements, especially shaping hands as if holding a ball, to tell stories of games that are akin to the rituals of dance. Further, ball games are an important means of enacting kinship, which energizes tribal networks and carries out role-play that is advantageous to diplomacy and political culture outside of Oklahoma Native communities. Therefore, these games, in Howe's words, "may signal our ever-returning presence on the land, just as cosmic solar and lunar events are ever-returning at earthworks sites. . . . Indigenous games and literatures written on the land are the embodied stories that reinforce our presence as ever-alive and ever-returning."[32] Time in *Miko Kings* is elastic, though not exactly the "rubber band reality" of the frog-man's (and perhaps a continental philosopher's) point of view. Instead, baseball performs Choctaw time and kinship. More explicitly than in *Shell Shaker*, the novel intertwines Native experiences across geographies of Oklahoma and the Gulf with non-Choctaws, particularly African Americans. This exploration of Native–African American kinship through the performance of baseball, not Mardi Gras, is another opportunity for Howe to foreground Choctaw epistemology in the story of New Orleans.

While Choctaw ball games are an unacknowledged chapter of American sports history, they are also fundamental to the culture of New Orleans and provide an effective bridge across time and space for Howe's characters. Native Americans and enslaved Africans in the city, particularly in the vicinity of Congo Square, played the sport *raquettes*, which evolved from Choctaw stickball and likely fostered enthusiasm for present-day Native ball playing in Oklahoma.[33] For main characters Hope Little Leader, Justina Maurepas, and Ezol Day, baseball counteracts erasure of their histories and provides a way forward in the face of further threats to their lives and lands. Learning about these individuals through her research on Indian baseball in present time allows Lena Coulter, like the contemporary characters of Howe's other works, to better understand relationships across cultures and generations that inform Choctaw ways of being. The importance of women to political and cultural strength is fundamental to these relationships, as are the overlapping realities that bring them together.

Hope Little Leader is the star pitcher of the Miko Kings all-Indian team, and though his baseball skills lead to his notoriety, his leadership (noted in his name) resonates beyond the field. Like Dixon Durant in *Shell Shaker*, Hope is a leader in his community and must negotiate the difficulties of Choctaw persistence after removal to Indian Territory. But while Dixon exhibits similarities to Bienville, Hope is compared to Pushmataha, the Choctaw chief who shepherded the tribe through several treaty negotiations, including the Treaty of Doak's Stand. Reflecting on his life from the bed of a nursing home in his old age, Hope likens pitching baseball to battle. It is not simply a comparison, however; it is evidence of Howe's rendering of baseball as an ecotone with both spatial and temporal significance. Telling the story of the game to his caregiver, Kerwin Johnston, Hope asks, "You know baseball is a game without limitations?" He then describes the pick-up system of substituting players as "a diplomatic solution for everything."[34] Presumably, Kerwin takes these comments at face value, yet they hint at Hope's experience of inhabiting the past through memories and of navigating Choctaw responses to colonialism through the game.

Baseball takes shape as Indian nationalism in the novel as the Miko Kings team is formed and battles non-Indian teams concurrent with statehood in 1907. Baseball allows Natives of Oklahoma, following their own traditions of intertribal stickball, to battle the U.S. Cavalry; the most important Miko Kings game is its contest with the Seventh Cavalry team from Fort Sill. But the Indian Territory League also reflects Choctaw business and diplomatic engagement that can be traced to Gulf homelands. Henri Day, league founder and mayoral candidate, believes that baseball will drive the engine of Choctaw and Chickasaw wealth in the growing town of Ada, Oklahoma: "A League of all Indian baseball teams will demonstrate that the people from different tribes can own something together. It will be the country's first inter-tribal business, an alliance that will spread across the whole U.S.

Maybe the whole goddamn continent. 'The Naholla can't take it away if it's owned outright by Indians,' says Henri softly, under his breath. 'And solvent.'"[35] The games are also a counterpart to the anti-allotment activism of Native women (Cherokee, Chickasaw, Choctaw, and Muscogee) in the Four Mothers Society, who frequently conduct meetings at the ballfield.

Henri fears allotment cannot be stopped, but in a dream vision of a Choctaw baseball field of the future, he is assured of Choctaw survival: "He saw a modern baseball field unlike any other. . . . The sign on the stadium read *Chahta Hapia Hoke*. We are Choctaw." Through her archival research, Lena confirms that the league and the Four Mothers Society are links to the actions of Choctaw ancestors. She observes: "Indians in the southeast had been organizing inter-tribally to play ball long before the Europeans ever arrived. According to historical accounts and archaeological reports, there are old ballfields along river bottoms and next to the mound sites. So Henri Day's new baseball league was based on something very old."[36] Howe's narrative enacts her theory of baseball as embodiment, particularly of Indigenous activism, which creates kin among Choctaws across generations and geographies as well as with other "teammates," or fictive kin, in other cultural groups.

The seeds of relationship between African Americans and Choctaws within the fictional world of *Miko Kings* are planted in the South at Hampton Institute, a historically Black university in Virginia. There Hope Little Leader meets and falls in love with a teacher's aide, Justina Maurepas, known later in her life as activist Black Juice. According to Lena's archival research, Hampton began its program to educate Native Americans in 1877, and it lasted forty years, until there was no more financial support for it from the federal government or Foreign Mission Board. As Howe explains in an interview with LaRose Davis, Native children were the drivers of General Samuel Armstrong's fundraising for Hampton, since the federal government would provide $127 for each child educated there. Yet Native students from outside Virginia, like the character Hope Little Leader, were never in place at Hampton, at a distance from their lands. For Native students the Hampton experience led to loss of family, which, according to Howe, is part of a colonial "replacement narrative," the ramifications of which are still "spinning out" in Native communities "just like a ball when it's thrown."[37] At Hampton, Hope and Justina are subject to this replacement experiment in the school's project of assimilating pupils into U.S. culture through industrial and domestic arts. Though a relationship between them, student and employee, would have been forbidden, their love blossoms. Their relationship is an example of kinship across overlapping time, space, and communities despite this replacement project.

Hope and Justina have individual histories of activism that fuel the romantic spark between them. Along with his assertion of Choctaw culture through baseball, Hope's refusal to submit to the assimilationist culture at Hampton, repeatedly running away and practicing Choctaw religion, provides common ground between him and Justina. Justina, older than Hope, later becomes known as "Black Juice," a Black nationalist who is credited with causing explosions in New Orleans that ended the Charles Riots of 1900 and coincided with the deportation of Marcus Garvey in 1927. In notes from an interview with Justina in 1969, biographer and professor Algernon Pinchot states that Justina has led a life full of "contradictions." Pinchot describes her ancestry as mixed—"Louisiana Indian, African, and French"—and credits her experience teaching Houma Indians in Louisiana in 1907 as transformational. He also learns (but doesn't believe) that she will not read or write in English and discovers that she will only converse with him in French. Apparently, like Choctaws, Justina does not have admiration for the English or their language. While Justina left Hope in 1907, in her older age she still names him as her one true love. Her daughter, Evangeline, born in Houma, Louisiana, in 1908, is theirs, and she is well acquainted with the importance of Hope, the "wild Indian," to her mother.[38]

Pinchot seeks to document Black Juice's prominence in Black nationalism in his book *Black Juice, the Martyr of Hope*, perhaps not fully realizing how much his title reveals about the importance of Hope to Justina's life, apparently above her association with Black nationalism. Hope and Justina's relationship signifies connections between Native Americans and African Americans across the South but especially in the Gulf region, prompting consideration of the possibilities and limitations of activism against white nationalism. In the same way that Hope, through baseball, embodies Choctaw resistance to statehood, Justina, in her role as Black Juice and connection to Marcus Garvey, has become a symbol to African Americans such as Professor Pinchot. Her original name, Justina, akin to the word *justice*, gives way to Black Juice, more strongly noting her association with Black resistance to Jim Crow segregation in New Orleans. But in her later years, though she is most frequently called "Madame Maurepas," she longs for Hope, whose nickname for her was "Dusky Long-Gone Girl." According to Pinchot, all of these identities are parts of the same woman, much as the relationships of Native Americans and African Americans are interwoven. At the end of her life, however, Justina turns away from her experience as a Black nationalist, calling herself "a heroine only of the imagination," and prefers to speak of her experience in Indian Territory as the lover of Hope.[39] In Pinchot's view, Justina's reputation and later isolation indicate the way that stories allow people to transcend time; her role as a Black nationalist heroine has frozen her in time, perhaps obscuring the person she truly was, but her telling of her experience with Native Americans allows her to inhabit another world.

Enacting the transformative power of storytelling, a prominent theme in Howe's writing, both Hope and Justina spend the end of their lives telling others of their experiences in the early twentieth century, in the years corresponding with the transformation of Indian Territory into the state of Oklahoma. Both communicate feelings of regret, with Justina bordering on bitterness after her exile from New Orleans in 1900. While their love demonstrates kinship across Choctaw, Houma, and African American communities, the pain of their separation echoes the disillusionment of statehood and the unrealized promise of Indigenous and Black nationalism. The end of the relationship occurs when Justina leaves due to her doubts that Hope is serious about much more than baseball or that she and Hope could build a future together. In her words: "There were many reasons, many justifications, but the truth is I ran away from him because I thought he was weak. What I mistook for his failings were indeed his strengths."[40] Howe describes Justina's view of the world as influenced by her age; after her time at Hampton, with a realistic understanding of racial divides and more life experience than Hope, she is led to take direct action against injustice in New Orleans, even when it complicates her love life. Howe explains that Hope "thinks that if he is a part of this team and he makes this difference, he is going to be accepted by her. She thinks, on the other hand, that once she is in the environment of New Orleans she has to make a difference."[41]

Hope reacts to Justina's lack of confidence in him by throwing the Miko Kings' game against the Seventh Cavalry, believing that the gamblers' bribe he accepts will allow him to provide a living for him and Justina. His plans, to buy a house and plant a crop, align with the aims of the allotment policy that the U.S. government is imposing across Indian Country and that will pave the way for Oklahoma statehood. Though Hope's decision foils the victorious legacy of the Miko Kings, it does not compromise his association with Choctaw leadership in his comparison to Pushmataha. Hope and other Natives in Oklahoma find themselves on the precipice of great change in the coming of statehood. In signing the Treaty of Doak's Stand in 1820 with Andrew Jackson at the Natchez Trace, Pushmataha signed over the bulk of Choctaw homelands in Mississippi and agreed to language that called for assimilation and eventual U.S. citizenship for Choctaws, outcomes that were devastating to his people. Yet Pushmataha's actions were responses to an overwhelming sweep of U.S. actions to undermine tribal sovereignty in the Southeast after America's victory in the War of 1812; limited in his options for resistance to these policies, Pushmataha's signing of the treaty may be understood as a gamble of his own. In this way Hope's compromise is the ecotone that baseball represents for Choctaws and other Natives. Not only is it a symbol of the defeat that statehood represents, but also it allows Hope—and readers of Howe's novel—fully to inhabit the experience of Choctaw histories of diplomacy, which are certainly marked by hard choices and regrets.

Like the relationship between the Choctaw and Haitian women of Howe's essay "The Chaos of Angels," the bond between Hope and Justina is a powerful reminder of the ties between Natives and African Americans that are compromised under a colonial "replacement narrative" that fuels alienation. This kinship is also formed in *Huksuba*, or chaos, which is both destructive and generative. Wielding dynamite in New Orleans, Justina may be perceived as inciting chaos in the city, but the world's perceptions of her do not align with her own understanding of her personal and educational connections to Native American communities. These connections depart from the imaginative assumption of Native identities and pasts that infuses masking traditions in New Orleans and instead spur her direct action.

But in her time, Justina's position at the juncture of overlapping worlds is not well received. Pinchot identifies her as profoundly isolated in her later years on Magazine Street; Justina's alienation likely stems not only from her loss of Hope but also from the way that the events of her life—and her identity—have been misunderstood. Pinchot explains that Justina's last husband, Gerard Louis Maurepas, died while she was in Haiti searching for her ancestry not long after they were married. In this suggestion of Justina's Haitian ancestry, Howe likens her to the Haitian woman—a descendant of unrecognized Choctaws—in "The Chaos of Angels." Justina sought to make a difference in New Orleans amid white supremacy that is disorienting not only in its segregation of and violence against African Americans but also in its erasure of Natives, and to her regret, her actions resulted in destructive chaos. Her daughter calls Hope "wild Indian," and her descendants apparently do not recognize their Choctaw heritage. So it is unclear to Justina or to others surrounding her how a fuller account of her life and legacy may be revealed. As the Grandmother explains in Howe's essay, isolation from relatives is "the worst horror we can imagine." Through these words the devastation of the final years of Justina's life becomes clearer.

Lena, however, tells the story of Justina and her relationship with Hope and thus, in the productive, creative dimension of *Huksuba*, subverts erasure of Choctaw kinship. Her telling of Indian Territory baseball, of course, is not just a recollection of "the Big Game" trope; it also collapses artificial divisions of time and space, allowing her, through an ostensibly simple story of baseball, to embody the stories, reasserting and even changing the history of the Miko Kings and their relations. Lena's discovery of the diary and newspaper clippings of Ezol Day in her home in Ada, accompanied by periodic chats with Ezol's spirit, facilitates her coming awareness of the artificial boundaries of Euro-Western time. As Patrice Hollrah notes, the materials of Ezol's that Lena consults—maps, clippings, drawings, and such—convey a visual dimension to tribalography, a Choctaw archive that is an alternative to the repositories of Oklahoma information that lack sufficient documentation of the Miko Kings.[42] Ezol recognizes time travel in a drawing she made at the Good Land Indian Boarding School, which displays an "eye tree," an image of a tree with an eye at its base and six more eyes gazing in multiple directions around the tree's branches. This image opens up the possibility for Lena to understand Choctaw temporality as built upon the experiences and perspectives of multiple kindred spirits across generations. For Ezol this insight led to social ostracization, but for Lena, who is lacking strong connections to Choctaw family members after the early death of her mother, this insight binds her to the Choctaw community. Lena's connection to Ezol becomes a literary collaboration; Lena asserts, "The voice speaking is my voice, but the voice of this story is hers."[43] This relationship across time also allows Lena to learn about and tell the story of Justina's life, further emphasizing the power of creativity to unite communities, especially of women.

Through her recovery of the history of the Miko Kings and, in turn, Justina's story, Lena achieves a deeper understanding of Choctaw legacies in New Orleans, counteracting the "ghosting" of Native peoples in the city and its surrounds, and reveals the ties between Oklahoma and this Gulf Coast geography. These ties are not only historical, however; they become ecotones, regions that overlap in the practice of baseball. Similar to Howe's description of baseball in "Embodied Tribalography," the philosophy of time Ezol captures in the eye tree involves embodiment, which she links to baseball. She compares ball players like Hope to *Alikchi*, or "healers working in collaboration with the earth's mathematical systems." She observes: "Time is like a majestic dance. . . . Observe how I can step forward or backwards or sideways and form multiple patterns that intersect." With baseball thus allowing geographical and temporal flexibility, Lena, who becomes "a moving body in Choctaw space," is empowered to change the game against the Seventh Cavalry into a victory for the Miko Kings, which presumably holds the promise of a future for Hope and Justina.[44] This ending is a fictive counterpart to tribalography that Howe sets forth in her essays; it is a means of recasting settler colonial histories that divide and relegate Natives to the margins of their own lands and stories. History, especially a revisited history, can, as Jill Doerfler argues, "be used to construct a future that unites us through relationships."[45] This alternative outcome to the novel does just that: it makes possible a closer relationship between Justina and her Choctaw kin and may prevent the destructive actions in New Orleans that she came to regret. Ultimately, baseball makes possible a reclamation of braided African American and Choctaw communities signified in the dancing—and ball playing—of Congo Square.

"Where It All Started"

Like LeAnne Howe, Joy Harjo locates Congo Square as inspiration for her creative and spiritual life, though in Harjo's case, Muscogee histories and musical legacies take center stage. Harjo, who has described her life as predominantly urban, reclaims New Orleans in her poems and songs for Muscogee communities, referring to well-known places in the city to tell of her people, despite the city's failure to recognize them.[46] In *Catching the Light* (2022), Harjo calls her first trip to New Orleans in her thirties a homecoming, "the closest I had come to traditional Muscogean tribal nation territory."[47] She also reorients histories of jazz to their foundations in Indigenous musical traditions, pointing out, like Howe, the dynamic relationships between tribal citizens in the area and African Americans. Similar to the way that Howe discusses baseball as a means of embodying and recasting Choctaw time, Harjo employs the saxophone to play and sing of Muscogee New Orleans, challenging, playfully at times, the presence of colonial interlopers there. Performance, for Harjo, highlights the essential, spatial relationships of humans to their surroundings (and the universe), just as kneading dough or playing ball games is for Howe's characters.

Also like Howe, Harjo asserts that the story of America is the story of her people rather than of colonists. She explains the importance of Muscogee origins of America in her tribute to the late Kaw-Muscogee saxophonist Jim Pepper:

> Last week I spoke to students at Santa Fe Indian School on Jim Pepper, the quintessential native jazz saxophonist. Only a few people in the audience had heard of him. None of the students had. I ended at Congo Square, the symbolic and real ground where jazz rose up, born of this North American, this native earth. Literally and metaphorically. For Congo Square was a Houma ceremonial grounds. And this is where it all started: stomp dance, jazz, the blues, rock, what is American in music. The Indian has been left out of the equation. So it makes all the sense in the world that jazz found its way back to the grounds with Jim's saxophone. All the sense in the world.[48]

These words tell a broader story of Native American place than is often recognized, one that, through grounding in New Orleans, places Muscogee people at the center of jazz, of quintessential American culture. This move undergirds Harjo's poems "New Orleans" and "We Were There When Jazz Was Invented" and her work in progress, a musical set in New Orleans and Tulsa that will revise jazz and blues histories.

"New Orleans," of the collection *She Had Some Horses* (1983), immediately destabilizes the settler colonial narrative of the city. The first words, "This is the south," provide geographic positioning, but in using a lowercase instead of uppercase *s* in the word *south*, Harjo clarifies that New Orleans is not most significant for its affiliation with the Confederacy, at least not the one led by Jefferson Davis. Instead, Harjo is looking for evidence of Creeks. Like Adair in Howe's *Miko Kings*, Harjo spatially reclaims New Orleans, looking for "tobacco brown bones" to appear on the streets of the French Quarter and spying a blue horse near the French Market. The horse, "frozen in stone," was brought by the Spanish in a journey akin to the Middle Passage, which led the horse to madness:

> They caught him in blue
> rock, said
> don't talk.

Intermingled with ivory and knives, other items of trade associated with violence, red rocks in a nearby shop suggest Muscogee claims to this land. Harjo writes:

> The man behind the counter has no idea that he is inside
> magic stones. He should find out before
> they destroy him. These things
> have memory,
> you know.[49]

According to Tracey Watts, these suggestions of madness and destruction indicate the "inherent fatality of the colonial project of New Orleans" because of its failure to acknowledge the full story of its geography.[50] But despite the city's shrouding of its Indigenous origins, signs of Muscogee continuance remain in objects and their memories.

Harjo's poem links the built environment of the city to the Mississippi River, a waterway so important to Indigenous communities of New Orleans as well as to the harrowing experience of removal to Indian Territory. In this turn to the natural environment of the city, Harjo counters a preoccupation with built structures that fuels lack of recognition of Indigenous urban experiences. She also de-emphasizes colonial building by referencing her memory through images of the body—of blood, skin, and feet—that are tied to the river. Turning from an impulse to find other Muscogees to her declaration of her own presence, Harjo asserts:

> I have a memory.
> It swims deep in blood,
> a delta in the skin.

Asserting her own presence in this place and in the poem's persona, Harjo's autobiographical poem continues the practice of oral literature so crucial to Indigenous cultures.

Craig Womack explains that this impulse is common in Indigenous poetry, not to be understood as "confessional poetry." For Native storytellers and poets, literature is performed, drawing on the speaker's own body movements, and is part of an individual's understanding of his or her place in a larger community.[51] Therefore, memories of the Muscogee collective are Harjo's memories as well. As in the poem's opening lines acknowledging "the south," this reference to the delta region situates Harjo and her people firmly on this land; they will always have an enduring bond to this area even from Oklahoma. Her memory of New Orleans sustains Harjo at the same time as it is a source of trauma, however. She writes:

> My spirit comes here to drink.
> My spirit comes here to drink.
> Blood is the undercurrent.

The river contains the stories of Muscogees who died during removal and thus is an almost holy place for remembering them, "buried beneath the currents stirred up by / pleasure boats going up and down." Like the spaces of the French Quarter, then, the river is also colonized. The flow of Harjo's memories makes her people appear again.

With her own memory a means of claiming this geography, Harjo also projects power over the river's colonizer, Hernando de Soto, despite the distances of time and space, through her memory. She notes that he is also buried in the river: "his bones sunk like the golden treasure he traveled half the earth to find." Like Harjo, other Muscogees knew de Soto even before his arrival and saw beyond his desire for gold. Harjo writes that they "knew he was one of the ones who yearned for something his heart wasn't big enough to handle." Harjo signals Muscogees' relationship to their land and to one another, which contrasts strongly with the mercenary inclinations of de Soto. She writes,

> Creeks lived in earth towns,
> not gold,
> spun children, not gold.

With Creek towns rebuffing de Soto's search for cities of gold, the poem suggests that madness is a next logical consequence, and the Muscogees' drowning de Soto in the Mississippi River "so he wouldn't have to drown himself" is an act of mercy. Community bonds to the Mississippi River and power over de Soto thus reassert Indigenous peoples within histories of the Gulf region and within New Orleans in particular, in contrast to familiar stories of dispossession.

While Harjo knows and experiences the force of her community in the area through her memory, her description of New Orleans in the concluding two stanzas of the poem highlight the city's erasure of Muscogee legacies nonetheless. Like the plot of any given murder mystery, Harjo is looking for a body to provide undeniable evidence to the world of what she knows to be true, "To know in another way / that my memory is alive." What she sees in New Orleans belies that truth in its lace and silk buildings, beaten silver paths, graves rising out of the soft earth, and shops selling black mammy dolls, all vestiges of colonial influence. The legacy of de Soto himself persists:

> I know I have seen DeSoto,
> having a drink on Bourbon Street,
> mad and crazy
> dancing with a woman as gold
> as the river bottom.

De Soto remains a ghost, haunting the city even today. Womack calls the persistence of memory central to Harjo's philosophy, both in its recalling of ancestral memory and in its reckoning with histories of genocide, even as Harjo imagines an alternative through her poetry. Perhaps others do not see de Soto, but Harjo knows—and shares—the truth about New Orleans through her poem.

Jazz, even as the soundtrack to de Soto's mad dance, serves as Harjo's performance of memory and futurity and is especially significant in her recent work. A poem from the collection *Conflict Resolution for Holy Beings* (2015) combines jazz with collective and individual memory across eras and geographies. The poem "We Were There When Jazz Was Invented" draws a parallel between memory and architecture, much as "New Orleans" does. The epigraph reads: "Each human is a complex, contradictory story. Some stories within us have been unfolding for years, others are trembling with fresh life as they peek above the horizon. Each is a zigzag of emotional design and ancestral architecture. All the stories in the earth's mind are connected."[52] In these words, Harjo intertwines human consciousness with the earth, emphasizing spiral, rather than linear, Muscogee time.

Harjo resituates jazz as an Indigenous creation by tracing Muscogee history, including removal from southeastern homelands, in the form of song. Like performance of oral history through storytelling, the song offers personal, collective, and spiritual significance, revealed in the repetitions of a chorus or bridges to other refrains. Rooted in the rhythms of music, the spiral of Muscogean philosophy emanates from the ceremonial practice of stomp dancing counterclockwise around the sacred fire.[53] The circular movement of the dance complements the fire's rising smoke, which connects the three worlds—Lower World, This World, and Upper World—of the Muscogee cosmos. Like the zigzag, improvisational quality of jazz, time and the cosmos are fluid in Harjo's poem, crossing from the Lower World of fish (chaos), governed by Tie Snake; to This World of humans (the present), guided by the ceremonial fire; to the Upper World of lunar and planetary orbits (order), referenced in images of the moon and of futurity beyond the present.[54] This movement also takes Harjo across a range of locations she's inhabited, with her jumping from "an island of fire and flowers" (Hawai'i); to Albuquerque; to Los Angeles; and finally to Tulsa, the place of her birth; followed by a leap to "the stomp grounds where jazz was born" (Congo Square, New Orleans). In a 2005 interview in *Triplopia*, Harjo describes music as being one with the body, experienced even before birth into present reality. She states: "My first experience of music in this world was through my mother's singing voice. I have a very, very faint memory of that experience while in the womb, and then it became the center of my world, especially in the formative years, when my mother was writing songs and singing for country swing bands, jukeboxes in truck stops where she worked, the radio, guitar players at the house. Music was and is my body. I don't think I ever felt a separation between music and my body. Words make bridges but music penetrates."[55] Throughout the stanzas of the poem, jazz is a Muscogee song, highlighting performance of both memory and futurity as well as Indigenous ties to the earth.

Robert Warrior and Mishuana Goeman have remarked on the theoretical force of Harjo's poetry, which, like Howe's tribalography, itself provides a framework for Native American literary theory. Warrior looks to Harjo's poetry as a guide for creative and theoretical work because of its commitment to embodiment. He explains: "For those of us committed to theoretical approaches that seek to address and make changes to the material realities that people in Native communities face, . . . Harjo's erotic poetry is a challenge to understand that our bodies, including our intellects, are connected to these material realities."[56] Warrior especially appreciates Harjo's emphasis on embodiment because it does not shy away from eroticism—key to one's power in seeking justice—and evokes the fullness of Native experiences, including reproduction as well as pleasure as means of inhabiting alternative and future realities. Warrior points out that this embodiment facilitates travel across fluid Muscogee boundaries. It is also important to recognize, in turn, that this travel is literal, not just metaphoric, and it conceptualizes Harjo's relationship to geographies that comprise homelands, including the South and Oklahoma as well as locations not typically associated with Muscogee lands. Further, as Harjo describes it, embodiment is inherently musical, with jazz, the art form so often named America's indigenous music (though without recognition of it as Indigenous music), providing the melody of this embodiment.

While Warrior connects Harjo's eroticism to literary theory, Goeman foregrounds mapping—and (re)mapping—as the heart of Harjo's alternative future making, which, as is the case in the works of many Native women writers, counteracts patriarchal spatialities. Goeman's *Mark My Words* (2013) tells of ways that women writers such as Harjo move beyond recovery of violent settler histories to imagine futures of possibility through literature, which evokes an alternative to settler heteropatriarchal space. Goeman determines that the Muscogee stomp grounds in Oklahoma are formed in Harjo's poems as "ongoing and connected to spatial forces across the planet" and (re)map the United States, including its cities of global capitalism, to bring Indigenous experiences to light.[57] Goeman discusses ways that Harjo employs jazz to connect local and global histories of survival that unite Indians in kinship with dispossessed immigrants. Introducing her edited collection on Indigenous performance, Goeman describes such performances as a dynamic way for Native artists and writers to "imagine different sets of power relations between Native people and settlers by presenting us with complicated visions that . . . produc[e] a visual sovereignty."[58] I bring together and extend Warrior's emphasis on embodiment and Goeman's discussions of remapping and performance to a centering of jazz—originating in the stomp grounds of New Orleans and then becoming a soundtrack for urban life in Oklahoma—as the primary method by which Harjo expresses and embodies alternatives to settler colonial space. These ties to the homelands of the South, including the urban culture of New Orleans, structure Harjo's writing about the origins of memories and her performance of them even in the post-Removal space of Indian Territory. Connections between the South and West guide her spatial relationships to other geographies.

Harjo's poem "We Were There When Jazz Was Invented" immediately introduces temporal and geographic zigzagging, with song as the primary link to Muscogee culture throughout. In the first stanza Harjo unites images of fish, fire, and rainbow (linked to Lower, Present, and Upper Worlds, respectively) in her recollection of periods of her life, from her young motherhood in Albuquerque to her years in Hawai'i. She chronicles her "19,404 midnights" as spent "in the quaver of fish dreams" or leaping from "a night rainbow, to an island of fire and flowers," which she calls "a holy / Leap between forgetting and jazz." At the beginning of the second stanza, the natural world of bears hunting salmon is a realm she can see "Beyond the door of my tongue," suggesting that words themselves may not be a sufficient entry into a space where, presumably outside of a global city like Los Angeles, creatures thrive. However, her dreams may yet allow her to "reconstruct that song buried in the muscle of urgency." Though she describes herself as "bereft / In the lost nation of debtors," song allows Harjo to leap back to the stomp grounds:

> Wey yo hey, wey yo hey yah
> hey. Pepper jumped
> And some of us went with him to the stomp. All night, beyond
>   midnight, back
> Up into the sky, holy

Singing unites the community at the stomp and a connection with the world of holy beings. Following Pepper, Harjo reconstructs song that originates in New Orleans, which she reclaims as an Indigenous homeland and identifies as entrée to experience in worlds beyond the limits of settler colonial space, putting the Indian back into the equation.

Having established the Muscogee origins of jazz emanating from the stomp at Congo Square, song is thus an answer of sorts to Harjo's bereft feelings; however, as is the case in her "New Orleans" poem, the trauma of removal cannot be disentangled from recognition of Muscogee histories in the South. Harjo chronicles the devastation of removal and relocation to Indian Territory (now-Oklahoma) in the language of music. She writes,

> Back there the ceremonial fire was
> disassembled, broken and bare, like chord breaks
> forgetting to blossom.

In succeeding lines she references mostly jazz song titles along with Muscogee song to provide the language of grief, injustice, and loss—as well as endurance in the face of those struggles—which are formative themes in the jazz tradition as well as in Indigenous histories. At the teardown of the ceremonial fire, Harjo watches prayers take root "Around midnight," with a nod to Thelonius Monk's "Round Midnight." Referencing Duke Ellington's "I Ain't Got Nothin' but the Blues," she explains:

I get jumpy in the aftermath of a disturbed music. I carried that
baby up
the river, gave birth
To nothing but the blues in buckskin and silk.

"Get Back," she says, evoking the Beatles in her call to homeland, while asking, "what bird / Have you chosen to follow in your final years of solitude?" signaling the lead of saxophonist Charlie "Bird" Parker. Accompanied by Muscogee song, the bear prophet urges her to

jump holy
Said the bear prophet. Wey ya hah. Wey ya hah. All the way
down to the jamming
Flowers and potholes,

indicating the reach of Muscogee song in the natural and built environments, even if removed from the birthplace of jazz. "There has to be a saxophone somewhere," he assures.

With music enabling the holy jump across worlds, Tulsa, the literal endpoint in Muscogees' forced migration to Indian Territory from the South, suggests both possibility and regret as revealed in song. Harjo writes:

Take me back
Or don't take me back to Tulsa. I can only marry the music; the
outlook's bleak
Without it.

The iconic western swing song "Take Me Back to Tulsa," written by Bob Wills and Tommy Duncan, is typically celebrated as an ode to Tulsa pride, but in Harjo's poem, the conflicted place of Tulsa in Muscogee history is apparent. The town where the ceremonial fire that was disassembled in the South was rekindled, first a Muscogee town, is also emblematic of the loss of homelands and the coming of settlers who eventually transformed Indian territory into the state of Oklahoma. The bleakness of the Muscogee endpoint, at least in linear geography, is coupled with the promise of another holy leap, however, which leads back to the stomp grounds of New Orleans. Again calling up Muscogee creativity in the form of music, Harjo turns from an ambivalent response to western swing to essential life force—breath, the heart of song:

> Breath
> Is the one. And two. And. Dream sweet prophet of sound, dream
> Mvskoke acrobat of disruption. It's nearing midnight and
> something holy
> Is always coming around.

Music documents the perils and promise of humanity, with the body itself creating its beat.

With another leap, images of birth and rebirth, alongside more song titles, conclude the poem in a return to the stomp grounds of New Orleans. Love is revealed in the

> Perfect neck of a woman who's given up everything for the
> forbidden leap
> To your arms as you lean over the railing to hear the music hopping
> at the jump,

calling to mind the balconies of Bourbon Street and the jump blues. With the turning of time to "the midnight hour" and the rhythms of Wilson Pickett, Harjo notes:

> I can hear it again; the blue moon caving in to tears of
> muscle and blood. Birth
> Of the new day begins less than one second after.

The two songs cited, "Blue Moon" (Richard Rodgers and Lorenz Hart) and "Sixteen Tons" (Merle Travis), both recall earlier lines in the poem that for Harjo link song both to the heavens and the body. With the surrender of the moon, the new day begins, an "incubation of broken dreams." But with the death of night, and presumably the death of Pepper, the new day leads back to the origin of jazz. Harjo writes, "It took forever for that bear of a horn player to negotiate the / impossible jump," suggesting a turn from the present to the next world. But alluding to the earlier image of a baby birthed at a river,

> water spirits will carry that
> girl all the way back
> To the stomp grounds where jazz was born. It's midnight.
> How holy.

Fittingly, the final song reference of the poem is Pepper's "Witchi Tai-To," which features the lines,

> Water spirit feelin'
> Springin' round my head
> Makes me feel glad
> That I'm not dead.

Even in his death, Pepper is the inspiration for singing of life, which is the song of jazz.

The Muscogee foundations of American music are a focus of Harjo's current work, in both individual projects and collaborations, which builds upon her previous poetic and musical achievements. Having released five albums, four solo and one with her former band Poetic Justice, Harjo also has created two performance pieces, *Wings of Night Sky, Wings of Morning Light* (2008) and *We Were There When Jazz Was Invented*. The latter production, a work in progress, is a multimedia performance of jazz, blues, and rock songs as well as stomp dance and an expression of the prominence of Indigenous musical traditions. Harjo introduced the piece in 2010 as part of the New Mexico Jazz Workshop series and has been commissioned by the Public Theater of New York to complete it as a musical play.[59] Her album project *An American Sunrise*, a companion project to her 2020 poetry collection of the same name, likewise links Muscogee song traditions with blues and jazz. Reflecting her authority on the subject of Native American music, Harjo has appeared in two groundbreaking documentaries, Sterlin Harjo's *This May Be the Last Time* (2014) and Catherine Bainbridge and Alfonso Maiorana's *Rumble: The Indians Who Rocked the World* (2017). In both, she comments on the significance of Indigenous song to cultural identity and to a complete understanding of the music of America. *Rumble*, like Harjo's poetic catalog of musicians in "We Were There When Jazz Was Invented," fills in unacknowledged gaps in American music history by recovering Indigenous ties to musicians at the forefront of blues and jazz. The film locates the "pre-blues" southeastern Indian music championed by artists Pura Fé and Rhiannon Giddens as an origin story for performers such as Link Wray, Charley Patton, and the Neville Brothers. Echoing the most prominent theme in her current work, Harjo names the Muscogean stomp dance at Congo Square as the origin of the call-and-response form of blues, rock, and jazz that these performers innovated. Harjo traces her genealogy as a poet and musician to Congo Square, calling it "her inheritance."[60] She returns to the Mississippi River as a nurturer or her ancestors and conduit for the stories that connect her to them. "That River," she says, "is a poem fed by the Arkansas that flows by my home south of Tulsa."

"Waking Up God"

Sterlin Harjo, like Joy Harjo, uses music to tell stories of Muscogee people, and all of his films are notable for their incorporation of compelling musical soundtracks to complement the emotional journeys of characters unfolding on-screen. His feature films focus on stories of Oklahoma, which he has named as his creative inspiration. Harjo brings the unique spaces of Oklahoma into focus, drawing connections between homelands, in both rural and urban locations, of Indigenous Oklahomans. Harjo grew up in Holdenville, attended the University of Oklahoma, and moved to Tulsa as a young adult. With the encouragement of N. Bird Runningwater, an alumnus of OU, Harjo received a fellowship from the Sundance Institute in 2004 and quickly began receiving more attention in local, national, and international communities. He remains committed to having a home in Oklahoma. In *This May Be the Last Time* Muscogee homelands both inside and outside of Oklahoma are united in the birth of American music.

This May Be the Last Time can be understood as fruitful counterpart to the poems and music of Joy Harjo, as it reveals connections between Muscogee homelands in the South and in Oklahoma. These connections tell the story of Muscogee people as a community as well as the individual story of the filmmaker himself. *This May Be the Last Time* documents the origins of the song of the same name, which for many is known only as a Rolling Stones tune. As is the case with much American music history (including the history of Congo Square), the song represents an unrecognized story, especially of Muscogee peoples in the South and their relationships with others amid settler colonial intrusion. The song "This May Be the Last Time" provides a fascinating link between American Indians, African Americans, and whites, and its evolution in language and rhythm tells a foundational story of American music that endures.

Harjo tells the story of "This May Be the Last Time" through a personal account of the disappearance and death of his grandfather, Pete Harjo, who went missing in 1962 after driving home to Sasakwa, Oklahoma, from a neighboring town. With no sign of Pete, his community gathered to search for him north of town in and surrounding the Little River, a part of the Mississippi River watershed. Searching for days, Harjo's friends and relatives gathered, camped, and sang hymns in their language. Finally, after damming up a section of the river and floating a felt hat of Pete's down his likely watery path, the body was found. Since an ambulance was unable to reach the scene, a group removed Pete's body from the river in a blanket while singing. This incident, a springboard in the film for an investigation of the roots of Muscogee hymns, brings to light this music as the first American music, rooted in the Indigenous cultures of the Southeast and evolving in gospel and blues traditions incubated in New Orleans. As Joy Harjo comments in the film: "Indigenous people have been written out of the story of America. It's right there in the face of American music but that story has been disappeared." This documentary, like the community's loving recovery of Pete Harjo in 1962, recaptures that story.

Echoing Joy Harjo's poetry, Sterlin Harjo documents ways that "This May Be the Last Time" is oral literature, expressed in words but also in the body through the performance of song. Several of the interviewees in the film indicate that Muscogee hymns are so important to them because in singing they experience and express their culture physically, without additional instrumentation, and feel a communion with others, past and present. Singer Wotke Long explains that when he returned to Oklahoma after some troubled times in his life, learning the songs was a way for him to re-home. He learned the songs to sing to his uncles, and now that his uncles have passed on, he says, "I know spiritually they can hear . . . sometimes I can hear them coming out of my voice." Pastor Jimmy Anderson says that while attending a funeral in an Athabascan community in Alaska, sensing the palpable grief of the deceased's family, he explained the importance of singing to his community in Oklahoma and offered a song. In that moment, he says, "I was singing this song for them, and voices were singing with me. And I thought, 'Do these Athabascan Indians in Alaska know this song? Do they know it? Are they singing with me?' And I looked up, and no one was singing. They were standing there with tears coming down their cheeks. And I closed my eyes and started singing again and I could hear voices singing with me. . . . And I thought, 'God's telling you, Jimmy, people back home are praying for you.'" Nelson Harjo offers a similar explanation of the how songs are embodied: "Even those who don't go to church realize God for the first time because . . . all the ones that are singing along with them . . . it's not sung with emptiness, but they actually *feel* it." The voice embodies Muscogee community across space and time, according to the singers, and so one's place in the larger community is evident even in times of separation, which is a fundamental function of oral tradition.

Images and comments about the Mississippi River are also important to Muscogee singing and to Harjo's representation of it in the film, further linking Pete Harjo's disappearance and recovery to the broader story of his people. In re-created episodes of the search for Harjo, images of community members appearing sometimes waist-deep, wading in the river and eventually carrying Pete's body, are interspersed with underwater camera shots. In several other scenes, Muscogee hymns accompany extended shots of the flowing river and the bridge above it. This watery theme connects with historic narratives that emphasize water crossings in trade and travel across cities and towns in the South as well as in Muscogee cosmology, and the care with which the images unfold suggests that the river itself is holy. In Christianity, wading in the water represents baptism, a ritual of rebirth, of acceptance of Jesus's grace and unity with the saints. These meanings have resonance for the hymn singers, many of whom practice religion in Christian churches of mostly Methodist or Baptist denomination. At the same time, the river is holy because of its relationship to Muscogee homelands in the Gulf region conquered by Andrew Jackson and the river's role in forced removal through New Orleans to Indian Territory (now-Oklahoma). Some of the same songs were sung along the removal journey and tell of Muscogee histories. Many tribal citizens died along the way, some drowning in the Mississippi River. According to Harjo, these songs tell of a river of death. The songs also tell of a day when all will be reunited, which may be understood literally as a reunification in Indian Territory at the end of the Trail but also resounds as a heavenly or spiritual reunion. Joy Harjo describes these feelings in the film as "carrying grief as well as this great love for the creator."

Though Muscogee hymns are connected in their words and tunes to songs that Scottish missionaries introduced in the form of hymn lining in missions to Indigenous communities of the Southeast, they also have a specific role outside of a settler context. In the film Hugh Foley recounts his role in connecting scholar and musician Willie Ruff with Muscogee singers for a conference at Yale with members of other communities who sing versions of "This May Be the Last Time," including an African American church in Alabama and a white church in Kentucky. While footage of comments at this meeting highlights the Scottish origin of this singing, it is important to note that in Harjo's interviews the singers emphasize that the songs are a gift from their Creator from the beginning of time. In cities, churches, and conferences like the one on-screen, the singers enact their right to their own histories, so often disappeared in these spaces, and in their fellowship, collaboration, and relatedness with whites and African Americans, they are part of a thriving, cosmopolitan production of art.

According to Wotke Long's father, Harry, who was a minister, the songs themselves are the theology of Indian churches; the people sing rather than speak their theology. Nelson Harjo describes the songs in the words of a pastor friend of his: "When we sing these songs, what we're doing is waking up God." These beliefs, described in a Christian framework, also resonate in ceremonial religion. According to Reverend George Harjochee, of Middle Creek #2 Indian Baptist Church of Holdenville, elders prayed and fasted in the woods to receive the songs as a gift from God. Pastor Houston Tiger explains in the film that rather than studying the Bible to prepare for his Sunday morning message, he goes to the woods to fast and pray. Harjo comments that during his teen years, hearing Tiger's singing at a wake service was the moment he first felt the power of Muscogee hymns. He felt something moving within the song. Calling the Indian churches "church grounds," Harjo states that as an adult, as he became more active at ceremonial grounds, he came to appreciate ways that aspects of ceremonies, including fasting and using Indian medicine, were integrated into churches and mixed with Christianity: "Our ceremonial songs have been with us since the beginning of time. For the most part they are hidden away and only sung at ceremony. They no doubt had an influence on these hymns."

"This May Be the Last Time" is, in Foley's words, "the first American music," as it threads through an intermingling of communities that together formed the United States. Harjo sketches out the evolution of the song as originating in Muscogee, becoming a slave spiritual in the 1800s, reaching wider notoriety in gospel and blues, and eventually being recorded by the Staple Singers in 1961 and Keith Richards in 1965. But he explains that the way the song is still sung in Muscogee communities today has not evolved; it is sung in the same way it always has been. While change is essential to survival, in this context the historical continuity of this song and similar hymns are ties, expressed through the body, to pre-Removal homelands and ancestors that influence contemporary Muscogee culture in Oklahoma to this day. In "waking up God," the singers enact their abiding relationship with their Creator and their agency in continuing that relationship despite settler colonialism. For most Americans "This May Be the Last Time" will always be a hit for the Rolling Stones, who were inspired by African American musicians and especially the music of New Orleans. They recorded "Time Is on My Side" the same year as Irma Thomas, Soul Queen of New Orleans, and incorporated elements of her version. Their original, offensive lyrics of "Brown Sugar" tell of rape culture and the slave market of the city. This history of British bands like the Rolling Stones profiting off of America's Indigenous music has been criticized as exploitative. Margo Jefferson writes in her 1973 essay "Ripping Off Black Music," "The night Jimi [Hendrix] died I dreamed this was the latest step in a plot being designed to eliminate blacks from rock music so that it may be recorded in history as a creation of whites."[61] As Sterlin Harjo's film, Joy Harjo's artistry, and the *Rumble* documentary remind us, eliminating Native Americans from the story of American music has likewise accompanied a trail of genocide that runs through New Orleans. Yet as the Muscogee singers of "This May Be the Last Time" show, this first American music has not been lost to the mists of time or disappeared into a melting pot; it remains a feature of dynamic Indigenous cultures whose members retain ties to their homelands despite the odds.

Whether through a mound of dough, a hurtling baseball, the bright sound of a saxophone, or the a cappella voicings of ceremonial hymns, Native American writers maintain bonds of community and culture between New Orleans and Oklahoma homelands in their works, creatively presenting experiences of both history and modernity. For Choctaws and Muscogees, New Orleans has been a site of trade and entrepreneurship, military strategy, kinship, celebration, and performance at the same time that it has brought the legacies of American colonialism—violence, Indian removal, and cultural appropriation—into stark relief. LeAnne Howe, Joy Harjo, and Sterlin Harjo all tell (and retell) origin stories that are rejoinders to these colonial legacies. These stories are powerful claims of the primacy of Indigenous peoples to the story of America and to the cosmopolitan gumbo that is the essence of New Orleans.

3

FINDING TALLASI

Native Tulsa in Literature and Film

As New Orleans is for Louisiana, Tulsa, the heart of what was once Indian Territory, is recognized as the arts and culture capital of Oklahoma. This standing is in no small part due to the thriving Native American arts scene in the city. Unlike New Orleans, Tulsa does not usually make lists of top tourist destinations in the United States. However, its cultural institutions, like the Crescent City's, are inextricably linked to histories of Native American commerce, politics, and arts as well as the dispossession of Native lands. Because of Tulsa's geographical importance in Indian Country, one of two large urban areas in a state that is home to thirty-nine federally recognized tribal nations, its relevance to studies of urban Indigenous experience should be obvious. Surprisingly, none of the research on urban Indigenous literatures discusses Tulsa in any detail even though it is a formative place in the lives of many Native writers, including U.S. poet laureate Joy Harjo.

Despite disorienting signs that disappear their rights to and histories of Tulsa, writers and filmmakers make Native experiences visible in the city, echoing what LeAnne Howe describes as tribalography, undertaken "to inform ourselves and the non-Indian world about who we are."[1] Tulsa's Indigenous art scene is in fact among the most influential in the United States. Gilcrease Museum, named for the Muscogee collector and museum founder, Thomas Gilcrease, houses the country's largest collection of western and Native American art, and Philbrook Museum, which hosted the Indian Annual from 1946 to 1979, are both pivotal in showcasing Indigenous art, especially of the contemporary era. The Greater Tulsa Indian Art Festival and Tribal Language Symposium is one of the nation's largest intertribal fine art markets. Well beyond these institutions, the participation of local tribes, including in arts, culture, and tourism, is vital to the Oklahoma economy, making a $10.8 billion impact statewide through tribal government and business operations, including gaming. Indigenous creativity fosters community with ancestors who established the city and with other kin who continue to live and create on their land, despite the transformation of Tulsa in the aftermath of Oklahoma statehood. This chapter links writing and media by Joy Harjo, Sterlin Harjo, and numerous other songwriters, journalists, and storytellers to studies of urban Indigeneity. Across media these writers express their rights to the city and their crucial role in the dynamic intersection of arts and activism.

"Oklahoma Never Leaves Us"

Joy Harjo honors her birthplace of Tulsa through music and song, with added layers of poetry and narrative. In "Oklahoma: The Prairie of Words," an essay she first published in Geary Hobson's anthology *The Remembered Earth* (1979), Harjo explains why this land of her birth pervades the imagination. She writes: "In a sense, we never leave Oklahoma, or maybe it would be better said that Oklahoma never leaves us. The spirit is alive in the landscape that arranges itself in the poems and stories that are created and the spirit takes many forms and many voices. . . . What is breathing here is some sort of dangerous anger that rises up out of the Oklahoma landscape. The earth is alive with emotions, and will take action on what is being felt. This way of seeing is characteristic of most native poets and writers of Oklahoma." Alluding to histories of violence and displacement in Indian Territory, Harjo draws attention to the many Oklahoma poets who inspire her, including Jim Barnes, Linda Hogan, N. Scott Momaday, and Carter Revard. This chorus of voices shares this place that has become a homeland, even while the land contains stories and histories of diverse peoples who have gathered here, many having endured painful journeys from original homes. The weight of this experience makes Oklahoma ever-present in the lives and words of its poets. Harjo says: "Even if they move away, they always return. They return, even if they have been sent miles away to school or leave to find jobs, and then come back with families and settle down. . . . And some return only in their hearts and voices, singing, again, and again—to Oklahoma red earth, a curving wind plain—to creeks and rivers that cross over and through the land. No one has ever left."[2]

Harjo expresses this sense of Oklahoma as home in several poems across her body of work, in some instances wrestling with the stifling conservatism she finds there and in others writing of this place with tender affection. In the prose poem "Sleepwalkers," Harjo describes her childhood creative inclinations being stymied at school in Tulsa, and she says that the pressure of conformity is a tempter toward sleepwalking, or hiding one's gifts. She writes, "My life revolved around a father and mother, two brothers and a sister, segregation of people and ideas and in a city that depressed me with intimate human cruelties, then astounded me with the sheer beauty of sunlight on dew." During a session of coloring at school, she is surprised by the similarity of the artwork of all the other students in the class. When she questions why they copy each other, they begin copying her drawing as well. She recalls: "Each of my many lives, from teenage mother to tribal-jazz-rock musician, is marked by similar incidents. . . . This dogmatic system of conformity proscribes the shape of thought, of everything in this Puritan-influenced country (especially the Bible Belt)."[3] Harjo writes in more detail in her memoirs, *Crazy Brave* (2012) and *Poet Warrior* (2021), about the trauma she faced in her home environment, but in this instance she gives voice to her experience of being starved for artistic mentors. The drive to express herself artistically in this conservative space far removed from the birthplace of jazz would later contribute to her decision to leave Tulsa for Santa Fe.

"The Flood," published in *The Woman Who Fell from the Sky* (1994), alludes to the turmoil of Harjo's childhood, drawing on the Muscogee story of the tie snake as a means to approximate the turmoil of a sixteen-year-old girl. The poem begins with the suggestion that the girl is considering willfully disappearing into the lake, knowing that "the story at the surface would say car accident, or drowning / while drinking, all of it eventually accidental." But the "watermonster," the snake at the bottom of the lake, is real: "This story is not an accident, nor is the existence of the 'water-snake' in the memory of the people as they carried the burden of the myth from Alabama to Oklahoma. Each reluctant step pounded memory into the broken heart and no one will ever forget it."[4] The images of dangerous waters in the poem reflect the Muscogee natural world in the Southeast as well as beliefs about bodies of water as portals to the underworld of chaos.[5]

Harjo explains that she has heard stories of the watersnake, "soaked into my blood since infancy like deer gravy," and in her imagining of the girl's fate, she has a memory of herself becoming the wife of the watermonster, ultimately disappearing with him in a storm. In this recollection Harjo channels the grief and desperation that remains in Oklahoma generations after removal: "When the proverbial sixteen-year-old woman walked down to the lake within her were all sixteen-year-old women who had questioned their power from time immemorial." The speaker then explains that the girl emerges from the lake years later, and she sees her in a convenience store. Harjo writes that she "hurried the cashier for my change as the crazy woman walked in, for I could not see myself as I had abandoned her some twenty years ago in a blue windbreaker at the edge of the man-made lake as everyone dove naked and drunk off the sheer cliff, as if we had nothing to live for, not then or ever." The piece connects cultural ancestry rooted in eastern homelands with the sexual awakening and growing independence of a young woman living at the end of the removal trail. Though it is not recognizable on the surface, or is not believed by those in Oklahoma who have stopped telling the story of the watersnake, the girl's power has real consequences: "It was beginning to rain in Oklahoma, the rain that would flood the world."[6]

The relationship between womanhood and artistry is a significant theme in much of Harjo's writing, and a source for creativity that would later drive Harjo's thriving career can be traced in several poems to Harjo's mother, who was of Cherokee ancestry, in Tulsa. In "The Last Song" (1975), from her first book, a chapbook of the same title, Harjo creates a conversation between her and her partner (presumably Simon Ortiz) during a trip home from New Mexico. He asks:

how can you stand it
he said
the hot Oklahoma summers
where you were born.

She responds:

it is the only way
i know how to breathe
an ancient chant
that my mother knew
came out of a history
woven from wet tall grass
in her womb
and i know no other way
than to surround my voice
with the summer songs of the crickets
in this moist south night air
oklahoma will be the last song
i'll ever sing.[7]

The geography suggested in these nighttime images is literally Oklahoma, but the references to "history woven from wet tall grass" and "moist south night air" bring to mind the ancestral lands of her people in the Southeast as well, with Harjo's mother, Wynema Baker Fisher, a bridge, through her body as well as her song, to the memory of her people and their homelands at a distance from Tulsa.

In her 2019 poetry book, *An American Sunrise*, Harjo's mother's body holds memory that facilitates peacemaking in the poem "Washing My Mother's Body." Harjo begins by explaining, "I never got to wash my mother's body when she died." Through the poem Harjo carefully and affectionately describes the act of tending to her mother before burial, observing items in her house that hold memories of her life in northeastern Oklahoma and the histories her people carried there from the Southeast. Harjo enters through the door: "I step in to make my ritual. To do what should have been done." She finds in the house her mother's white enamel pan for bread and biscuit making, which she also used to bathe Harjo and her siblings in their infancy in Tulsa. She then prepares to use the same pan for this bathing ritual, testing the water to ensure it's the temperature one would use to bathe a baby. A stack of washcloths reminds Harjo of the life her mother made in this place, striving for plenty after going without basic needs for so long. In her mother's face, Harjo sees remarkable beauty, which reminds her of the generations of Cherokee women she is descended from. An iron pot is a tangible reminder of this connection between homelands in the Southeast and here:

> My mother had the iron pot given to her by her Cherokee mother,
> whose mother gave it to her, given to her by the U.S. government
> on the Trail of Tears.
> She grew flowers in it.

Harjo imagines her mother's spirit taking flight, visiting places she loved, including this house, as well as the local bar where she was "shuffleboard queen." These images, revealed through everyday objects, of Wynema's connections to her Cherokee women ancestors and to her roles as both mother at home and playful expert at shuffleboard, contain a history of survival and love in this city. Here she has made a life for herself that profoundly impacted her daughter. Through memory her spirit will endure, Harjo says: "I cannot say goodbye yet. / I will never say goodbye."[8]

Along with these comments about the home Wynema built for herself and her family, Harjo includes painful episodes from her mother's life, visible in marks on her body, that capture her struggle of poverty and abuse so common for so many women but also empower Harjo's awareness of the strength of her own body. A burn scar on her mother's arm prompts a recollection of the "cruel boss / who insisted she reach her hand into the Fryolator to clean it." Harjo writes,

> That scar always reminded me of her coming in
> from working long hours in restaurants,
> her uniform drenched with sweat, determination and exhaustion.

Harjo finds a journal with notes about the lives of her mother's friends and coworkers, including "a Jewish woman who treated her kindly" who has cancer. These events, carrying the grief as well as the purpose that Wynema found in her life in Tulsa, point toward the resolve following loss that being from this place represents for Oklahoma's Native peoples. Harjo offers gratitude to her mother's body for endowing her with this legacy:

> The story is all there, in her body, as I wash her to prepare her
> to be let down into earth, and return all stories to the earth.
> My body memories rise up as I wash.
> I recall carrying my two children, rocking them,
> and feeding them from my body.
> How I knew myself as beloved Earth, in that body.

As she completes her act of washing, Harjo is able to let her mother go, fittingly while singing. She offers her

> one of those old homemade heartbreak songs
> where there's a moment of happiness
> wound through.[9]

Take Me Back to Tulsa . . . or Don't

Harjo's recent projects emphasize the importance of jazz, also expressed through the body, as cultural and historical memory as well as futurity, and as discussed in the previous chapter, she asserts the Muscogee foundations of jazz through her writing about New Orleans. In her poems about her childhood in Tulsa, Harjo's rendering of homelands in the Southeast is never far from the endpoint of removal to Indian Territory. Harjo writes in more detail about her hometown of Tulsa, indicating with love as well as pain the interrelatedness of her personal experiences with the broader history of her tribe in the city. In "Dear Tulsa," a letter; her memoirs; and selections from her forthcoming jazz musical *We Were There When Jazz Was Invented*, Harjo expresses the city's complicated past with tribes, with African Americans, and with settlers, which has influenced her own relationship with Tulsa as she has left and returned.

"Dear Tulsa" is a letter Harjo composed for Al Letson's Peabody Award–winning podcast, *State of the Reunion*. In her letter to home, Harjo calls the city her "mother town," where she "entered the human story." As in her poem "We Were There When Jazz Was Invented," in this letter Harjo highlights musical ties between Congo Square and Tulsa, describing "the Arkansas River up which blues and jazz traveled, set up and jammed." She names herself as a Tulsan who took her place among other Tulsans in a grand experiment. She writes: "We were Creek, or Mvskoke Indians and the other four of the Five Civilized Tribes. We were many other tribes moved west by the U.S. government, European settlers who followed behind them carrying whiskey, bibles and fiddles, and the African and African-Americans who came with everyone, enslaved, and often on their own. Tulsa, you are part of the grand experiment of a trickster god to see what will happen with such a mix of humanity." In this description of the Tulsa populace, Harjo indicates the unique diasporic position of tribes in Indian Territory as having been relocated from homelands far elsewhere. While loss of land and separation from homelands are fundamental to the experiences of tribes after colonization, Oklahoma's amalgamation of such a diversity of Indigenous nations, many of which, due to forced relocation, are at a great distance from the lands of ancestors of just a few generations past, indicates the relevance of cosmopolitanism for describing this place. The legacy of Indian Territory and its transformation into Oklahoma is hard to come to grips with: "I was your difficult child, like one of S. E. Hinton's 'Outsiders,'" Harjo writes. "When I came of age, I fled you and didn't look back. I could not reconcile the theft of lands, the largest race riot in the country, the inequities of economics and religious rigidity." For Harjo, being in place, or at home, in Tulsa is simultaneous with unease because of the city's fraught history.

Music is at the heart of Harjo's return to Tulsa, however, with Bob Wills singing the anthem of a prodigal daughter. She writes of her return "to the city of country and country swing, square dance, round dance, stomp dance, gospel, hymn, powwow, rock and roll, blues and jazz and rhythm and blues. Food, laughter, crying, and deep mythic roots accompany every story of music, and each carries the story of humanity." For Harjo this musical story is a dance of creation, destruction, and change, even when things seem to stand still. Appropriately, then, she concludes her letter with a reference to the western swing song "Take Me Back to Tulsa," which she associates both with her personal family story and with the broader Tulsa family story. Named in her "We Were There" poem, which comments in a similar way on the city's history of conflict, this song represents both a recovery of Native people in the story of jazz and a meeting of regions—South and West—that can be heard in western swing. As in her writing about New Orleans, this letter to Tulsa emphasizes that this place is Indian Country: "I most likely will leave my last breath here, Tulsa, in your leafy, Indian town arms." Yet the reference to the Bob Wills song also indicates kinship between Natives and others, especially African Americans, who have their own stories of coming to Tulsa, freely or by force, only to find themselves disenfranchised by the United States, by the state of Oklahoma, and by southern tribes such as the Muscogee Nation.

The song "Take Me Back to Tulsa" is one more example of the way that histories of people of color are disappeared in cities, with artists such as Harjo countering that disappearance creatively. Tulsans are fond of "Take Me Back to Tulsa" as a chorale of their hometown's "indigenous" western swing music, but not often mentioned are western swing's connections to minstrelsy. Like the masking traditions of Mardi Gras Indians in New Orleans, the roots of western swing reflect a cultural mediation, most often discussed as joining jazz typically associated with urban (read: Black) areas and the "hillbilly" music of rural (read: white) dance halls of Oklahoma and Texas. When in 1929 he won a contest with a fiddler in a traveling medicine show, Wills got his big break in music, allowing him to leave his job as a barber in Turkey, Texas, to join the show as a musician and blackface comic. The distinctive performative style that Wills perfected in his regular show at the Cains Ballroom is the subject of some disagreement. According to his biographer Charles Townsend, members of the band believed that the showmanship Wills displayed proceeded directly from his years as a touring minstrel performer. Townsend notes, however, that Wills himself remarked that his years as a blackface comic were not the source of his style; instead, he asserted that "he grew up playing with and living close to Negroes and that part of his style came *directly* from them. His work in these minstrel shows gave him an opportunity to express the folkways and folk music of the Negroes he had grown up with in East and West Texas."[10] Wills here appears to be claiming cultural knowledge akin to the way that many non-Native performers of "Indianness" also claim authenticity, and it is difficult to discern where Wills (or his biographer) draws the line between influence and appropriation. Still, though western swing performances went hand in hand with segregation in the South, as Jean Boyd reminds us, the music is "a crossroads for diverse cultures, including Native American, Mexican American, Anglo American, German, French, Cajun, African American, Czech, and Polish."[11] As such, a Bob Wills song is a fitting soundtrack for the histories of Tulsa—of creation, destruction, and change—that Harjo brings to light in her work.

Harjo's memoir *Crazy Brave* extends this representation of the fluidity between individual and family stories, deeply entwined with music, that for Harjo begins in Tulsa but also reaches to other geographies: her ancestral homelands in the Southeast and her creative homeland in Santa Fe. Harjo describes her first hearing of jazz, around the time that she first acquired language, as changing "the spin of the world." She recounts:

> We were driving somewhere in Tulsa, the northern border of the Creek Nation. . . . I became acutely aware of the line the jazz trumpeter was playing (a sound I later associated with Miles Davis). . . . I don't know how to say it, with what sounds or words, but in that confluence of hot southern afternoon, in the breeze of aftershave and humidity, I followed that sound to the beginning, to the birth of sound. I was suspended in whirling stars. . . . My rite of passage into the world of humanity occurred then, through jazz. The music was a startling bridge between familiar and strange lands. I heard stomp-dance shells, singing. I saw suits, satin, fine hats. I heard workers singing in the fields. It was a way to speak beyond the confines of ordinary language. I still hear it.[12]

In this passage Harjo tells a jazz creation story, "the birth of sound," from within the Muscogee Nation, with music as an entrée to other places and communities. Ceremonial songs from the stomp grounds combine with the spaces of jazz clubs and fields of labor to transcend time and space. She remarks that the music that led her to earth also endowed her with responsibility to carry "voices, songs, and stories to grow and release into the world."[13] Among the voices she hears are leaders of her people, family relations (including the Afro-Muscogee mother of Osceola) who resisted U.S. encroachment, as well as singers from Congo Square who espouse the spirit of New Orleans ceremonial grounds. Music also allows Harjo a voice even when, as a child, language is insufficient, both because of the limits of language itself and because of the difficult, abusive family life she experienced.

Music not only serves as a birth story for Harjo, but it also is an accompaniment for her understanding of family, on earth and in the spirit world, as she grows from childhood. Harjo explains that her mother's singing is what attracted her from the land of spirits through the doorway into earth. Harjo's mother was a western swing musician who filled her home with singing, crooning to the music "threading the atmosphere" of Tulsa and jitterbugging with her daughter across the kitchen floor. Harjo describes her mother's life through musical language: "I heard the soul that was to be my mother call out in a heartbreak ballad. I saw her walking the floor after midnight. Though she was crazy in love with my father, she sensed the hard road ahead of them. I heard Cherokee stomp dancers in the distance. They were her mother's people. They danced under the stars until the light of dawn."[14] Music is integral to the courtship of Wynema by Harjo's father; they swing danced at their first acquaintance at the Casa Loma dance hall in western Tulsa. Wynema's music is quieted, however, due to the abuse she endures from Harjo's father and stepfather. Harjo recalls that her father's alcoholism led to a climate of fear in the household. This tension only intensified after her mother's second marriage.

Harjo's stepfather targeted Wynema's musical life out of a desire to keep his wife (and Harjo) in check. After he sexually assaulted Wynema while Harjo listened from her bedroom, Harjo's stepfather kept tight control over the household, and Wynema stopped singing. The incident that solidified Harjo's feeling of alienation from her own home was her mother's performance with Leon McAuliffe (later a member of Bob Wills's band) and His Cimarron Boys. Having accepted an invitation to sing one of her original songs with the western swing band, Wynema, nervous at first, found her voice, and Harjo "felt her spirit reach up and touch the sun."[15] Rather than celebrating her accomplishments, however, Harjo's stepfather belittled Wynema, and upon their return home, she went to her room, signifying surrender in her retreat to sleep. From that turning point, Harjo was aware that her creative life, as well as her growing sexual maturity, must remain hidden. Creativity, especially singing, represented an escape from the "domestic prison" of the home, but once Harjo was beaten after playing her records and singing too loud, like her mother, she stopped singing entirely.

When she began Tulsa's Will Rogers High School, Harjo was granted permission by her mother to inquire about trying out for the school play; Harjo had found in performance "an escape from the hard reality of the Oklahoma of stolen Indian lands and the self-righteous religious right." However, beaten once again by her stepfather, Harjo was bereft and turned to self-destructive behaviors. Increasingly desperate, even considering running away to a life of prostitution in San Francisco, a feeling of knowing, or an alternative understanding of God, led Harjo to request that her mother enroll her in Indian boarding school. Planning at first to attend Chilocco Indian School near the Kansas border, the agent at the Bureau of Indian Affairs office in Okmulgee suggested the Institute for American Indian Arts in Santa Fe. A new chapter, an escape from Harjo's "emotional winter" of childhood, began in New Mexico.[16] It would be many years until Harjo returned to music or to Tulsa, her mother town.

"We Were There When Jazz Was Invented, or a Love Song for Justice Fields," a short excerpt from Harjo's jazz musical in progress, mirrors the association of music with birth and with the responsibility of storytelling that is presented in Harjo's memoir. The play begins with the words of a Story Helper who has been summoned by the spirit of American music to help it complete its story. The Story Helper at first questions her usefulness. "But I am not the most likely, not a lettered scholar of original American music, or a renowned player of profound jazz interpretations, or a touring blues diva," she says. Her grandson Justice is troubled and under the influence of drugs and racism. Like the sixteen-year-old girl of "The Flood," who was contemplating disappearing into the lake, Justice is threatening to jump off the top of the Mayo building in downtown Tulsa, a skyscraper built to capitalize on the need for office space that emerged after the development of the Glenn Pool oil field. Story Helper asks, "How can I fix the American music story when I need to help my grandson?" to which the spirit replies, "It is the same story." Completing the story of American music, reframing it as Indigenous music, promises to save Justice.

As Harjo herself experienced, Justice is feeling alienated from this Tulsa homeland because of its history. As he contemplates jumping, Justice types into his cell phone:

> Take a good look America, this is the last stand of Justice.
> Tulsa's homegrown Creek Indian homie on stolen Creek Indian land,
> The son of disappearing act Rabbit Leroy Fields
> And devoted mother soon without son, June.

As a chorus of hecklers chants at Justice from below, Story Helper warns, "You are in a dangerous place in your story," to which Justice replies, "Being Indian in this town is always dangerous." Justice's struggle with feelings of alienation capture the layered relationships to the city expressed in the work of Tulsa's Indigenous writers. The history of Indian removals, which separated southeastern tribes from their homelands in the East, is an ever-present influence on being in place in Indian Territory. Tulsa is an Indian town, as Harjo reminds us, but as other reminders of dispossession pervade like the "Indian ghost stories" that dot the city's landscape, feelings of despair are hard to escape. That despair, that intergenerational trauma, was devastating to Harjo's own father, as it apparently is for Justice's father and for Justice himself. Creativity, however, is a means of healing as well as for honoring the Indigenous families whose lands form the city. For Harjo, jazz is a performative and philosophical counter to settler colonialism. Music, this Indigenous music, is the song of survival, of life.

With Justice counting down the moments until he leaps to his death, Story Helper tells of his birth, which is described as Justice's blues song. Story Helper explains that his arrival on earth occurred, appropriately for Oklahoma, during a tornado, which picked up his parents' car and spun it into a field of wildflowers. At that moment Justice gave his first cry song, his first blues. Moved by her family's survival, Justice's mom sang a lullaby that imbued the parts of his body with beauty. Justice's father, a musician, left the family "to catch a gig in some city on the blues trail." Apparently not able to recover from this abandonment and also coping with the death of his Kiowa girlfriend, Janey, Justice is still set on suicide, imagining what he will find in the afterlife, whether his Mvskoke relatives or a vengeful Christian God who punishes him for his suicide. But as he and Story Helper, who reminds him of his aunt who lives near the New Tulsa ceremonial grounds, contemplate how his story may end, another in a long list of teenage suicides, Justice hears a stomp dance caller. Suddenly he is aware of his grandfather close by. Story Helper shares that this turn is Justice's own story "making a noisy effort against a heavy moment of time." A barely audible Muscogee hymn, his grandmother's favorite, disarms Justice, causing him to pause from his destructive plans. Story Helper replies: "Rest here for a moment, grandson. There is plenty of time for playing with death. Tell me about the music. Tell me about Janey." The reality of stolen land persists, but music, in the form of a hymn, also nourishes a connection to ancestors and family members across time and geography so that Justice may find his place.

Another selection from the musical, a song called "An American Sunrise," reprinted in Harjo's poetry collection of the same title, creates voices that are similar to the voice of the Justice character, this time rendered in a send-up of Gwendolyn Brooks's poem "We Real Cool." In the tradition of call-and-response and combined with jazz instrumentation, the last words of every line of the piece together form lines of Brooks's iconic ode to the bravado of young Black pool players. In Harjo's version, young warriors meet the sunrise, "surfacing the edge of our ancestors' fights, and ready to strike." Music enables their orbit beyond this world, reflecting Muscogee understandings of the cosmos: "And some of us could sing / so we drummed a fire-lit pathway up to those starry stars." Like the subjects of Brooks's poem, the youth are pool players with plans. Their actions and attitudes reflect the swagger of jazz:

> Sin
> was invented by the Christians, as was the Devil, we sang. We
> were the heathens, but needed to be saved from them—thin
> chance. We knew we were all related in this story, a little gin
> will clarify the dark and make us all feel like dancing. We
> had something to do with the origins of blues and jazz
> I argued with a Pueblo as I filled the jukebox with dimes in June,
> forty years later and we still want justice. We are still America.
> We know the rumors of our demise. We spit them out. They die
> soon.[17]

In Brooks's original poem, the pool players assert their presence, together repeating *we* at the end of each line as they gather in a pool hall on the south side of Brooks's hometown of Chicago. Harjo's version is also presumably in an urban setting; it could be in Tulsa or any other place with an Indian bar, and while this version also echoes a collective "we," the *I* pronoun intervenes and comments more directly on the interplay between individual and community experiences that is a common theme in Harjo's work.

Like LeAnne Howe's story "The Chaos of Angels," Harjo's rewriting of "We Real Cool" emphasizes the power of kinship, especially among African Americans and Natives. "We knew we were all related," Harjo asserts; dancing together, while on one level simply a logical progression after consuming gin in a bar, is also a reminder of the ceremonial importance of dancing. Throughout Harjo's recent writings, dancing, traced to Congo Square, is the heart of creativity and a powerful reminder not only of the Indigenous roots of jazz but also of community making among diverse peoples to resist settler colonialism. A Pueblo person at the bar needs this reminder from the poem's persona, who fills the jukebox to keep the music going in June (also the name of Justice's mother). "We are still America," then, is an idea that comes straight out of music formed on Muscogee land, whether in New Orleans or in Tulsa, at the beginning of time or in the present. This sense of determination against the odds is another legacy of jazz, an affirmation of life. So in Harjo's poem, the "We / Die soon" conclusion to Brooks's "We Real Cool" is countered with: "They die soon." In this reworking *They* could refer to rumors of demise or to the colonizers themselves; either way, the people who were there when jazz was invented are still here seeking—and singing and dancing—for justice.

Joy Harjo's relationship with Tulsa resonates in both personal and spatial terms in her writing, with jazz the driving force for telling the story of her own creativity. Similar to Howe's story of America, or tribalography, Harjo finds in jazz the Muscogee creation of America. Uniting and making visible her homelands in the Southeast and in Oklahoma, Harjo's writing also honors the power of music for reconciliation. Removal to Indian Territory, followed by statehood, presents loss for Muscogee people that will endure, and Tulsa's shameful history of racism, epitomized by the Tulsa Race Massacre of 1921, contributes to the disorienting experience of living in a place where visible reminders of attempts to disappear peoples of color pervade. Like the "Kilroy-is-here" sentiment that Brooks expressed, Harjo, in her poems, songs, and narrative, makes clear: "We were there."

The community making that "An American Sunrise" and other poems present is a meaningful entrée into Harjo's service for three terms as U.S. poet laureate. The COVID-19 pandemic disrupted Harjo's in-person events and projects; however, her presence in the spaces of virtual and digital worlds has made her poetry more accessible to an array of audiences in these years of uncertainty, despair, and upheaval. Bringing to mind Arjun Appadurai's discussion of new media as vernacular and connective, public and imaginative, Harjo's signature project, "Living Nations, Living Words," is an interactive story map of forty-seven contemporary Native poets across the country housed freely online with the Library of Congress.[18] Referring to her appointment as poet laureate for a third term, Harjo stated: "Poetry has provided doorways for joy, grief, and understanding in the midst of turmoil and pandemic. . . . The story of America begins with Native presence, thoughts, and words. Poetry is made of word threads that weave and connect us."[19] Harjo orients the virtual tour of the story map "as in Muscogee Creek tradition" with the East, "the direction of becoming," then moves to other directions. She comments on her own experiences in various geographies alongside representations of poet colleagues across the country in locations that each identifies as his or her "place." Harjo takes care to make Native American poets visible in urban sites among many states and regions. She explains in the introduction to the project, "I want this map to counter damaging false assumptions—that Indigenous peoples of our country are often invisible or are not seen as human. . . . Our common language of English, or sometimes Spanish, is a crossing place, a place to meet many from all over the world. . . . Though we may venture far from our origin story, we are bound by genealogy, by land, even by instinct."

Now Tulsa is again home for Harjo. She explains: "I moved back to Oklahoma after my mother passed from this earth. I returned to my family here, to my Muscogee Creek people where I belonged, just as my spirit told me I would years ago. I married Owen Sapulpa, a Muscogee Creek citizen whom I had met years ago when we were young Native artists working for justice in New Mexico at the National Indian Youth Council. I returned with him to *Oce Vpofv* ceremonial grounds, my family's home grounds, though I had long been made welcome at *Tvlahasse Wvkokaye* ceremonial grounds. I finally made it home."[20] In print, in sound, and in the virtual world, then, Harjo identifies Tulsa as a place of homecoming while telling the broader story of her people and of America.

Tallasi through the Lens

Seminole-Muscogee filmmaker Sterlin Harjo, like Joy Harjo, brings to the fore urban Indian stories, showing on-screen relationships to place that counteract the ghost stories that city landmarks tell. Harjo has enjoyed remarkable success on the film festival circuit with his groundbreaking representations of contemporary Indigenous life, especially his artful and affectionate perspective on Oklahoma landscapes. With Cherokee photographer Jeremy Charles, he founded a film production company, FireThief Productions, which produces *Osiyo: Voices of the Cherokee People*, and several other Oklahoma-based video and film productions. In early 2020 Harjo was invited to join the Academy of Motion Picture Arts and Sciences.

According to Harjo, stories of Oklahoma are his creative inspiration. "I love all the stories in Oklahoma. It's overflowing with unique history," he says, "I love dirt roads and the countryside. Tulsa is perfect because it's not too big and it's not too small. You can get a good cup of coffee, but you can also get to the country pretty fast if you need to."[21] His films, *Goodnight, Irene*, *Four Sheets to the Wind*, *Barking Water*, *This May Be the Last Time*, and *Mekko*, and his hit television series, *Reservation Dogs*, bring the unique spaces of Oklahoma into focus, drawing connections between Indigenous homelands in both rural and urban locations. In *Four Sheets to the Wind* and *Mekko*, Tulsa emerges as a center for contemporary Indigenous life, a hometown that holds great promise as well as tragedy. In these two works, Harjo presents the cosmopolitan experiences of Indigenous Oklahomans while also recognizing the Muscogee foundations of the city, countering all-too-typical notions of dislocation between urban Natives and their homelands. The two films convey Indigenous participation in the human, lived—not abstract—everyday life of the city, which resonates beyond the architecture of objects to transformative encounters in beauty and in art.

Like their ancestors, the characters within these films find grounding as Indigenous people within the city while connecting with relatives and other, more rural landscapes of Creek country. *Four Sheets to the Wind* places the Muscogee and Seminole Smallhill family in the overlapping landscapes of Holdenville, Wewoka, and Tulsa, creating a synchronicity between rural and urban environments that also reflects the relationships among towns that are distinctive to the Creek Confederacy. Harjo's rendering of Tulsa is Indigenous, a place that is, though apart from rural homelands in southern Oklahoma, an appropriate location for the film's protagonist, Cufe Smallhill, to find love and to reach insight into the family dynamics that have led to his sister Miri's troubles. By depicting Cufe's maturation amid Tulsa landmarks such as the Blue Dome district, the Cain's Ballroom, and Cathedral Square, Harjo creates a sense of home for Cufe that parallels the homeplace evoked in rural Muscogee towns of Oklahoma and sets the stage for Cufe's final decision to travel more widely.

Thus, Harjo constructs characters not inherently marked by loss of or disconnection from culture in the city, as some earlier writers of the Native American Renaissance have done. Instead, in Harjo's works Indigenous characters challenge typical notions of authenticity, creating fluidity among various places, rural and urban, that are significant for understanding self, community, and culture. This fluidity renders an alternative Indigenous space, unsettling urban settler imaginaries. In fact, one of the most remarkable things about the premiere of *Four Sheets to the Wind* in Tulsa's Circle Cinema independent theater was the audience's response. In the lobby afterward, amid the racially, economically, nationally, and generationally mixed crowd, I could hear over and over again comments that expressed a common sentiment, that this Oklahoma was recognizable to its people. Harjo's film, accordingly, both depicts and creates experience, asserting a right to the city. Within the language of Indigenous studies, this accomplishment is also an act of visual sovereignty. Michelle Raheja, in her foundational study *Reservation Reelism* (2011), amplifies Maori filmmaker Barry Barclay's articulation of Fourth Cinema, shaped by Indigenous subjects and aesthetics, and relates it to early Native filmmaking in North America.[22] Raheja notes that importance in visual sovereignty of presenting films to local communities. Kristin Dowell deepens this study of the relationship to community in her *Sovereign Screens* (2013), arguing that such an act not only recasts images of Indigenous peoples on-screen but also creates and negotiates community off-screen.[23]

Harjo's Oklahoma mirrors the diverse, multi-tribal, non-reservation, heavily Indigenous-populated dynamics of the state that do not often see the light of day in popular culture, especially movies. Cufe's community extends outward from Holdenville but also from Tulsa and includes peoples from a variety of backgrounds. Cufe's experience of kinship is driven by his relationship with his Muscogee father but is inclusive of and informed by people of other tribes and other races. In Holdenville and Wewoka (the capitol of the Seminole Nation, adjacent to the Muscogee Nation), Seminole and Muscogee peoples interact, and Cufe and his friends and relatives create kin with whites, African Americans, and other tribal citizens, achieving intimacy in some instances and confronting racism in others. The situation is much the same in Tulsa, where encounters in bars, health clinics, and eating establishments almost directly correspond to similar scenarios and scenes in the rural locations. These parallel scenarios and scenes of conflict, hardship, love, and reconciliation across Tulsa, Holdenville, and Wewoka demonstrate that life in these urban and rural locations is connected and reciprocal, further confounding state formations of settler and Indigenous space.

The opening scenes of the movie reveal this parallelism. The film begins with the image of Cufe dragging his deceased father, Frankie Smallhill, who has died by suicide, down a dirt road, through woods marked "private property," and into a pond, where he gives his father a watery burial to fulfill his final wishes.[24] From the scene of the pond and surrounding trees, Harjo transitions to images of dirt roads, then to a shot of the town of Holdenville, then to a picture of the landscape viewed through a barbed wire fence. After Cufe walks across a cattle guard, the audience sees a passing train, a storefront church, several oil pump jacks, an overgrown basketball court, some broken-down cars, and finally Cufe's house and dog. Later, when Cufe heads to Tulsa to visit Miri, the series of images—evoking natural elements as well as manufactured items associated with transport—is parallel. The audience sees a railroad yard, the Tulsa skyline, a bus station, a kitty, and Miri's apartment complex. In this catalog of images, not only is this Oklahoma landscape in its natural appearance significant for Cufe, most obviously in the association between his father and the pond, but also the material items, the trains, cars, scooters, and cityscapes, are visible reminders of "progress" and its problematic as well as invigorating implications. It seems that upon his arrival in Tulsa, Cufe has literally seen it all before.

Miri's and Cufe's plotlines, though leading to different outcomes, are also parallel. Whereas Miri's Tulsa experiences following her failed attempt at an acting career in California seem to be mostly negative, revealing her desperate and empty existence in the city, Cufe's Tulsa experiences spur his honest communication about his father with his first serious girlfriend, a young white woman named Francine, and seem to give him the confidence to consider making a road trip with her to California. In this way the movie hinges on the contrast between Cufe's and Miri's experiences of space, which for both characters involve leaving Holdenville and traveling to Tulsa and California. From the beginning of the film to the end, Cufe leaves Holdenville, goes to Tulsa, returns to Holdenville briefly, and then leaves, apparently for California. Miri, on the other hand, has already been to California, begins the film in Tulsa, and finally returns to Holdenville. This contrast between Cufe's and Miri's spatial encounters transforms typical representations of urban Indigenous peoples by highlighting a fluidity between rural and urban and representing these spaces as Indigenous. These images counter settler colonial whitewashing of urban space.

In most literature and film up until the 1990s, urban Indigenous experiences are marked by ambivalence, usually accompanied by "hybrid," or mixed-blood, identities, which, if not leading to tragedy, lead to eventual flight from urban locations that are environmentally and spiritually problematic and return to reservations or rural towns. Indigenous-authored literature that has received the most critical acclaim, especially texts from the 1960s and 1970s such as N. Scott Momaday's *House Made of Dawn* and Leslie Marmon Silko's *Ceremony*, emphasize reservation over urban experiences, especially the religious importance of returning to these locations after time overseas and/or in cities. William Bevis calls this phenomenon "homing in," explaining, "In Native American novels, coming home, staying put, . . . is a primary mode of knowledge and a primary good."[25] Joanna Hearne describes how, in the realm of film, Indigenous peoples typically appear only "at a certain historical moment in the mid- and late nineteenth century, or . . . are chronically incapable of navigating a modernity imagined as the sole purview of urban dwellers—the audience of the movies themselves, who are imagined as homogenous white settlers."[26] Based on narratives such as these, readers and audiences may thereby conclude that being authentic necessitates living in a predominantly Indigenous community, usually on a reservation, and rejecting urbanization, a process equated with assimilation.

In Harjo's film Miri's character ultimately returns home, echoing the homing plot just described; however, Cufe's path suggests another option, transforming this narrative convention. Significantly for theoretical approaches to Indigenous studies, though Cufe presumably leaves Oklahoma to travel and pursue a relationship with Francie away from his ancestral home, the implication of his choice is not a turning away from a particular Muscogee identity. Cufe's father narrates his son's story at its beginning in Holdenville and at its end at the start of Cufe's travels, speaking in the Muscogee language and integrating Cufe's experience into traditional tribal stories. Cufe, whose name in Muscogee means "rabbit," thus is part of the story of rabbit, who as Frankie Smallhill explains, was able to trick the bear into entering his stomach in search of honey, rendering him satisfyingly full. By the end of the film, viewers get the sense that Cufe is likewise full. As Lee Schweninger argues, though Frankie is dead, his influence endures, his voice critical to the revelation of the characters, which is an important revision of Hollywood's vanishing Indian convention.[27] As Frankie narrates, the night before his departure, Cufe sleeps well, full of dreams of love and travel. Cufe's story buoys tribally specific cultural frameworks while also incorporating other nationalities and even faraway places into that model, suggesting, as Renya Ramirez, Mishuana Goeman, and others have theorized, that Indigenous mobility across borders, landscapes, and culture are not prohibitive of identities strongly connected to tribal homelands. This understanding of cosmopolitan Indigeneity has implications for urban space itself, as Indigenous writers like Sterlin Harjo reclaim cityscapes for their communities. In the film the privileging of space over histories of tribal peoples that viewers might expect is apparent in an encounter between Cufe and a white partygoer in Tulsa. Reflecting his almost comical (but typical) obsession with "Indians and time," he won't stop asking, "Where have all the Indian gone?" His question indicates his assumption that there are no Indians in the present, especially in this urban environment. Understandably, Cufe responds with confusion and incredulity.

In Frankie's narration, communication, even in unexpected ways, emerges as the most important factor in becoming "full" in urban space, as Cufe does. The day that Cufe leaves, after Miri, Cora, and Cufe spend their last night together in Holdenville, Frankie explains: "I know something wonderful happened that day in Oklahoma. . . . It was a silence that everyone shared . . . and I know . . . it resembled something like love." He continues: "People come around in circles. Never ending circles. But you're never that far from home." As Francine places a picture of Cufe in a frame in her Tulsa apartment, Frankie asserts, "You always come back." As Cufe leaves Holdenville for the final time, he returns to the burial pond where he fished with his father and takes a fishhook with him on his travels. Frankie ends this final act by saying: "All my life people have said, 'You never talk.' I just like listening I guess." Cufe's actions to share Muscogee community, whether through overt communication or through shared silence, maintain a constant connection to family and culture.

Harjo's feature *Mekko*, like his first, portrays a protagonist who eventually reaches self-awareness against the backdrop of Tulsa landmarks. And also like *Four Sheets*, Muscogee language is the source of narration as the film begins and ends, this time representing the main character's own thoughts. Inspired by fellow Oklahoman Richard Ray Whitman's *Street Chiefs* photographic series, Harjo seeks through *Mekko* to bring to life the stories of homelessness in the city, stories of a community that he realized was noticeably Indigenous upon moving to Tulsa. Like *Four Sheets*, *Mekko* portrays an urban environment that for some characters only mounts feelings of hopelessness. But also like the earlier film, there is not a clear dichotomy between rural and urban. The rural homeland away from Tulsa is not the clear guidepost to redemption, at least not uncomplicatedly so. Instead of privileging a timeline of events in Mekko's life, the film emphasizes sites across landscapes of Oklahoma as locations for his reflections on his past and his relationships to family and community.

The film begins with Mekko's articulation in Muscogee language of sickness, brought from *estekini* (a shape-shifting "witch") to his rural community. Accompanying this voice-over are images in black and white of an abandoned small town, with rows of homes that look like tribal housing commonly seen in Oklahoma. Mekko explains that his grandmother instilled in him the importance of striving against the sickness, a special responsibility for him in his role as a seer who could "see the darkness coming." Oakhern is the fictional town for this sequence, but the filming locations are Maud and Picher, two Oklahoma towns with histories of violence (Rutland). Maud is today mostly known as the birthplace of rockabilly star Wanda Jackson. But the town is also notorious for a horrific lynching. Resting on the pre-statehood dividing line between Oklahoma and Indian Territories, in 1898 it was the scene of the lynching of two Seminole teenagers who, in the wake of the murder of a white woman (presumably by an Indian), were dragged into Oklahoma Territory and burned at the stake at a Baptist church.[28] Picher, located in far northeastern Oklahoma within the jurisdiction of the Quapaw Tribe, is now a ghost town due to its designation, along with the town of Cardin, as the Tar Creek Superfund Site in 1983.[29] The site, one of the most toxic in the United States, was subject to federal buyouts due to contamination from lead and zinc mining. Mining, which drove the Indian Territory's transformation into the state of Oklahoma, poisoned Tar Creek and left a multitude of chat piles (mining waste). These chat piles caused elevated levels of lead in Picher's children, along with other adverse health effects such as chronic lung disease in the population as a whole.[30] The connection between these communities indicates the connections between urban and rural that are fundamental to Henri Lefebvre's articulation of the urban fabric. The industrial exploitation of Picher demonstrates the dependence of areas outside of built cities on the urban. *Mekko*'s foreboding opening emphasizes a shared experience of homelessness in the protagonist's community, in Tulsa and beyond, an experience that prepares him (and the audience) for empathy with the inhabitants of Tulsa's streets.

Mekko's release from prison begins the action of the film, and his first move is to head for Tulsa in the back of a pickup truck. Though the reason for Mekko's imprisonment is not revealed until later in the film, Mekko explains that he continually thinks of his grandmother and cousin John, with ever-stronger visions that drive him to drink and make him afraid to return home, highlighting Mekko's history with John as a source for his torment. Echoing the significance of water in *Four Sheets*, the first Tulsa location that Mekko visits is the Arkansas River. Like the Loachapoka who established Tulsa near the river, Mekko orients himself to this waterway, and against that backdrop the audience learns that he took John's life, though the circumstances are not immediately known. From the river Mekko walks to the gallery (appearing in the film as the Great Plains Gallery) of Cherokee Wes Gan, a longtime collector of Indigenous art in downtown Tulsa. There Mekko is again reminded of John, an artist. Next Mekko heads to Coney Island, a mainstay in the city for over ninety years, and savors a plate of Coneys at one of the small wooden desks so familiar to Tulsans. Affected by these touchstones that evoke a strong sense of place, Mekko visits another cousin, to whom he explains that he misses his family, has been left behind, and is ready to make amends. But he is rejected.

Though having found meaningful connection with Tulsa landmarks, this rejection from family leaves Mekko without a place to lay his head. As night falls, he stares at the Tulsa skyline rising over the expressway, and as the motion of the cars lights up the sky, Mekko is standing still. Walking into the darkness, he senses that he is being followed, the sound of an owl adding to the disturbing atmosphere. But despite this menacing moment, the next day Mekko finds a kindred spirit at another Tulsa institution, Brownie's Hamburger Stand, known for its excellent coconut pie. Tafv, a waitress, has her own troubles, like Mekko; with her mother struggling with addiction, she is responsible for her little sister's care. Her empathy with Mekko fosters an avuncular relationship between the two that makes Brownie's a lighthouse of sorts for Mekko. After leaving Brownie's, Mekko arrives in the Kendall-Whittier neighborhood, where the city's homeless gather at Whittier Square across from the art house Circle Cinema. There, finding a new family, Mekko joins the homeless camp, where he first sees Bill, an embodiment of the *estekini* figure that he has been dreading. It is soon clear that Bill has several of the characters under his control, dealing drugs to them and demanding payment. Mekko connects with an old friend in the camp, Bunnie, who leads Mekko to the Circle Cinema, pointing out the sidewalk tribute to Will Sampson and letting him in on a free popcorn hookup via an exasperated employee. Again, Mekko finds a level of solace in a legendary Tulsa location, even as a familiar (and literal) demon follows him.

Bunnie's relationship with Mekko is a noteworthy bridge between the spaces of Oakhern and Tulsa and ultimately between conflicting sides of Mekko's character. The two discuss their upbringing, musing about the decline of their small town. Bunnie reminds Mekko of the devastation of lead mining that forced people to be evacuated. Immediately following this discussion, scenes of Bill's evil impact on others are revealed. Bill calls himself a warrior of the streets who protects people, but it is obvious that he is bent on destruction. Bunnie and Mekko sleep next to the river, and in the night Bill provokes Mekko by stealing his favorite hat. When Mekko asks, "Who does he think he is?" Bunnie utters the prophetic words, "He's one of us." As Mekko circulates with Bunnie among sites in his new community—the Coney Island, the Beehive Lounge, Brownie's, the Admiral flea market—Bill, who by this point is emblematic of Mekko's own spiritual darkness, haunts him. Still, Bunnie keeps hope for spiritual renewal alive for Mekko. At the flea market, Mekko finds one of John's paintings and purchases it for $1.50. As the two admire the piece, Bunnie confides that he has been dreaming about the sweat lodges, a means of cleansing evil. In a confessional moment back in camp, Mekko explains the accidental circumstances that led him to kill his cousin John: a drunken altercation in the parking lot of a bar. Bill reappears, this time provoking Bunnie. When the two friends sleep for the night in front of Ziegler's Art Supply store (significant in light of John's artistic talent), Bill attacks them both, killing Bunnie. With this climactic event, the stakes of Mekko's responsibility to his community, and to his better nature, are abundantly clear. In light of his conversation with Bunnie, Mekko is aware that Bill is not just a reflection of his own personal demons; he also can be traced to the exploitation of their home community. Bunnie can no longer be cultural memory or compass. Mekko is responsible for setting things right to prevent further violence.

Mekko recovers in the hospital, buoyed by hymn singers and the care of Tafv, and from this point forward, Mekko endeavors to exorcise Bill, his literal and figurative antagonist. Remembering the warning contained in the stories, that one can't run from an *estekini*, Mekko returns to the river, where his resolve is clear. Harjo signals the significance of this Tulsa location by including in the shot graffiti on the Twenty-First Street Bridge that reads, "Motorcycle boy reigns." This message is a nod to Francis Ford Coppola's *Rumble Fish*, a film based on the book by Tulsa novelist S. E. Hinton, which was filmed on location in the city. Motorcycle Boy is a character with a dark past who feels stuck in a deterministic future yet seeks a way out for his younger brother. The way ahead for Mekko is unclear, but key to his redemption is his ability to relate to and care for others, especially Allen, a young newcomer to the streets. With no money (which means no Coneys!), Mekko heads to Iron Gate soup kitchen, a gathering place for Tulsa's homeless residents, where Harjo recruited several of the individuals who appear in the film. At Iron Gate, Mekko breaks bread with a Native lady who, like Tafv, offers him comfort and empathy. Near St. Francis Xavier Catholic Church, Mekko finds Allen, a former OU student who is in danger of overdose and exposure. Recognizing Allen's sickness, literal and spiritual, Mekko listens to his story of loss, in which he expresses a desire to be reunited with his grandmother and cousins, a story that Mekko can certainly understand. Mekko offers words of wisdom to this rendering of his younger self, stating, "Welcome to manhood." As Bill eavesdrops, Mekko urges Allen to recognize that the sickness can enter when darkness takes over one's spirit. Looking at John's artwork, Mekko recalls that when the sickness retreats, his people will return, and he determines, "I can make them well."

The conclusion of Mekko's journey leads to vengeance and redemption, symbolized in the presence of water in both urban and rural locations. As Mekko walks down Greenwood Avenue, in the historically Black neighborhood devastated during the 1921 Tulsa Race Massacre, a Native individual plays a hand drum while Bill follows, confronting Mekko by yelling his name. Mekko reacts by chasing Bill down and stabbing him, carving out his heart, immersing it in the river, and washing his hands clean. Mekko and Allen then return to Oakhern, where the two camp out and build a fire. An elder assures them that the fire represents the fire that continues to burn in the hearts of their community despite their trials, and it also calls to mind the fire that Loachapokas started in Tulsa from the cinders they carried during Removal. Mekko, having shown Allen the mentorship he couldn't express for John, is confident in the message of the stories of his childhood. He knows now that the people will come back, and he believes "we'll have a big victory dance." Committed to keeping the fire going, Mekko decides, "As long as I breathe, I will fight to the end." Finally, he and Allen enter the abandoned house of his grandmother, where he sees a vision of her and his cousin John. "I'll be here, cousin," he says. "I'll be waiting for you." Immediately, an aerial view of the river in luscious color, a stark contrast to the film's bleak opening, leaves viewers with a sense that the sickness has retreated.

While *Mekko* certainly paints a grittier portrait of Tulsa than *Four Sheets to the Wind*, its depiction of the city is nonetheless affectionate, highlighting a right to the city amid the struggles of homelessness and asserting a prominent role for Indigenous peoples in the city's creative and artistic oeuvre, or product of spatial and social relationships. Though Mekko leaves Tulsa for spiritual renewal at the end, explaining that he "had to get out of the damn city," framing the story as a typical homing plot would be a misreading. It is the experience of finding an alternative family at Whittier Square that allows Mekko to become a mentor, fulfill his obligations to his tribe, and be assured of his community's renewal. As in *Four Sheets*, homelands and waterways are present across rural and urban locations, with the threat of dislocation—and the opportunity for reconnection—available in both.

Oklahomans have been enjoying Sterlin Harjo's work for many years, but with the success of Harjo's hit series *Reservation Dogs* on the Hulu streaming service, a much wider audience is learning about him. Created in partnership with Taika Waititi and developed with an Indigenous cast, directorship, and writers' room, the series is also shot within the boundaries of the Muscogee Nation, including in Tulsa. It is appropriate that the title (a nod to Quentin Tarantino's *Reservoir Dogs*) foregrounds this place as a reservation. Since statehood, tribal jurisdictions in Oklahoma have had a different legal status than reservations elsewhere in the United States, with state law applying in the prosecution of crimes committed by tribal citizens within these jurisdictions. But in 2020 the *McGirt* decision ruled that the Muscogee Nation's reservation had never been disestablished and that tribal and federal law—not state law—should apply in these cases. With the major backing of the television network FX, Harjo finally has the resources to tell the story he wants to tell about Oklahoma, specifically the Muscogee Reservation—in his words, "to sell the magic that butts up against the reality."[31]

As the first full-time, scripted series to film an entire season in this state, the show broadcasts to the world that Oklahoma is Indian Country, just as other projects, such as the film adaptation of *Killers of the Flower Moon* (which wrapped up filming in Pawhuska and Tulsa in 2022) and NBC's *Rutherford Falls*, have been bringing more attention to Indigenous stories and experiences. The highly anticipated premiere of *Reservation Dogs* occurred in 2021 in Tulsa at the Circle Cinema just as Harjo's narrative films have, with the Los Angeles premiere following a few days later. At the packed Tulsa event, Muscogee chief David Hill praised the project for its illustration that "representation matters," and the Nation pledged a scholarship in Harjo's name to support future Native filmmakers. The mood of celebration, in Oklahoma and beyond, for what the project has already achieved and how meaningful it is for Native people, is truly moving. In the words of Apollonia Piña, "Being in a movie theater full of 'stecates is why I can't leave Oklahoma."

Reservation Dogs introduces us to a group of friends who are committing crimes on the Muscogee Reservation to save enough money to move to California, but as the series continues, viewers are treated to a wide array of characters who provide a glimpse into the web of kinship that is common in Native communities and leads the young friends to think twice about leaving. This large cast contributes to scenes that pull at the heartstrings, addressing subjects such as youth suicide, fractured families, grief, poverty, and historical trauma. At the same time, these scenes are infused with humor, particularly insider humor that is delivered without explanation to Indigenous audiences. Waititi and Harjo came up with the idea for *Reservation Dogs* during a conversation about how excited they would be to have a show about Indigenous people that was not depressing, that acknowledged and told experiences of hardship or trauma but through the lens of humor.[32] This humor appears from the outset through the character Spirit, named William Knifeman, a buckskin-clad warrior, played by comedian and activist Dallas Goldtooth, who cracks dirty jokes and exposes the ridiculousness of stereotypes about Native Americans commonly present in film westerns. *Reservation Dogs* is led by actors mostly unknown outside of Indian Country but also creates opportunities for seasoned Native actors to play characters unlike any that have appeared on-screen. Gary Farmer, Wes Studi, and Zahn McClarnon all get to play their own brand of crazy uncle, countering the stoicism or seriousness of roles they are known for, and expertly deliver generational humor imbued with an undeniable sweetness.

As with his films set in Tulsa, in *Reservation Dogs* Harjo shows the relatedness of urban and rural homelands in Oklahoma, of Tulsa and the fictional Okern, a thinly veiled version of Okmulgee, capital of the Muscogee Nation (population roughly twelve thousand). In several episodes, characters mention traveling to or visiting relatives in Tulsa. Relations among Natives of diverse backgrounds, common in cities like Tulsa, are among the many topics of importance to Indian Country in Oklahoma and beyond that the show features. For the purposes of this discussion, I reference two episodes: "F*ckin' Rez Dogs" (season 1, episode 1) and "Run" (season 2, episode 2).

The series premiere begins with an aerial view of the Muscogee Nation accompanied by the voice of Cvpon Bruner, a deejay from K49 Territory Jams, giving a shout-out to everyone in "Indian Territory, Oklahoma" and introducing weekend programs called "Southern Drum Saturday" and "old timey gospel" on Sunday. This opening is a clear reference to the beloved Morning Traffic Report introductory scene voiced by Randy Peone (John Trudell) in the 1989 Chris Eyre–directed *Smoke Signals*. But in this opening shot, the landscape is green and lush, and the tunes signal the southern cultural roots of this part of Oklahoma. Immediately, the Reservation Dogs—Bear (D'Pharaoh Woon-A-Tai), Elora (K. Devery Jacobs), Willie Jack (Paulina Alexis), and Cheese (Lane Factor)—appear, carrying out a scheme to steal a Flaming Flamers chip truck while the Black truck driver, Mississippi Miles (Rhomeyn Johnson), makes a delivery to Rob 'n' Cleo's convenience store, a spot the group frequents for Cleo's expertly prepared fried catfish. As with all of Harjo's work, the soundtrack in this episode and in the series overall is carefully curated, featuring Native musicians such as Link Wray, Halluci Nation, and Mato Wayuhi and bands with Oklahoma ties such as Samantha Crain, Broncho, and Labrys (with many fitting into both of those categories). The presence of hip-hop is also immediately striking, with characters Meeko and Mose (played by an Oklahoma City-based Christian duo, Pawnee performers Lil Mike and Funny Bone) sharing with the friends their latest rap and Jackie (Elva Guerra), a new arrival from the city and member of a rival neighborhood gang, wearing a Wu-Tang Clan T-shirt. The Wu-Tang Clan's "Protect Ya Neck" plays in the background, while Bear shares a velfie of the friends' hideout in an old abandoned brick building near downtown, where Willie Jack has been practicing her graffiti art. These examples connect the small-town rez setting of Okern with urban culture. As the episode proceeds, we learn that the friends have a plan, originally envisioned by their now-deceased friend Daniel (Dalton Cramer), to head to California, and they need money to get there.

As the first season continues, the highly romanticized ideas that the friends, especially Willy Jack, have about what is possible in California help explain the allure of Okern. However, the most visceral motivation is escape from the grief that still haunts them one year after Daniel's suicide. Late in the "F*ckin' Rez Dogs" episode, Bear is racked with guilt over the consequences of their carjacking for Miles. While snacking on catfish, the friends have overheard Miles share with Rob that the thievery caused him to be fired and then for his wife to leave him. Bear and Elora have a difference of opinion about their culpability. Bear asserts: "We are the bad guys. You gotta see that," to which Elora replies: "This place is shit. . . . That's why Daniel's gone. This place killed him. I'm not letting it kill me. I'm getting the fuck out, with or without y'all." Evidence of the town's decline and the poverty that pervades it is apparent in shots of the public housing where the characters live and the abandoned buildings where they hang out. The next morning, Elora comes by Bear's house and suggests that they try to give the money back to the scrapyard in exchange for the truck, which they will drop off at Rob 'n' Cleo's (an unsuccessful plan, since the truck has already been stripped). At the episode's end, after the friends complete an emotional tribute to Daniel, Bear proposes a rebranding of themselves with a new purpose as the "Reservation Dogs"; rather than being criminals, they will protect their homes, more like vigilantes. In succeeding episodes, this impulse toward care for community is reinforced with lessons (albeit comical) from William Knifeman; Big, the tribal cop (Zahn McLarnon); Willy Jack's father (John Proudstar); Elora's Auntie Teenie (Tamara Podemski), who herself left home for the city; and others. Bear especially becomes less enthusiastic about leaving for California, while Elora remains determined to go.

The carjacking episode that is integral to the plot of the premiere prompted criticism from some viewers about the representation of Indigenous communities of eastern Oklahoma, where Afro-Indigenous people, including Freedmen descendants, and others of African ancestry are prominent in the area's population. In the show some Native characters use African American Vernacular English and enjoy hip-hop (by Indigenous as well as African American artists), but there are few African American or Afro-Indigenous characters. The Reservation Dogs' treatment of Miles, which gives only Bear a sense of regret, seems to indicate that the friends have no qualms about exploiting an innocent Black man, which is ironic considering their love of African American pop culture.

On social media, many pointed toward the pervasiveness of anti-Blackness in Indigenous communities and saw the inclusion of hip-hop in the comedic framing of certain characters as reinforcing racism. This criticism continued with the airing of episode 4, "What about Your Dad." In that episode Bear's dad, Punkin' Lusty (played by Muscogee tattoo artist and rapper Sten Joddi), flakes out on a planned visit to Okern from Los Angeles; he was to be the entertainment at an anti-diabetes conference. The episode contains a comical rap video, *Greasy Frybread*, which to some viewers reinforced stereotypes and appropriated African American culture.[33] It was revealed in screenshots on Twitter that Sten Joddi has used the N-word in his own Twitter posts, and he was not invited back to the show for the second season. Harjo explained in an interview with Melanie McFarland for *Salon* that some episodes he planned, including one devoted to Rob 'n' Cleo's catfish spot, had to be cut but that the second season would be returning to their story. He also announced that the writers' room was expanding for the second season and would include Afro-Indigenous writer, comedian, and filmmaker Chad Charlie.[34]

The follow-up to the introduction of Rob, Cleo, and Miles comes in the second episode of season 2, "Run." In the second season, Elora and Jackie have teamed up to take the California road trip, leaving the second-guessing other Rez Dogs back in Okern. But Elora's grandmother's car is not up to the trip, and almost immediately, car trouble leaves the duo on foot. Elora is grappling with grief dreams; she was the person who found Daniel's body. A restless Daniel appears before her in her dreams, at times interspersed with visions of Bear. Elora and Jackie wander onto the property of a recently divorced white woman, Anna (Megan Mullally), who feeds them and provides a place for them to sleep, along with a large dose of unsolicited advice. The two sneak out of her house, stealing her truck. Out on the road, in a scene parallel to the exchange between Bear and Elora after the carjacking in the series premiere, Elora asks Jackie: "Do you feel bad? . . . Everyone was just trying to help us." Jackie replies, "I don't feel bad about shit." In the meantime Willie Jack has carried guilt of her own; she placed a curse on Jackie but has a suspicion that it has unleashed chaos on her community. She enlists the help of Uncle Brownie (Gary Farmer) and Bucky to release the curse, culminating in a hilarious scene at the water's edge, where the two elders sing Tom Petty's "Free Falling" for their ceremony. In the distance William Knifeman chants along, assuring the elders that the curse is gone, as long as the young ones also let go of their guilt.

Back at the convenience store, Rob and Cleo (Cleo in a T-shirt that says "Oklahoma Freedmen") are marveling at the number of catfish that Bear is consuming. Bear shares that he is looking for a job, but Rob and Cleo are incredulous, considering all that the Reservation Dogs have stolen from the store. In walks Miles, and Bear is immediately embarrassed. The three men burst out laughing, Miles telling Bear that he knows that he and his friends stole his truck. He, like the elders in the previous scene, has a message to share: "We don't need no more young folk in jail. It's easy to tear things down, but a lot harder to build them up. . . . Build things, boy.

Don't tear 'em down." Miles reveals that Rob and Cleo have the theft on video and played it on "Facebooks" but decided not to turn Bear in. As a thank-you, Bear helps Miles unload his delivery. It seems that Bear takes Miles's words to heart; in the next episode he begins work roofing houses.

At the end of the episode, Jackie and Elora make a stop at Jackie's mom's apartment in Tulsa to borrow gas money. Jackie greets her friend Johnny Boy outside, and he comments on how Jackie up and left him (a reminder of how Elora left Bear). Inside, Jackie's mom (DeLanna Studi) is herself overwhelmed with depression, and viewers learn that Jackie was sent to Okern to live with her aunt Bev (Jana Schmieding) for a chance at a better life away from the city, an interesting reversal of Elora's feelings about the possibilities and pitfalls of city versus small-town life. While Elora's explanation to Bear in the series premiere about why she is so desperate to leave Okern is delivered against the backdrop of small-town decay, with the friends' hideout located in an abandoned building, Jackie's home suggests urban blight; Johnny Boy seems to spend a lot of time in this parking lot, and though the details are unclear, Jackie may have been sent away because she was getting into trouble there.

The comparison of these two episodes shows ways that the characters, their friendships, and the show itself continue to evolve. It seems as if, in time, Elora sees herself in Jackie, who at the beginning of season 2 shared that she is grieving, having lost her brother. Willie Jack softens her animosity toward the Indian Mafia (the rival gang of Jackie's), especially after she learns about Jackie's brother in a later episode. Bear finally takes action in accounting for his transgression against Miles rather than quietly feeling guilty, which paves the way for his own introduction to the hard labor of a job and a later encounter with Daniel's bereft father. The easy assumptions that the characters have made about each other are tested, including their beliefs about the communities they live in, whether in Okern or Tulsa, and these two geographies, especially through the stories of Jackie and Elora, are shown to be parallel and related, contributing to the complex representation of Native communities in Oklahoma that is so groundbreaking.

Black and Afro-Indigenous characters have more of a presence in the second season, though certainly not as fully developed main characters; it is heartening to see that Mississippi Miles is not simply a victim, Cleo appears more often, and Marc Don (Chad Charlie) is introduced as one of

Bear's roofing construction mentors. In a 2021 article for *Ethnomusicology Review*, Afro-Indigenous scholar Kyle T. Mays, author of *Hip Hop Beats, Indigenous Rhymes: Modernity and Hip Hop in Indigenous North America* (2018), addresses Black representation in *Reservation Dogs*, highlighting the global ubiquity of Black culture, including Black language, and instances of its appreciation—not appropriation—in the show. At the same time, he cautions that Indigenous artists should welcome criticism as well as praise. He writes: "Even if season two of *Reservation Dogs* includes more Afro-Indigenous peoples—and I think it should—then what? We have to create art that is not meant for the white gaze, without defining our experiences as an 'Other.' Nevertheless, we also have to deal with how Indigenous artists respond to critics. . . . If Indigenous cultural producers want to continue to create important, groundbreaking art like *Reservation Dogs*, then we need to accept criticism—an NdN cultural criticism—that features those who criticize for a living and from the communities you claim to represent with your art."[35] Mays's last point, about criticism from the communities represented, gets to the heart of the controversy; it raises important questions about how Indian Country, in all of its diversity, should be represented and how viewers with varying degrees of cultural knowledge may interpret what they see.

Through Black and Afro-Indigenous characters as well as the racially ambiguous White Steve (is he a non-Native friend or a tribal citizen who has a light complexion?), the writers, I believe, seek to portray the heterogeneous population that comprises the Muscogee Reservation; adding more characters who purposefully draw attention to this racial diversity would be true to the composition of both Okmulgee (Okern) and Tulsa. In the abandoned buildings of Okern's downtown area, I also recognize the sites of once-thriving businesses, schools, and hospitals that were developed in Okmulgee almost entirely by Afro-Muscogee and African American families in the early part of the twentieth century, a situation parallel to Black Wall Street on Greenwood Avenue in Tulsa. When the Reservation Dogs discover that their hideout in one of these buildings, where they've kept a memorial to Daniel, is being destroyed in the first episode of season 2, a construction worker explains that a Texas rancher bought the building to transform it into a megachurch. Texas ranchers also show up on land where Willie Jack and her dad go hunting in episode 6 of the first season, the ranchers mumbling to each other a list of complaints, including: "Mexicans. Cancel culture. Taxes. Wokeness. Government overreach. Don't forget the gays!"

This needling of Texas ranchers is welcome comic relief, but it also speaks to the shared experience of divestment and land loss that those of African and Indigenous ancestry have endured in Indian Territory (now-Oklahoma). An influx of settlers attached to the oil industry in both Okmulgee and Tulsa started in the early twentieth century, and even in the present, property investors from outside the state drive gentrification there. With its mockery of conservative rancher hegemony, *Reservation Dogs* is subversive; it turns attention to the diverse peoples of the Muscogee Reservation and also to the structures underlying their experiences. In its representation of flows across homelands of Okern and Tulsa, the world of *Reservation Dogs* is urban and cosmopolitan, highlighting relatedness across cultures and spaces of the Muscogee Reservation despite the oppressive conditions of its containment within the state of Oklahoma.

Appadurai's discussion of the possibilities new media affords for liberatory imagination can also inform the debates about representation in the show. While for some *Reservation Dogs* must do more, Mays is skeptical: "It's not freedom to have accurate portrayals for mainstream society. In this way, even asking *Reservation Dogs* to create more liberated representations in mainstream media can only lead to disappointment." At the same time, as is clear in the enthusiastic response to *Reservation Dogs*, much of the power of film and television for audiences is the relationship cultivated between storytellers and audiences, the shared, imaginative experience that a show can create both as a final product and through its production in a community. The progression of season 2 suggests that Harjo and his team of writers are continuing with an aim of relationship, listening and responding to those whose stories they seek to tell.

Sterlin Harjo documents and envisions an Indigenous cityscape that is rooted in Muscogee stories and culture and extends outward to people of other nations and backgrounds and even to Indigenous homelands that are at a distance from built urban environments. He thereby complicates the "homing in" theme, suggesting that for his characters, fulfillment comes not from an in-between identity or from a choice between rural and urban but rather from locating and transforming Indigenous identity within an urban landscape. This creative act undermines settler colonial impositions of urban-rural divisions of Indigenous space. It also reflects the importance of Indigenous production of space, which can be understood as creative and meaningful experiences of community in the urban present that counter ideologies rendered through civic monuments. The impact that Harjo's films have in creating community both on- and offscreen also shows the power of art to reclaim urban Indigenous space, echoing Lefebvre's celebration of the right to the city and disrupting settler colonial erasure of Native claims to urban lands. A critical approach to Harjo's representation of Tulsa (Tallasi) that links Indigenous studies and urban studies methodologies is thus a productive way to foreground Tulsa's history as Indigenous homeland as well as its significance as a center for Indigenous creativity. Throughout *Four Sheets to the Wind*, *Mekko*, and *Reservation Dogs*, Indigenous Tulsa comes into focus as communitist and transformative, with Muscogee culture at its center.

"Representation Matters"

Along with programs such as the Tulsa Artist Fellowship, tribal arts incentives have supported Indigenous creatives in Tulsa who are asserting greater authority over narratives about Oklahoma. The Osage Nation, of which celebrated prima ballerinas Maria and Marjorie Tallchief were citizens, hosts a ballet school that performs *Wazhazhe*, a production that recounts the history of the tribe. The Osage Tribe was also heavily involved in Martin Scorsese's adaptation for film of David Grann's *Killers of the Flower Moon* and provides an annual arts incentive grant for Osage artists and arts organizations to promote their culture creatively. The Cherokee Nation has launched a new film office to attract and support filmmaking across the fourteen counties of its jurisdiction and is setting up shop in Tulsa, asserting its mission with the tagline "Representation Matters." With podcasts and online entertainment streaming exploding in popularity and influence, this is an unprecedented time for Native writers to share their work with new audiences. Indigenous journalists are playing a critical role in shaping the narrative of Oklahoma, specifically Tulsa, as Indian Country.

Elisa Harkins, composer and visual artist, who is also a Muscogee citizen, is just one of many artists who make their home in Tulsa while exhibiting nationally and internationally. A member of the 2018 class of Tulsa artist fellows, Harkins, originally from northeastern Oklahoma, pursued her arts education at Columbia Institute of Chicago, CalArts, and the Skowhegan School of Painting and Sculpture before returning to Oklahoma for the fellowship. In her short film and performance piece *For Hellen Woodward*, Harkins makes visible the Muscogee history of the former "Perryman's Pasture" that is hidden to most. Describing the driving concept of her work as "Performing Life," in which performance intersects with lived experience, Harkins employs music, sculpture, and the body to honor Woodward's memory.[36] In the piece Harkins and Oglala Lakota artist Suzanne Kite foreground natural and created sounds to respond to and unearth stories that proceed from Hellen Woodward's land and the oil mansion (now the Tulsa Garden Center) that was constructed upon it.

In the opening scene, the land itself takes center stage, with fallen green and brown leaves appearing to the accompaniment of atmospheric sound. Immediately, Harkins appears, wearing a blanket and singing into a microphone in the Muscogee language as she walks in front of the Travis Mansion, looking to the sky and the trees that form the natural space of the surrounding park. According to the informational note posted with the piece online, the song is "about the relationship between Hellen Woodward, her father, and the land." She then walks into the mansion, where Kite "map[s] the site-specific sounds onto her body," connecting the walls and windows of the home's music room with sounds and movements that suggest entrapment and discord. At the end of the piece, Harkins and Kite stand at first apart in the south room, each expressing through their physical movements the alternating force of both jarring, discordant and natural, calm sounds. Kite covers her ear in response, while Harkins lets her blanket fall to the floor. Finally, Harkins retrieves the microphone and walks the floors of the mansion, singing amid the cacophony from room to room. Circling back to the front of the room, where Kite is standing, the two women meet and face each other in front of the fireplace, ending the piece with a gradual quieting of sound. In Harkins's words, "The piece is about honoring land with our musical expression . . . about histories that are unearthed and experienced collectively." Through their movements the two artists indeed excavate and sing of history that remains buried in Tulsa, coming together in a spatial reclamation of the mansion as well as of the natural area surrounding it, joining built and natural environments of a city that is Indigenous to its core. As in Joy Harjo's and Sterlin Harjo's work, this reclamation of Muscogee history and community is felt and expressed in the body, which is fundamental to the oral culture of the people.

Begun as a project of the Tulsa-based FireThief Productions and funded by Cherokee Nation Businesses, *Osiyo: Voices of the Cherokee People*, an Emmy-winning documentary series, tells the stories of the people, places, heritage, history, and culture of the Cherokee people. In newsmagazine style, journalist Jennifer Loren, show host and writer, introduces Cherokee language instruction, profiles of artists, history lessons, and reports on cultural events and initiatives. Along with segments about Cherokees who are keeping practices in traditional crafts going, stories of citizens who are finding success on the national stage in the entertainment industry, in modeling, indie songwriting, mixed martial arts, and acting, emphasize ways that Cherokees are expressing their culture in the modern world. Writers such as Daniel H. Wilson, Mary Kathryn Nagle, Brandon Hobson, Jessica Mehta, and Adrienne Keene speak of what inspires them to write within the worlds of science fiction, the theater, literary fiction and poetry, and academia. In addition to the diversity of perspectives offered, *Osiyo* also showcases the diverse geographies that form the Cherokee Nation; episodes filmed in Tulsa communicate to viewers the ways that Cherokees enrich the cultural life of the city.

A few representative segments of the show bring the cityscape of Tulsa together with conversations about how the creative process honors Cherokee ancestry. Chef Bradley Dry, for example, is filmed riding around the Kendall-Whittier neighborhood on his ten-speed, with voice-overs of his comments about how making food reflects his love for his Cherokee family. Originally from the town of Kansas, Oklahoma, populated with just a few hundred people, Dry explains that in Tulsa, traveling everywhere by bike allows him to find and harvest local foods from Native plants growing within the city. Scenes of Dry shopping in the produce section at the grocery give way to a demonstration of foraging for poke, garlic, and acorns in Kendall-Whittier Park, making use of plants in contrast to the fetishizing of nature that is common in urban parks. Against the backdrop of the Tulsa skyline, Dry rides to his job at Chimera, one of the city's trendiest coffee shops. Inside, he prepares Native dishes with the fruits of his urban harvest. He shares how to make Indian tacos using an extra-hot pizza stone instead of a fryer, explaining his intention to innovate in his cooking in order to support those in his community who struggle with chronic conditions like diabetes. Dry concludes the episode by articulating ways that feeding people, even strangers, allows him to feel a connection with his family and to honor the memory of his grandmother, who taught him how to cook. "Being able to represent the Cherokee Nation with what I do," he says, "I feel like I would be making our Nation proud."

Multimedia artist and musician Kalyn Fay Barnoski is the focus of another Tulsa-based *Osiyo* segment. Barnoski's story begins with footage of her entering the art building at the University of Tulsa. From the studio she explains that she plans a career in academia in order to use her artistic passions to help others. The focus of her printmaking and design work is "trying to interact with other people who are dealing with being Native and being white and trying to fit in." She explains: "It's different in Oklahoma than it is anywhere else because there are thirty-eight plus affiliated tribes in Oklahoma. So many of the people you run into are going to be a little bit Native." Her academic project is a study of the dual influences of her dad's Cherokee spirituality and her Christian upbringing, a subject that also impacts her songwriting. Like Dry, Barnoski is inspired by her grandmother, a Cherokee language speaker who always encouraged her artistic passions. Noting that her musical career really began when she moved to Tulsa, Barnoski discusses her album *Bible Belt* as being devoted to Oklahoma. The title track contains the lyrics "Don't remember much about that house on Broadway, that town in the Southeast. Trees are swaying around as if they had a secret. Wish they would've told me. . . . Can't explain just how I felt, living in the Bible Belt." As these lyrics, which refer to traces of southern heritage that are remembered (if faintly), play in the background, Barnoski is filmed in key locations in the Tulsa music scene, including the stage at the Guthrie Green urban park and the overpass just adjacent to the Cain's Ballroom. The episode ends with Barnoski's words about what being Cherokee means to her: "For me, Cherokee means community . . . always being appreciative of your history . . . not letting it die but also not being scared to keep progressing."

Another story that asserts Cherokee contributions to music in Tulsa and beyond centers on western swing legend Tommy Allsup. A native of the Tulsa suburb Owasso, Allsup, who died in 2017, played on hundreds of hit records by musical celebrities including Tammy Wynette, George Jones, and Charlie Rich as a session guitarist. Western swing was the formative music for Allsup, as it was for Joy Harjo. Marrying string band music with big band, swing, and blues, this musical style was associated with Bob Wills, whose many Tulsa performances earned the venue the nickname "the House That Bob Built." From the glowing neon sign outside the venue to the portraits of musical legends on the interior walls and the vintage stage that musicians from near and far call hallowed ground, scenes of the Cain's Ballroom make clear in the episode the role that this Cherokee citizen had on shaping American music history. In their narration of the episode, Asleep at the Wheel's Ray Benson and local music historian John Wooley argue for the reach of Allsup's influence as he headed west to Los Angeles because of his expertise as a music insider, skills at production, and role in forming rock and roll. Echoing a repeated theme in the *Osiyo* series, Wooley asserts Allsup's generosity in mentoring other musicians such as Leon Russell. He concludes, "Tommy Allsup is one of the most unsung musical heroes not just in western swing but in all of popular music."

A final story of urban Indigenous Tulsa on *Osiyo* emerges in a segment devoted to lawyer and playwright Mary Kathryn Nagle. Nagle explains that successful lawyers tell stories well. A descendant of John Ridge, who signed the 1835 Treaty of New Echota that led to Cherokee removal from their ancestral homelands, Nagle wrote the play *Sovereignty* in 2015 to tell a story of her family that would resonate with the heart as well as mind and give a fuller historical context than is possible solely through legal records. Nagle staged a reading of the play that included descendants of the Ross and Ridge families. John Ross, principal chief from 1829 to 1866, staunchly resisted removal, putting him at odds with Ridge, and this political divide would endure for generations. In bringing together these descendants, therefore, Nagle created a powerful space for healing.

In the segment, while Nagle comments on the impact of historical trauma, she is shown looking out the window from her legal office in a downtown Tulsa skyscraper, making the case that her story of the past is still relevant to this city in the present. She also comments on the ways that being in Tulsa impacted her research for the play. Upon consulting with colleague Dr. Duane King of the Gilcrease Museum while working in the Ross papers archive, she had the opportunity to visit the exact location where Ridge was shot, which made the play real to her in a way she hadn't experienced before. The episode concludes with Nagle's comments, "Anyone who is a citizen of a tribal nation is here today because at some point along the way, someone in their lineage sacrificed his or her life so they could be here today. So no matter what you do, whether it's write plays, or fight cases in the court, or practice traditional art, or make food, or raise families, whatever you're doing, I think that we all feel . . . that pressure of 'I'm here today, I've got to do something with that.'"

Like *Osiyo*, the series *Invisible Nations* offers a diverse collection of profiles of individuals, but its style is more investigative in its recovery of the stories of Indigenous Tulsa. Hosted by Xolon Salinan journalist Allison Herrera, the show is a combination of video, radio, and live events and is created as a collaboration between Localore, KOSU Radio, and FireThief Productions. According to its website, *Invisible Nations* investigates and explores the lives of Native people in Oklahoma who "live in communities where no lines are drawn by reservations or boundaries" and "tells stories that go beyond, as one subject put it, 'powwows, gambling and diabetes.'" One report in particular, "Glory in All Things Creek," addresses the disenrollment of Freedmen from Muscogee citizenship rolls and the racial divisions within the tribe that have broken families. Tulsa activist Eli Grayson, named for his father and grandfather of the same name, is a descendant from a prominent Muscogee family that held slaves. In his conversation with Herrera for *Invisible Nations*, Grayson explains that he moved to Oklahoma after living in New Orleans and California, and during a visit to the Muscogee preservation office, he heard a librarian there tell an African American woman and her children that they had to leave the premises. Reacting to his puzzled expression, the librarian referred to the woman and her child as an annoyance because "those Freedmen, they think we owe them something." That incident sparked Grayson's desire to learn who these Freedmen were, and upon further research, he discovered a history of exclusion that he is now passionate about correcting within his tribe. He explains that a culture of silence surrounds the status of Freedmen in Oklahoma: "We could talk about Custer and we could talk about the crap that the U.S. government did to western tribes all day long, but we cannot talk about the Freedmen."

In referring to the status of the Freedmen, Grayson is commenting on a vote that the Muscogee Nation took in 1979 to adopt a new constitution that stripped Freedmen of their rights as citizens. A mandate of the tribe's Reconstruction-era treaty with the United States in 1866 had been to emancipate those enslaved in their tribe and grant them citizenship. In 1979, however, during an era often viewed positively because of its association with Indian self-determination in America, the new constitution that was ratified limited citizenship to those who could prove Muscogee lineage by blood as documented in the Dawes rolls. Because the Dawes Commission had imposed racial classifications in line with American "one-drop" perceptions of who was Black and who was white, leaving out any recording of Blacks' blood quantum and because these classifications also corresponded to how land would be distributed in Indian Territory, the Dawes rolls were notoriously inaccurate, placing some close family members on different registries, some as Freedmen and some as "Creeks by blood." Many who were of mixed ancestry could not neatly be classified in this system and had their identities recorded as "Freedmen" with no acknowledgment of their kinship, the impact of which was an act of paper genocide. With the 1979 vote, African Americans, some descended from mixed Muscogee families and some descended from non-Native enslaved people, were disenfranchised. In 2018 a group of Freedmen sued the tribe, calling for an abolishment of the constitution due to noncompliance with the 1866 law, but the case was dismissed in federal court. Meanwhile, a group organizing as the Muscogee Creek Indian Freedmen Band maintains that they have legal grounds for citizenship and have even applied for federal recognition as their own tribe. Grayson, in a recent opinion piece for the Tulsa-based *Oklahoma Eagle*, the longest-running Black-owned newspaper in Oklahoma, made the case for a call to action in response to the Black Lives Matter movement not only from whites but also from Natives in Oklahoma. He writes: "The Five Civilized tribes cannot have it both ways. They cannot on the one hand claim they are victims of discrimination and participate in BLM rallies yet discriminate against Freedmen by denying them suffrage and other rights of tribal citizenship under the guise of sovereignty."

Grayson's call for alliance between Oklahoma's Black and Native populations is timely; America once again grapples with racism and terror against African Americans that Tulsans know well. Among the many names of African American men and women who have been wrongly killed at the hands of police is Tulsan Terence Crutcher. While unarmed, Crutcher was killed in 2016 on a street in North Tulsa by white police officer Betty Shelby. Though Shelby was charged with manslaughter, a jury found her not guilty. Crutcher's twin sister, Tiffany, has been a tireless advocate for justice for her brother and police reform in alliance with the Tulsa chapter of Black Lives Matter and her attorney, Freedmen descendant Damario Solomon-Simmons. As the Black Lives Matter demonstrations of spring 2020 erupted across America in response to the killing of George Floyd, Tulsans of all backgrounds organized and marched over several days, the wounds of the Crutcher tragedy still fresh. On Interstate 244 a pickup pulling a horse trailer drove through a crowd of protesters, causing a thirty-two-year-old Cherokee and Choctaw man, Ryan Knight, to fall from the overpass and break several vertebrae, paralyzing him from the waist down. According to Knight's brother Randy, showing up to support Black Lives Matter was an important act of solidarity: "The murder of George Floyd has ignited this newest round of protest, but we've been in that same vein for a while, the parallel history of Native Americans and blacks is not lost on us." On 23 July 2020 the Tulsa district attorney announced that no charges would be filed against the truck driver.

This renewed focus on intersectionality goes hand in hand with a commitment to Indigenous sovereignty in Oklahoma that is now a part of the national conversation due to the 9 July 2020 Supreme Court decision in the case *McGirt v. Oklahoma*. In 2019 Cherokee journalist Rebecca Nagle (sister of Mary Kathryn) hosted an award-winning podcast, *This Land*, documenting developments in the case and providing its historical framework. The case hinged on whether the state of Oklahoma had the authority to prosecute a major crime by a tribal citizen within the jurisdictional boundaries of the Muscogee Nation. Oklahoma argued (and had long been operating under the assumption) that Muscogee lands had been disestablished as a reservation. The court decided in favor of McGirt, determining that Congress had never terminated the reservation or transferred federal jurisdiction to Oklahoma. Ultimately, because of multiple existing treaties with the United States and the lack of an act of Congress to transfer authority over Muscogee land to Oklahoma, the court concluded, in an opinion written by Justice Neil Gorsuch: "Today we are asked whether the land these treaties promised remains an Indian reservation for purposes of federal criminal law. Because Congress has not said otherwise, we hold the government to its word." As Nagle confirms in her podcast episode with arguments from the minority, especially Justice Brett Kavanaugh, the dissent from the decision hinged on the racial composition of eastern Oklahoma, where many whites reside in Tulsa, within the Muscogee Nation. As legal scholar Matthew Fletcher explains, in the history of Indian law cases, no matter the logic, courts continually find against sound claims of Indigenous sovereignty because of their incredulity at the idea that Indians could have authority over whites. It is the flawed racial logic of the Dawes rolls that determines, at least in the U.S. government's eyes, who is an authentic Indian, and the framework of blood quantum—not law—is inescapable in the settler mindset.

If the primacy of law—not race—is the foundation of Indian Country, then for the descendants of Freedmen, the treaties of 1866 that provide some of the basis for the Supreme Court's decision also ensure their rightful standing as citizens of their tribes. Through her podcast and her writing for publications such as the *Atlantic*, Rebecca Nagle uses her platform, her legal knowledge, and her understanding of the significance of the moment we are living in to argue for an end to racism within her tribe and others. Coinciding with a larger national movement to remove monuments to racists, the Cherokee Nation, in the summer of 2020, removed statues of its leaders who were allied with the Confederacy from its courthouse square in Tahlequah. Writing for *High Country News*, Nagle asserts: "Throughout our history, Cherokees have taken things from Europeans, adapted them and made them ours. . . . But some of the things that we took from Europeans serve neither our tribe nor our people. From white society, we adopted racism—plain and simple. That *is* our history. Rooting out the visible ways that racism still exists within the Cherokee Nation is not erasing our history, but building a better future for our tribe." With writers and activists now speaking out more strongly about the need for Native and African Americans to stand together, the potential for healing in this wounded city is encouraging.

Tulsa is an Indian town, even while signs of urban ideologies that disappear Indigenous peoples from their rights to this land appear throughout the city. These disorienting signs are apparent especially in locations, from Owen and Woodward Parks to Greenwood, that are civic landmarks, treasured by the wider populace and marketed for tourist purposes. While these locations are, ironically, on home sites of Indigenous citizens who were Tulsa's first city leaders, they contribute to a false narrative of homelessness for the first peoples of Indian Territory. Joy Harjo, Sterlin Harjo, Elisa Harkins, and others all address in their work these experiences of homelessness, either literal or metaphoric, that Native peoples have endured in Tulsa. However, their writings also recover the landscape of Tulsa as an Indigenous place, spiritually connected to other Indian towns both in Oklahoma and in the Southeast. Through the power of creative expression, in visual art, sound, and song, these artists continue to grow the Indigenous arts community in Tulsa and bring stories of Oklahoma Native life to national and international stages.

4

"THE CITY DIFFERENT"

Writing Oklahoma in Santa Fe

Santa Fe, like New Orleans, is a destination town. For those with a passion for art, especially those of the leisure class, Santa Fe is an idyllic retreat, a place to experience (and purchase) a slice of Americana that is steeped in the mystique of the area's many Indigenous nations. Santa Fe is a compelling emblem of sorts for the settler dynamics of occupation, tourism, and commerce that collide with artistry and creativity in America. At the same time that monuments to Indigenous displacement are visible across the city, Native people for whom the city is a homeland as well as Native people from elsewhere are continually drawn to Santa Fe to market their work and participate in a thriving creative community. The histories that have shaped Santa Fe's growth into a magnet for Native arts connect with histories of Louisiana and Oklahoma that, beyond these civic markers of Indigenous absence, provide a glimpse into the unique experiences of Indigenous peoples who have roots in Indian Territory. From the Santa Fe Indian School to Indian Market to the Institute of American Indian Arts, Indigenous Oklahomans have been at the vanguard of Santa Fe arts, spurring its national and international renown. Oklahoma writers in particular have a history of participation in the Santa Fe writers' scene. For well-known writers, including Lynn Riggs and Joy Harjo, as well as a new wave of writers with Oklahoma ties, Sterlin Harjo among them, Santa Fe is both a refuge and a staging ground for critique. These writers reveal traces of Oklahoma's historical and creative influence on Santa Fe, demonstrating the unique geographies and histories of Oklahoma's Native nations at the same time that they subvert the myth that Santa Fe tells of itself.

"Art Never Thrives in a Sophisticated Hothouse"

Accompanying trends in American arts, non-Indian writers have continually found a "Native" and regional turn to be a palette of sorts for breathing new life into their own work and rejuvenating American letters. This literary form of Dean Rader's "Indian action figures" has likely created confusion as well as opportunity for Native writers, especially those of the early twentieth century, including Darcy McNickle, Zitkala Sa, Mourning Dove, John Joseph Mathews, and Lynn Riggs. Writer colonists of Taos and Santa Fe, Alice Corbin Henderson, Mable Dodge Luhan, Witter Bynner, Mary Austin, and others, contributed to a nationwide settler fascination with Indigenous aesthetics (or their perceptions of them) and believed that their patronage of arts institutions and individual Native artists and writers was socially and politically just. But Leah Dilworth describes their writing as an expression of non-Indian desires to "assume, temporarily, an Indian identity."[1] She notes that Austin's enthusiasm for American Indian literature and translation, evidenced in her own writing, was simply a means of energizing Euro-American literature rather than celebrating Native writing for its own sake. Marta Weigle identifies Luhan's motivation as a convenient occupation for alleviating her own boredom and depression.[2] Into this tight community of often misguided patronage and boosterism, Cherokee poet and playwright Lynn Riggs found the inspiration and support that contributed to the success of his writing career, even while his writing shows a clear-eyed treatment of Santa Fe.

Arriving in Lamy, just south of Santa Fe, in 1923, Lynn Riggs, Cherokee citizen and native of Claremore, Oklahoma, couldn't have known just how much his life and career would change as a result of his move west. He had had a less-than-inspiring experience as a student at the University of Oklahoma, but a new relationship with poet Witter Bynner, who had been in residency there, spurred his desire to relocate to Santa Fe, Bynner's adopted home. Bynner encouraged Riggs to seek treatment for his poor physical and mental health in Santa Fe, and they continued their relationship.[3] In just a few short years, Riggs would become a fixture in the literary and arts communities of the area, where he quietly acknowledged his queer identity. Though already well traveled before his stint at OU—he had worked in Chicago, New York, and Los Angeles—his Santa Fe years were a time of great literary productivity in several genres, no doubt because of the creative community he found there. While his problematic home life and feelings of confinement in the former Indian Territory are well documented, Riggs nonetheless returned to Oklahoma often as a setting for his work, in evidence most prominently in his play *Green Grow the Lilacs* (1931), which Richard Rodgers and Oscar Hammerstein adapted into the musical *Oklahoma!* (1943).

In Riggs's work can be found a productive relationship between the Santa Fe and Oklahoma of Riggs's experience (and imagination). Riggs shared with regionalists a desire to capture and express authenticity in the characters he created, and writing the songs and speech of Oklahomans was his signature technique for doing so. In addition to his position in the city's literary arts scene, his engagement with settings, characters, and personas of Santa Fe was also an important way of exploring the conflicts—political, geographical, and social—that pervaded his writing. Through analysis of Riggs's Santa Fe poems, play, and film, I argue that Riggs is one of several Oklahomans who have contributed to (and critiqued) the city's significance as an Indigenous urban enclave informed by settler and Indigenous histories. Riggs's Santa Fe experiences, while inspiring remarkable creative output after a lackluster period in his native Oklahoma, also galvanized his critique of settler colonialism in Oklahoma and beyond.

In Riggs's move to New Mexico, he was following a trail already established by homesteaders, arts colonists, and Okie migrants that would see even greater traffic thereafter and which left its mark on literature of the 1920s and 1930s. Riggs's career was akin in some ways to those of Mary Austin and her peers, who craved authenticity, challenged industrialism and consumerism, and advocated for cultural preservation (at least as they understood it). When, in 1921, New Mexico senator Holm Bursum introduced a bill to Congress that would have allowed settlers to claim title to Pueblo lands after proving residency for ten years (an iteration of allotment policies that the United States had long been advancing), the Santa Fe and Taos arts and writing communities allied with Pueblo leaders and future commissioner of Indian Affairs John Collier to lobby against it. They launched a national public relations campaign to protest the bill.[4] In 1924 the Pueblo Lands Board Act was passed, which upheld Pueblo communal land titles and prioritized their claims in disputes over land title. The efforts of the artists and writers were thus helpful for staving off further legal alienation of Pueblo people from their lands; however, these allies also had their own interests front of mind, particularly tourism and the growing marketplace for collectors. Riggs would grow close to many of these individuals even while keeping a critical eye on Santa Fe's creative class.

Benjamin Botkin, an associate of Mary Austin, was a young faculty member at OU during Riggs's time there and became a key mentor and friend to him. Over his career at OU and later as chairman of the Federal Writers' Project, Botkin conducted the most thorough existing research on the American play-party tradition. He drew heavily upon Oklahoman participants and spent the later part of the 1920s documenting play-parties in the eastern part of the state, where Riggs was from, publishing in 1937 his findings as *The American Play-Party Song: With a Collection of Oklahoma Texts and Tunes*.[5] Riggs's plays, most of which were set in Oklahoma, were also distinguished by the playwright's desire to reveal the artistry of folk speech and song. Speaking of sources for *Green Grow the Lilacs*, which he wrote while in Paris, Riggs stated, "Oklahoma folk of thirty years ago talked poetry without any conscious effort to make beautiful language."[6] Riggs, like many artists, left home while remaining driven to write about it, perhaps benefiting from keeping his distance. But at the same time that Riggs's creative impulses converged with those of some non-Native writers and researchers whose fascination with Oklahoma or the Southwest can now be understood as imperialist nostalgia, Riggs was both an insider in the Santa Fe colonists' scene and an increasingly pointed critic of harmful settler mindsets.

Riggs is one of many Native writers and artists from Oklahoma who have helped shape Santa Fe's unique urban culture, but he was also a newcomer to the place, with roots east rather than in local Pueblo nations. In his Santa Fe works, Riggs critically engages with urban spaces and their histories, which in civic imagery most often sidesteps Indigenous participation. Primitivism, so typical of Santa Fe aesthetics, is complicated in Riggs's life and works. Riggs was a fixture in the dinner and cocktail parties of non-

Native writers and artists—for example, paying tribute to the visiting New England regionalist Robert Frost in 1935 for his renderings of "the gracious earth and its people."[7] Riggs socialized with southwestern enthusiasts and published with them in little magazines such as Spud Johnson's *Laughing Horse*, which featured writing and illustrations based in Taos and Santa Fe. At the same time, Riggs was honing his own socially committed agenda in his body of work, which Kirby Brown describes as progressing from a tone of nostalgia to anticolonialism. Brown calls attention to Riggs's cosmopolitanism: "Riggs moved in some of the most influential artistic and intellectual circles of the period, including Mable Dodge Luhan's Santa Fe literary salon and experimental theater companies like the Provincetown Players and the American Laboratory Theatre; he also ran with some of Hollywood's biggest stars, including Bette Davis, Joan Crawford, Gary Cooper, and Clark Gable to name but a few."[8] Riggs's cultural legacy is clear; undoubtedly, his participation in the southwestern arts scene as well as his residencies in Hollywood, New York, and abroad fueled his accomplishments and his reputation.

The ways that Riggs's cosmopolitanism converges with regionalism are key to his literary prominence, and more than simply a setting for his works, the unique place of Oklahoma can help explain this convergence, uneasy as it may have been for Riggs. Scholar of regionalism Robert Dorman has uncovered in his books, *Revolt of the Provinces: The Regionalist Movement in America, 1920–1945* (1993) and *Hell of a Vision: Regionalism and the Modern American West* (2012), some shared modernist assumptions between urban(e) avant-garde movements (such as the Harlem Renaissance and the *Partisan Review*) and regionalists of the early twentieth century, who are typically linked to rural locations. His assessment of the region as a framework for "new kinds of cities, small-scale, planned, delimited, and existing in balance with wilderness and a restored and rejuvenated rural economy" is helpful for explaining why affiliates of artist colonies retained their ties to metropolitan areas and were not invested in adopting fully rural lifestyles. Dorman argues: "Regionalism must be considered not only as a critique of modernization, and not only as a noteworthy contribution to the historic dialogue over pluralism, but also as marking a significant stage in the still-unfolding history of conservationism, preservationism, urban planning, and environmentalism. . . . the personal landscape of the region began to assume for a long line of artists and intellectuals a certain utility as a device for art, social commentary, and political expression." Dorman notes that regionalists were more invested in specific "places" (uniquely American ones) than cosmopolitans, which in turn gave the regionalist movement a more nationalistic character, which cosmopolitans rejected. Dorman's study of the West and its allure in American history and culture foregrounds the role of regionalism in empire building despite whatever intentions to democratize culture its proponents may have had. For the residents of artist colonies, aesthetics were fundamental, as they were to many cosmopolitans, but Native Americans were especially revered as primitive embodiments of art itself: "The most ancient cultures of the West, as construed by an array of artists and intellectuals from the 1900s to the 1930s, became the most avant-garde. Rather than the 'Indian problem,' they were the 'Indian solution.'"[9]

Echoes of LeFebvre's urban theories surface in these threads concerning aesthetics, the avant-garde, and reimagined places, as do debates in Indigenous studies about the relationship between the regional, national, and cosmopolitan, which inform Lynn Riggs's life and writings. For LeFebvre the urban is not limited to a particular scale of built cities; instead, primarily through ubiquitous consumerism, the urban, empowered by the state, extends to all areas, including the region, where nature (and Indigenous culture) is fetishized. Considering the ways that Lynn Riggs lived and wrote in many environments—rural, regional, urban—and the ways that Oklahoma has been defined by its ties to other regions (or in turn, perceived to have a lack of connection to a specific region) is fruitful for understanding Riggs's legacy. Like many Oklahoma Native authors, Riggs moved within and found success among so many communities but was also able to perceive and articulate the problematic settler mindsets that pervaded these places. Relational regionalism, which Tol Foster applies to the work of Will Rogers (another Cherokee), touches on the remarkable experiences of Indigenous creatives from Oklahoma, who are of necessity related to those within their own and other Native nations as well as to the plurality of communities in the state and beyond. Foster argues that Rogers's worldwide influence is an example of an "outward-looking, dynamic cosmopolitanism based in notions of relation" that is broader than tribal nationalism has been understood to be.[10]

I propose a reframing of this conversation with regard to Native writers from Oklahoma, bearing in mind the relationship between the regional, the urban, and settler colonialism. Rather than understanding Riggs as necessarily "outward-looking" or simply making a break for it in response to the closed-mindedness of typical Oklahomans, Riggs's work in Santa Fe and in other cities in the United States and abroad is following a defining path of mobility for Indigenous Oklahomans and reflects a creative production of urban space that complicates the artistic primitivism that non-Native regionalists projected. In the Santa Fe of Riggs's day (and today), certainly distortions and abstractions of Native cultures were everywhere, signifying ideologies that separate Native peoples from contemporary urban cultures even while primitivism made Native cultures oh-so-avant-garde. But in Riggs's artistry one can find the writer's creation of an Indigenous Santa Fe that is informed by his Cherokee background, his critique of primitivism, and his participation in a cosmopolitan, urban art scene.

Craig Womack's extensive attention to Riggs's work highlights ways that Riggs explored queer subject matter, with varying degrees of subtlety, and made intentional choices to set his plays in Oklahoma. Womack discusses representations of intimacy as evidence of Riggs's ambivalence about Oklahoma and notes his reluctance to spend much time there after he left home.[11] I contend that we can connect Riggs's writing about home and beyond to the work of other Native writers from Oklahoma who likewise do not conform to the modes of American Indian writing that literary studies have determined to be authentic (celebrating homecoming to reservation communities, for example). Part of the reason, of course, is the unique history of Indian Territory, which creates an always-already situation of being at a distance from ancestral homelands for the majority of Oklahoma's tribes. This reality informs the work of Indigenous creatives, who are in a unique position, therefore, to concern themselves with relationships to space and cosmopolitan communities despite whatever limitations Oklahoma's conservative culture may present. In my study of Riggs's Santa Fe–based poems, film, and play, I reveal the ways that Santa Fe's environment prompts urban-based critiques of settler colonialism as well as sustained engagement with aesthetics that shape the work of Native writers from Oklahoma who, like Riggs, have found success on national and international stages.

Riggs first gained confidence as a writer through poetry, publishing in little magazines such as the *Palms* and the *Laughing Horse* and ultimately releasing *The Iron Dish* in 1930. In these early forays into publishing, Riggs presents observations about and critiques of the world he entered in his move to northern New Mexico. Interestingly, while Riggs turned a critical eye to his fellow newcomers in some instances, the *Laughing Horse* itself advertised tourist attractions and curio shops in its pages. The magazine, which publisher Spud Johnson dedicated to writing and art from the Southwest, typifies the intersections of the urban, regional, and primitive in the early twentieth century. According to Daniel Worden, though the *Laughing Horse* projects a regional modernism, marked by its romanticization of the West, it also was part of a larger, transnational network of print cultures that celebrated the merging of art with everyday life, which was central to the avant-garde of urban art centers.[12] In my reading of a few representative poems of Riggs's early career, I uncover both the western landscape that inspired him and the urban life that informed his growing artistic sensibility.

Several of Riggs's nature poems feature iconic images of the West that stir his poetic voice without the sense of nostalgia that non-Indian primitivists displayed. While most enthusiasts knew the American West only in the imagination, Riggs, who became a skilled horseman while growing up in Oklahoma and appeared as an extra in cowboy movies, was no poser.[13] The poem "Bootheels" immediately calls to mind the trek of a cowboy across distances: "Bootheels go over the mountains, / Bootheels go over the sea." For the persona (presumably Riggs), these distances are at first unsatisfying: "And no birds rise from the fountains / And no songs rise from me." It is a trip over the "rose-colored / Cliffs," typical of the New Mexican landscape, that Riggs finds, "I can laugh!" A western, unforgiving climate that would have been familiar to Riggs in both Oklahoma and New Mexico is fundamental to Riggs's "Santa Fe Sonnets," a pair of poems titled "Spring" and "Summer." In "Spring" the speaker seeks to "heal my brain in water quieter / Than a mountain stream." He seeks solace from "lightning," "sharp rain," and "wind in the alfalfa" and wishes to gaze at "marigolds asleep / In water barely warm, and not too deep." In "Summer" the coming of autumn is likewise associated with harsh imagery: "Poplars will flame again; the lion head / Of the wind will roar among the alfalfa sheaves." The poem ends with foreboding: "Autumn will come too soon, and winter's breath / Shrivel the meadow grass; and after death. . . . . ?" The severe descriptions in "The Arid Land" are apparent in buzzards circling around "willows plunging / Their bloodless roots in air," "treeless wastes," and a sunny land that is "arid, desolate, and defiant." Together these representations of northern New Mexico, while beautiful, challenge the idea that Riggs was necessarily finding respite or escape here; the aesthetics of this landscape may indicate freedom, but they also suggest a turn inward. Published shortly after Riggs's abrupt departure from the University of Oklahoma and his stay at the Sunmount Sanitorium in the foothills of the Sangre de Cristo Mountains, these short lyrics suffuse a hardscrabble landscape with emotional intensity, pointing the way toward the struggles and dramas of characters in the plays he later became famous for.

Along with these nature poems, Riggs published several pieces in which the persona dwells in or walks along streets of Santa Fe. In these poems, living in the city is a moody affair—Riggs is often solitary or having chance encounters with others who are up early. Nature and architecture connect here and evoke an emotional response, and Riggs's careful and detailed attention to this connection of art, nature, and the everyday counters the abstraction of space that Lefebvre warns is a damaging result of capitalist consumption. Notably, where other writers of the Taos and Santa Fe colonies draw Indigenous characters as parts of the scenery, in Riggs's poems the speaker seems to ponder his own presence in the scene, in some instances coming across as self-conscious and in others appearing more at home. Three of this set specifically describe walks: "Morning Walk: Santa Fe," "Spring Morning: Santa Fe," and "Acequia Madre."

In "Morning Walk: Santa Fe" Riggs is alone in Burro Alley, "hours before the sun." This alley in the city's center was historically a place where sellers of firewood would do business, trucking in their wares on the backs of burros. This wasn't the only business venture there; the street was also the home of saloons, casinos, and brothels. Riggs's presence there in the wee hours suggests his participation in a culture of urban recreation and desire that has been fundamental to queer culture in cities. Alone in the alley, Riggs focuses on the adobe walls "leaning down like waterfalls" and the "weedy patios, / No longer gay with strumming beaux." In the next stanza, he is on Don Gaspar Street. He describes a processional, "its shoulders tall" and "red with brick," and words that "Rose and soared thereon like birds." Heading down the Alameda, a cottonwood-lined promenade near the Santa Fe River, Riggs encounters a man who

> looked at me without surprise
> Although I carried no pail of food
> Nor drove a burro lashed with wood.

When he sees burros making their way on Canyon Road, Riggs "looked at them as anyone should," seeming at ease with the inhabitants and routine of the city. In the final stanza, as dawn nears, Riggs's journey is complete. He states, "On Monte Sol I met the rain; / Dripping, he brought me home again." It's not a stretch to read a queer subtext in this ode to strolling home after a night of partying, with the rain personified as an escort. Riggs finds in these quintessential streets of the adobe city an intersection of nature and the everyday with an urban social scene that inspires him.

In "Spring Morning: Santa Fe" Riggs again finds poetry in the early-morning streets, similarly marking time with natural images joined with city scenes. In the first stanza, he calls the first hour "a word the color of dawn"; the second features a personification of poppies standing, "Backs to a wall," as a mockingbird sings shrilly. In the next stanza, Riggs describes water dripping from the acequia, a ditch irrigation system of the arid climate that has ties to both Pueblo and Spanish colonial farming practices. By 9:00 a.m. watery clouds lift, and the sun makes a stronger presence: "Gold fired the pavement where the leaves were shifting." In the next hour, Riggs notes the women in black shawls moving along the Alameda as burros recline; he hears a song. The conclusion of the sonnet is a couplet that signals the end of morning: "And the great bells rang out a golden tune / Words grew in the heart and clanged, the color of noon." This portrait of walking the streets of the central city, as with the other walking sonnet, displays the writer's feeling of being in place, with a poetic voice arising from the beauty of those streets. This example includes stronger representations of Hispano culture in its references to the black-shawled women, burros, and bells ringing (presumably from the Catholic church). No Anglos are present, and though Riggs doesn't insert himself as prominently into this walk as he does with the other example, he is a participant rather than a

10. Burro Alley, Santa Fe. Photo by the author.

detached observer in this street culture. His descriptions are not those of a pastoral poem; there is nothing soothing or idyllic here, with sounds that are shrill and clanging. The poet thereby avoids a primitive-civilized binary in these images of Santa Fe. The rhythms of the city—its streets, its walls, its gutters—are in concert with its inhabitants, human and nonhuman.

In a third walking poem, "Acequia Madre," Riggs emphasizes in his stroll alongside the main irrigation ditch of the city the appearance of the earth. The second line includes "patches of red, over squares of magenta earth," highlighting the red soil of the path. The fence separating the acequia from property lines is irregularly configured, turning "this way for a ditch" and "That way for a corner of yellow roses." The Acequia Madre, adjacent to where Riggs lived, reminds the poet of the fruit trees at El Hogan, where "There must be bees humming," and apples "Covering the ground below the smooth red branches." The final stanza repeats the poem's first two lines about walking over the red earth along the acequia and concludes, "And I think of apples sweetening under the fruit trees / Where the bees hum." As with the other walking poems, nature and city are entwined in these lines, but "Acequia Madre" connects Riggs's experience in town to his residence at the El Hogan Ranch, where, according to Phyllis Braunlich, he formulated his philosophy of writing. In a letter to writer Betty Kirk, a fellow Oklahoman who also moved to Santa Fe, Riggs concluded that he would write realistically about life: "I am no longer ashamed of healthy delight, emotional, even to tears. . . . Art never thrives in a sophisticated hothouse."[14]

Two additional examples of Riggs's poems that concentrate on his residence in the city, "The Choice" and "The Shaped Room," depict interiors rather than the outdoor cityscape. In the short, two-stanza poem "The Choice," Riggs hints at his realistic approach to writing. He explains:

Let those who will go seeking
Beyond the dim seas
For goblins and golliwogs
And slim fairies.
But I shall sit here
In quiet by the door—
Earth's are the people
I care for.

"The Shaped Room" describes his dwelling in more detail. In it he describes a relationship between the adobe structure and recognition of his solitary existence, yet along the way he also seems to indicate intimacy with another. Riggs sets a welcoming scene with a guitar hanging on an adobe wall, a nearby stove "tongued with pinion wood / less for the spirit than the skin." In the second stanza, "honey light" of a lamp and messy tables on the edge of "waxen night" portend a good time: "man cannot work who cannot play." Up until this point in the poem, Riggs seems to be suggesting a quiet night, observing the hominess of an adobe room. He resists romanticizing the scene, however. Piñon, though an important medicinal and ceremonial plant for Natives of the area, does not come with the promise of spiritual reward here.

By the middle stanzas of "The Shaped Room," the images become more strongly sexual, with the suggestion that someone else is being invited into the room. The third stanza contains the lines

11. Acequia Madre, Santa Fe. Photo by the author.

12. (*below*) Lynn Riggs's home, Santa Fe. Photo by the author.

Pause if you must (and mustn't one?).
Plumb precision with a pole
thrust at the point of star or sun,
else wake to wallow in a hole.

The mention of a pole in an interior room in this context brings to mind a wooden beam, or viga, which in adobe architecture supports the weight of a roof. At the same time, the double entendre of this pole thrusting upward is hard to miss. In the next stanza, drawing into the room seems to be an invitation to someone: "Foot and ankle / captain the heart—look where they lead you." This invitation culminates in sensory bliss in the fifth stanza:

Aware of waves of little blisses,
the nerves receiving what they can
of titillation and some kisses—
this is the ultimate, this is man.

With the final stanzas of the poem, Riggs mentions another room, this one "not lyrical." "The wall is hardly there to see / within that inner utmost lair," Riggs writes. He requests of his companion, "Step in, and if you will, with me, / or if alone no one will care." Again, this is not exactly the stuff of romance, even if Riggs imagines that this turn inward could be journeyed together. His final lines point toward his identification with and inspiration by this space, coexistent with his stark realism about solitude:

Alone you must be in the end;
the inner room appends unto
whatever wood or mud you bend
to shape of room whose shape is you.

Two more of Riggs's Santa Fe poems provide commentary about what he observes of the cultures of Santa Fe. "Sanitarium" is a prose poem that crafts a portrait of a woman under care, presumably in the Sunmount Sanitarium, where Riggs himself began treatment in 1923 for his depression. The woman has "hair the color of corn-shucks" and has so much

13. Lynn Riggs, self-portrait. Claremore Museum of History, Claremore OK. Photo by the author.

pent-up energy from being bedridden for over three months. It has not all been bad however because of the "million-dollar view." Riggs pokes fun at the woman's impression of the community she finds in the common areas, composed of other newcomers to the area. While she bristles at the behaviors that she perceives to be common and gauche, Riggs is clearly exposing her own rudeness. "What an undistinguished company!" she thinks, even while she murmurs to someone named Lucy, who waits on the guests, about the possibility of her getting indigestion. Riggs exposes her response—"awfully plebeian!"—to a "fat woman with . . . rolling-pin arms." He notes her own biases toward an orthodox man and a woman with "a Jewish face," whose name she has a hard time recalling. She doesn't find the social scene she desires by the latter part of the poem: "Such a bore for everybody having TB. . . . Restful, of course, except for Thanksgiving parties where every one talks about 'temps' and 'hems' and New York. O dear!" The woman's "corn-shuck" hair becomes unkempt, and frustrated and uninspired, she heads upstairs to fix it: "Don't save a place for me at this—what do you call it?—Bunko game." Now suddenly weary and tired, she leaves the room "dismally." Riggs cleverly ends the poem with the following response to her departure: "Shucks!"

While Riggs satirizes the bourgeois Santa Fe set in "Sanitarium," he writes of the Santa Domingo Pueblo with honor and admiration. In a series of five-line stanzas, each capturing a portion of the scene of an annual feast day, Riggs highlights in "Santa Domingo Corn Dance" the spiritual and personal significance of the green corn dance, emphasizing the relationship between the participants and the Creator. Riggs describes the beauty of dancers:

Bodies
Reddened, and gourds
Rain girdles, ornaments,
The skins of foxes—what should please
You more?

With the dancers, who "stamp the ground" and "shake the doors of earth," anticipating green corn, Riggs notes their efficacy, as shadows begin to form in the clouds. The Koshari, or sacred clowns, "glide, halt, grimace, grin, and turn," and Riggs turns to the perception of a child dancer, whose eyes are focused on ceremonial spruce. Toward the conclusion of the poem, Riggs concentrates on the mountain "Beyond / The baking roofs," which points "Still higher, though its feet are white / With bloom." The final stanza, titled "Rain," is the culmination of all these prayers in motion, with Riggs himself participating. He writes:

> One drum—
> Note more, one voice, One slant of bodies,
> And my tears will fall like rain
> Upon this ground.

Presumably, the rain, expressing "my tears," is personified here, but in keeping with Riggs's other poems, the poet is also contributing to the action. While the dramatic conclusion of this piece, with rain suggesting Riggs's own tears, may suggest melancholy or regret to some readers, I interpret this reaction to be the kind of positive emotional release Riggs described in his letter to Betty Kirk. Green corn ceremonies are important for many tribes, including Cherokees. Riggs, unlike other writers of the Santa Fe scene, avoids representing Pueblo peoples as in need of saving or as artifacts. Instead, though the Santa Domingo corn dance draws thousands of tourist observers annually, Riggs writes about the feast not as a mysterious or fascinating display; each component is meaningful, and he connects authentically with its purpose.

In 1931 Riggs and a young Santa Fe filmmaker James Hughes created *A Day in Santa Fe*, a short film that would premiere early the next year at the La Fonda Hotel, with several notable artists and writers in attendance. Framing activities one might observe in the city within the span of a day, the film brings Native, Anglo, and Spanish colonial cultures together into scenes that approximate the energy of Santa Fe with a playful tone. James Cox, whose research recovers the mostly forgotten film for Indigenous film history, cites Bruce Posner's inclusion of the project in the *Unseen Cinema* anthology as critical to placing *A Day in Santa Fe* within a history of avant-garde American cinema, which in the 1920s and 1930s took inspiration from the American Southwest. Cox argues that *A Day in Santa Fe* is "a meditation on Indigenous representation and the politics of modernist primitivism."[15] He divides the film into parts 1 and 2, suggesting that the filmmakers create a dramatic juxtaposition of colonial dominance and Pueblo sovereignty in the earlier and later parts. While I agree with Cox that the film is an early example of Indigenous filmmakers' foregrounding Native ways of being and knowing, I also seek to uncover ways that *A Day in Santa Fe* may be understood within both Riggs's larger body of Santa Fe writing and urban Indigenous studies. In compelling ways, the film mirrors Riggs's Santa Fe poems in specific images as well as in its overall project of capturing urban life. I place *A Day in Santa Fe* within a tradition of Oklahoma Indigenous writing that depicts Santa Fe as both cosmopolitan and foundationally Native.

In spirit and form, *A Day in Santa Fe* follows the first American avant-garde film *Manhatta* (1920), by painter Charles Sheeler and photographer Paul Strand. Walt Whitman's "Mannahatta," an ode to the New York borough published in 1871–72 in *Leaves of Grass*, inspired *Manhatta*. The poem features Whitman's signature mix of romanticism and urban scenes; Whitman begins by explaining, "I was asking for something specific and perfect for my city, / Whereupon lo! upsprang the aboriginal name." Sheeler and Strand's *Manhatta* provides vignettes of New York city life over the period of a day, drawing attention to the artfulness of streets, skyscrapers, and transit hubs, along with the waves of commuters making their way in the bustling cityscape. The film includes intertitles of lines from Whitman's poem, an innovative and impressionistic departure from the typical explanatory intertitles of silent films that adds to its novelty as the first poem film. Whitman's nod to the Indigenous name of Manhattan reflects his general interest in Native American legacies that in his creative (and problematic) perspective contributed to America's vitality, authenticity, and democratic potential.[16] Whitman's nod to Indigenous cultures as inspiration for American artistry is of course an interesting precursor of the primitivist agendas espoused by the Santa Fe and Taos arts colonists. With *A Day in Santa Fe* likewise taking the form of a poem film, in this case with Riggs's own poetry accompanying vignettes of Santa Fe, one may find Riggs's signature occupation with the intersection of nature, the everyday, and avant-garde urban arts along with critique of typical primitivism.

Riggs described the composition of his film as a "symphony," an intention typical of the montages of early avant-garde cinema in America and a helpful description of how the various communities and actors of Santa Fe society converge in *A Day in Santa Fe*. "City films" like *A Day in Santa Fe* were a robust component of film art of this period, and Riggs and Hughes's contribution was screened in New York City as part of the burgeoning art film movement there. According to Jan-Christopher Horak, American city films emphasized the relationship between man and nature, with *Manhatta* serving as one example of their mix of modernist formalism and romantic sentiment.[17] Horak also notes a shift in tone toward metaphor and parody with the coming of the 1930s. In his own words about *A Day in Santa Fe* in *Cine-Kodak*, a magazine for amateur moviemakers, Riggs describes this symphony as having "movements, with recurring themes and rhythms, with variety, with humor, and with a conclusion prepared for and demanded by everything that preceded it."[18] *Cine-Kodak* articles were a kind of advertisement for making home movies about one's own town with Eastman Kodak cameras. According to Jeffrey Ruoff, home movies were foundational to avant-garde film of the later twentieth century.[19] Within this context of *A Day in Santa Fe*'s moment in film history, its opening can be understood not only as a gesture toward the town's settler colonial underpinning but also as a formal reference to such American city films as *Manhatta*. Riggs's film highlights the artfulness of the built environment and its relationship to nature and, with a healthy dose of parody, deepens our understanding of the links between modernism, the urban, and regionalism in Indigenous studies.

A Day in Santa Fe, like *Manhatta*, reveals careful composition of images with a photographer's skill and perspective. Just as *Manhatta* begins with shots of skyscrapers towering over New York harbor at the start of a new day, *A Day in Santa Fe* opens with sunrise over the hills near town, accompanied by Riggs's lines:

> Dawn silence fills
> The domed tremendous
> glowing sky.
> The veils of dark begin
> to die.

The lens turns to Santa Fe's own version of skyscrapers, the towering Cross of the Martyrs and the spires of the Cathedral Basilica of St. Francis of Assisi, before providing a view of a street in town and of the Plaza from the Palace of the Governors. Cox points toward the Cross, erected to memorialize twenty-one Franciscan friars martyred in the Pueblo Revolt of 1680; the cathedral, constructed in place of other churches destroyed in the revolt; and the palace, emblematic of secular colonial authority, as evidence of the filmmakers' amplification of the imposing authority of the Catholic Church and isolation of Indigenous presence in part 1 of the film.[20] I agree with Cox that the impact of these images is in keeping with Riggs's acknowledgment and critique, in his Santa Fe writings and elsewhere, of settler colonial histories. I also want to draw attention, however, to the way that this opening's shot of the deserted street indicates a nod to the everyday in addition to the more striking landmarks. Riggs's attention to everyday scenes as well as the home movie style of his work signals an aesthetic of the urban avant-garde informed by Riggs's position as an Indigenous writer within the art world of Santa Fe.

My analysis of *A Day in Santa Fe* brings to the fore a bond between the city, its diverse inhabitants, and the natural world that surrounds it. The first frames of *A Day in Santa Fe*, tracing the emergence of daylight, turn from the arches and angles of city structures back to the expanse of the Sangre de Cristo Mountains, with a long, panoramic scan of the brilliant sky above. In some of the film's first intertitles,

hill and valley,
town and flower
Stir

symbiotically, followed by several shots of wildflowers. A burro, which Riggs names as the principal character of his film, appears still and alone on-screen, and the camera then follows him as he begins his journey, laden with wood, to the city center, which calls to mind the images Riggs develops in the poem "Morning Walk: Santa Fe." Creatures, human and nonhuman, begin to stir, and from the morning's quiet beginning, the film shifts to the speed of activity—"evolved acceleration," in Riggs's words—of a steam whistle, cars, a galloping horse, and a bike coasting down the street.[21] Like in "Spring Morning: Santa Fe," black-shawled women make their way down the street, some of a number of people "going with the sun" as the day progresses. A Mexican laborer is building a new structure, slinging adobe onto bricks. Santa Fe's creative class is then introduced, with a painter (Jozef Bakos, one of a collective known as "Los Cincos Pintores") emerging from his home and entering a casita that functions as his studio.

With the film's introduction of writers, artists, and tourists of the city's art world, Riggs once again treats the Santa Fe bourgeois with a satirical tone, yet his integration of nature, the built environment, and the "characters" that reside there is key to his emphasis on the symphony of these features of his adopted home and community. After Bakos enters the casita, the camera pans across the structure, becoming fixed on its window, which is reflecting the landscape. Inside Bakos looks from the window, sun streaming onto his face, to his canvas and the landscape scene he is creating. The camera then cuts to the opposite vantage point within the room; now the window is luminous, its square angles in sharper focus as everything else is darkened, and the artist's silhouette is in focus on the window's left side. From the interior of Bakos's studio, the view then turns to a Mexican man who emerges from a darkened doorway into daylight; he leans against an adobe building, sun streaming onto him. Next the lens turns to the plaza, where a white man (in a white suit) encounters a Native American man selling jewelry on the corner. The white man imposes, touching the jewelry maker's necklace and rings, and then removes one large ring, places it on his own finger, and negotiates its purchase. In this exchange, the white man appears to be confident in his own power, touching this stranger with no hesitation, emboldened by the cash in his pocket. Cox calls this scene "fraught," pointing toward its enactment of colonial encounter, of acquisition as conquest, to support his reading of part 1 of the film as primarily a commentary on colonial dominance.[22]

Though I agree that the buyer's expression of dominance is telling, I also want to draw attention to the jewelry maker's position as an artist—not just a cultural representative—in this series of shots that depict the Santa Fe arts community. I turn to the work of Deirdre Evans-Pritchard and Karl Hoerig as a reminder that Native Americans do view themselves as artists with agency in the tourist market of the city, and though the white man (and perhaps some viewers) presumes that he takes advantage of the jewelry maker in this situation, the maker's own body language—his waiting at the corner for a potential buyer, his shaking his head no during the negotiation, his smile when the deal is made, and his apparent satisfaction with the money he receives—suggests that perhaps he is the one in control of the situation. After this transaction, the camera turns to a succession of feet belonging to individuals—a Mexican, a Native American, an Anglo girl, and a cowboy—walking along a sidewalk, their shoes signaling their ethnic and occupational uniqueness. The lighting of this sequence, with the sun creating long shadows of the full statures against the adjacent building, creates an impressionistic view of each. The burro makes his way down a sidewalk as well, heading into town after pausing to graze on some nearby foliage.

In keeping with Riggs's comments about the recurring themes and rhythms in the film, the whir of a mechanical pencil sharpener echoes the earlier steam whistle and introduces another sequence with Anglo colonists encountering Native cultures. Alice Corbin Henderson emerges from her home to recline on her porch for a writing session, concentrating on the poem "Cundiyo," which she published as part of a collection of "New Mexico Folk Songs." Another woman entertains her dog. Turning to the busy commerce of the city center, the camera captures a stream of cars circling the Plaza. Six shoppers enter the Spanish and Indian Trading Post, where Riggs himself worked for a time after leaving the Sunmount Sanitarium.[23] The shop was founded in 1926 by Henderson's son-in-law, John Evans (the son of Mabel Dodge Luhan), along with Witter Bynner and others of the arts scene, its purpose to collect, promote, and sell Indian and Spanish crafts.[24] Viewers then see a kind of artistic exhibit: a succession of three paintings by Velino Shije Herrera, kachina dolls positioned in a chair, and finally a sculpture of a burro casting a long shadow against a wall. Cox argues that these shots "have put the 'primitive' on display" and that the "staging obscures the Indigenous artists and removes the works of art from Indigenous cultural contexts," ultimately representing Indigeneity "primarily as a cultural object in Part I."[25]

Citing J. J. Brody's *Pueblo Indian Painting: Tradition and Modernism in New Mexico, 1900–1930* (1997), Cox mentions that Herrera was an important painter in the "new tradition" of Pueblo painting early in the twentieth century, which focused on religious and social dances and daily activities. It is important to keep in mind the greater context for Herrera's work: this Pueblo easel painting was groundbreaking, a shift from exclusive attention to artwork with a utilitarian purpose for Pueblo communities. Herrera and other young people who were mentored by white teachers such as Esther

Hoyt, Elizabeth Richards, Elizabeth DeHuff, and Dorothy Dunn—all affiliates of the Santa Fe Indian School—were provided with watercolors and art supplies and encouraged to paint about their lives, violating the U.S. government's curriculum of craft work instruction (to serve a market economy) that was divorced from cultural and religious practices. The flat colorful style that became a signature of this easel painting movement itself came to be understood as overly restrictive by the time Oscar Howe (trained by Dunn) and other modern artists departed from this style in the 1950s and 1960s. Still, the desire to represent and advance Native culture through painting remained consistent over time, regardless of western influences and artists' responses to them.

Thus, this appearance of Herrera's pieces in Riggs's films is significant in my analysis not only for its representation of the Anglo-dominated tourist market but also for its opportunity to showcase the work of an innovative Native artist. The kachina dolls, positioned in ways that mirror the poses of the figures in Herrera's paintings, likewise connect the artistic and cultural significance of the items, and the burro sculpture, harks back to the scene of Santa Feans whose shadows dance artfully across a nearby adobe structure. All of these characters contribute to the everyday urban social scene that Riggs found so inspiring for his own artistic endeavors. With a shot of a clock face set to the noon hour, parallel to the earlier steam whistle and pencil sharpener, Riggs and Hughes introduce a leisurely wind-down to siesta, with a small gathering of diners enjoying Instagram-worthy New Mexican dishes al fresco while a goat and some dogs have a snack of their own. The burro pauses, and a few individuals relax into sleep as "the curtains close against the day."

The latter part of the film corresponds closely to Riggs's Santa Fe poems, as the filmmakers bring together views of spectacle, leisure, and performance with the familiarity and warmth of home. From the start of siesta, Riggs and Hughes transition to a dance at a nearby pueblo, with intertitles drawn from Riggs's "Santa Domingo Corn Dance" poem. The lower half of dancers appears, and as is the case earlier in the film, sunlight creates long shadows aside the figures' legs and feet; the segment serves as a live enactment of the scenes in the paintings and kachina displayed at the Spanish and Indian Trading Company. The camera angle widens to a full, aerial view of the dancers in motion, watched by a large gathering of spectators, before returning to the closer view of legs and feet dancing. As the intertitles suggest, this dance corresponds to rain provided by the Creator, and the camera switches repeatedly between an aerial shot of dancers and the gathering storm clouds and windblown trees above. At that point the view turns again to the nappers, human and animal, who must move inside to avoid the rain that is beginning to fall, creating shadows, waterfalls, and rushing water across the streets and sidewalks below. Transitioning away from the corn dance poem, intertitles then signal the sudden emergence of the sun as the rain ends. Now the viewer regards a series of close-ups of Santa Feans—Anglo people, a pet dog, and even a peacock, whose attention turns skyward to a circling plane overhead. As the burro again begins his journey, a young boy directs him to a sign above, ACEQUIA MADRE, the city's main irrigation ditch mentioned in Riggs's city poem of the same name. The burro strolls along the sidewalk, where a woman who has been waiting for his arrival finally unloads from his back the firewood that she is purchasing. A group of revelers—obviously with extra time on their hands—celebrates the afternoon with cocktail hour, bringing "the liquid sound . . . of laughter."

The return of the steam whistle signals the last movement of the film, which moves the action to homeward and interior scenes. A little girl enters her playhouse, a Mexican man who has been leaning against an adobe structure all day returns inside, and someone can be seen switching on a lamp through a window. The camera turns skyward to the darkened Cross of the Martyrs and then follows the burro home to the mountain. Back at the Plaza, "Moonlight and music / shimmers down": cars proceed at a slower pace with headlights on, and parallel to earlier scenes of Indigenous artistry, in a courtyard a mariachi band plays. The camera turns back to the mountains, capturing the sinking sun. Like Riggs's poem "The Shaped Room," the last scenes of "A Day in Santa Fe" evoke the warmth and beauty of home, particularly in an adobe interior, as the burro's customer lights the firewood he delivered. The camera lingers on the dancing light emanating from her fireplace, and then the viewer sees the burro being reunited with his creature family: "he goes home / to love and food." A cat yawns, preparing for night. The film ends with a slow, fading shot of the fire's gathering strength.

A Day in Santa Fe is a fascinating record of the cultural convergence of "the city different," as well as the innovations of avant-garde film, in the early twentieth century. I want to complicate the way we understand modernism with regard to Native writers and artists such as Riggs. Dorman's study of regionalism, which notes that some of regionalism's strains—faith in social art, artistic innovation, and cultural pluralism—parallel those of modernism, is helpful for identifying ways that *A Day in Santa Fe* reflects its unique time and place, which, though certainly different from large cities like New York, nevertheless launched the careers of so many artists, including Native Americans like Riggs. Horak observes in American early avant-garde film "dread" at the separation from nature and "lament at the separation from the country," with elements of parody surfacing by the 1930s.[26] Scenes and elements of nature are certainly prominent in Riggs and Hughes's film, but rather than exhibiting the kind of angst at separation that Horak describes, their film incorporates nature into the rhythms of the day, complementing the mechanization signified in the steam whistle, pencil sharpener, clock, and circling airplane. I identify these "movements" in the "symphony" that Riggs calls his structure as key to understanding the film's contribution.

Within these movements, Riggs and Hughes weave diverse human characters (Anglo, Mexican, and Indigenous) as well as nonhuman creatures into the rhythms of Santa Fe life. The humorous tone underlying the framing of the burro as the industrious main character and the humans, especially the Anglo characters (many of them friends and associates of the filmmakers), as decidedly less productive as they nap and drink supports a critique of the usual power dynamics of the Primitivist art scene. In this social world, who are the true primitives?

The filmmakers' rendering of urban aesthetics is also significant, as locations such as the Cross of the Martyrs, plaza, palace portal, cathedral, alleyways, sidewalks, studios, and shops are artfully drawn with nature—the sun, the mountains, the rain—always paramount. Finally, while these locations contain colonial history, they also stage art and performance, in which Riggs himself participates; this creative production of urban space complicates the artistic primitivism of non-Natives. Rather than reading, as Cox does, the Indigenous artworks depicted in the earlier part of the film as Riggs's exposure of the damaging abstraction of Native cultures, I suggest that the sale that the Pueblo jeweler makes, the featuring of Herrera's paintings, and the positioning of the kachina dolls asserts Indigenous agency in Santa Fe arts, a subversive move that sets the stage for the rain that proceeds from Pueblo dancing later in the film. Overall, in keeping with the city poems, *A Day in Santa Fe* reveals ways that Santa Fe energizes and inspires Riggs, even as it also offers fodder for critique.

Riggs's plays of the later 1930s and 1940s address more pointedly the continued force of settler colonial histories of the Americas, and as Kirby Brown notes, a clearer anticolonial voice emerges in these writings. Santa Fe was where Riggs's playwriting began in earnest.[27] There he wrote *The Primitives: A Satirical Comedy in Three Acts* (1925), a play based in New Mexico that he later destroyed. Without access to this play, it is unclear how Riggs shaped this satire or whom he was portraying as primitive, and we can only speculate about why he felt the need to destroy it. But Riggs's later longest-running play on Broadway, *Russet Mantle: A Comedy* (1936), the final text in my study of Riggs's Santa Fe writings, follows a pattern of critique in its representation of Anglo newcomers to Santa Fe in an unflattering light. As Jaye Darby, Courtney Mohler, and Christy Stanlake argue in their recent study of Riggs's plays, *Russet Mantle* "upends the traditional European theatrical form of comedy to expose mainstream hypocrisies."[28] First performed at the Masque Theatre in New York City in 1936, the play was staged by Alexander Dean with a set composed of adobe-style interiors to complement the script's commentary on the Santa Fe of the 1930s. *Russet Mantle* presents several themes, including a critique of American materialism and restrictive sexual mores and an assertive (if playful) treatment of the role of the poet, that follow the topics he explored in earlier pieces. Additionally, Riggs brings together Anglo, Mexican, and Native American characters to highlight the region's converging cultures as well as the fumbling racism of an older generation of Santa Fe upper-class whites.

Riggs's directions for set design in the introductory notes to each act of *Russet Mantle* draw attention to aesthetic interests he displays in his city poems and film, particularly an interplay of light, plants, and adobe structures. The aesthetics support a productive relationship between humans, nature, and urban spaces. In the introductory notes to act 1, Riggs creates a scene on the ranch of the wealthy Kincaid family, where the view looks out across a portal supported by Mexican corbels, sunlight streaming down just beyond the covering. Several furnishings give the impression that this is a home of well-to-do enthusiasts for the Southwest, from the strings of chilies hanging from the vigas to the hand-carved front door, from the tin Mexican sconces and adobe bench to the "Indian pot" and rustic leather and painted Mexican chairs. Several plants, including hollyhocks, potted geraniums, and a cottonwood tree, round out the composition of the autumnal set, with Riggs writing: "The place is magic with peace and beauty. Mottled sunlight, gold and luminous, ripples over everything."[29] This staging hints at Riggs's own affection for the region in which he found a creative home for so many years, even as the action of the play questions the motivations of Anglo settlers like the Kincaids.

The white characters of Riggs's play represent several regions of the United States and allow Riggs to connect each character's plans for life in Santa Fe with America's foundation in colonialism. Horace Kincaid, which Riggs describes as "grizzled, a little absurd, dour and fifty," comes from Philadelphia, a businessman occupied almost obsessively with the status of stock market reports, though he also has a passing interest in his apple orchard. His wife, Susanna, and sister-in-law Effie Rowley are from Louisville, and Susanna, "in rough clothes and a silly straw hat," feigns expertise in rearing Wyandotte chickens. Effie, a great beauty in an organdy dress, injects the play with what Riggs calls "mindless cheerfulness"—and comic relief—during her stay with the Kincaids, as she navigates her daughter Kay's promiscuity with the same level of engagement as her hosts' attention to apples and chickens.

This older generation inhabits Santa Fe with prejudices against people of color in their adopted community, including their servants, that support their upper-class standing. Effie in particular is a mouthpiece for the voyeurism of Anglo newcomers, especially tourists: "Will I see any Indians while I'm here on my visit? . . . Real live redskins? . . . Indians are all alike! Red and bloodthirsty. I'll be scared to death when I see one. Savages, they are."[30] With his flagrant materialism and anxiety about the onset of economic depression, Horace reflects the legacy of the industrial Northeast. The class consciousness and hollow agrarianism, not to mention the racism, of Susanna and Effie indicate a South in decline. The regional histories that these characters bring with them to Santa Fe hint at the problematic history of white settlement in the area, and the gap between the attitudes of these characters and their younger counterparts provides much of the social commentary that underlies the comedic tone of *Russet Mantle*.

At Kay Rowley's introduction, she is immediately associated with behavior considered unbecoming in her hometown of Louisville, and her eventual love interest, John Galt, also departs from the expectations of Effie and his employers, the Kincaids. Kay is first mentioned when Manuelita, the Mexican maid, inquires of Susanna whether she should wake the young woman; apparently, no one has yet noticed that Kay has not had breakfast or joined the family's activities. Effie casually states that Kay has likely not come home at all after a night out with a cowboy named Scoot, whom she met at the Plaza. This revelation shocks Susanna, particularly because Effie has shared this information in front of the servants. Effie cheerfully calls her daughter "wild" and "the scourge of Louisville," seemingly having abandoned the will to mentor Kay, regardless of how she feels about the safety or appropriateness of her behavior. When Kay appears along with Scoot, Riggs writes that she is wearing the "dirtiest pair of dungarees in New Mexico," and he calls her "young and handsome, dark, vibrant, superbly alive." When Horace presses her for details about her actions, Kay reveals that she sat with Scoot on the portal late into the night. She listened to him sing cowboy songs while playing guitar, a moment that mirrors Curly McLain's singing in Riggs's 1931 masterpiece, *Green Grow the Lilacs*. She then provides her own singing performance before explaining that she and Scoot tended cattle in the arroyo and rode horses after sleeping in a bed shared with the young Mexican cowhand.

While Kay's night out actually seems innocent enough, the reaction of Horace and Susanna contributes to a theme of fertility throughout the play. Susanna and Horace continually note that they have no children, and Riggs uses phrases such as *poor bereaved mother* and *pseudo mother* to describe Susanna as she frets over Kay. The audience eventually learns that before Susanna married Horace, she was in love with "a dreamer," an unworthy prospect because of his lack of wealth who moved to Spain.[31] The relocation of Horace and Susanna to New Mexico after the stock market crash was at Susanna's urging, and Horace fears their adopted home allows Susanna to keep her poet-lover of the Old World alive in her heart. Kay eventually becomes pregnant by John Galt, another newcomer to Santa Fe, and John and Kay become a double of sorts to the older couple, contrasting their ineffectual old ways with a new generation's hope.

John Galt, a native of Kansas City, arrives at the Kincaid Ranch shortly after Kay's exploits with Scoot are discussed, and he becomes a mouthpiece for the intergenerational debate that exposes the failings of Anglo-settler attitudes. Galt explains that he journeyed to the ranch along the Alameda, the thoroughfare Riggs features in his city poems and film. In his first conversation with Horace, he expresses his admiration for the apples of the Kincaid trees along the acequia, which immediately ingratiates him to the family. Horace and Susanna learn that Galt is well traveled and has worked a variety of jobs, in manual labor, agriculture, and education. When Horace tries to pinpoint any notable family connections, Galt says he has no family to speak of, that he came to Santa Fe "to think," and that he also writes poetry, leading Susanna and Effie to assume he will be a dreamy man like Susanna's rejected lover.

When John claims that he knows a thing or two about chickens, Susanna makes him her chicken-rearing assistant and offers him a room in the chicken house along with the job. As Susanna has described her chickens as broody, with their minds on sex, wanting "to set all the time," this arrangement hints at what is to come. During his first meal with the family, John makes it clear that his views put him at odds with his hosts. He is not dreamy after all; instead, his interest in poetry fuels his realistic view of the state of the world. When the conversation turns to the Depression, John identifies as "an alien in [his] own land" and focuses on the misery, avarice, and cruelty of America: "You can't cancel the economic root and the rotten tree. They have to be dug up."[32] Having already locked eyes with Kay at his arrival, it is not long before John and Kay are secretly sharing a bed in the chicken house.

The chicken house is the setting for act 2, which brings Mexican characters more strongly into the action of the play and continues references to sexuality and fertility established from the beginning. Riggs's stage directions emphasize the bed in the corner of the adobe room, illumined by electric lights "in glowing pools" that "make a strange, half-unreal mood in the place, as if anything might happen there." Guitar music enhances the scene, which calls to mind Riggs's careful descriptions of relationships between intimacy and adobe interiors in the poems "The Choice" and "The Shaped Room." When act 2 begins, Pablo tells John his reasons for rejecting the kind of white-collar work—being president of a bank, for instance—that Horace embraces. Instead of sitting inside a bank, in a "cage with wire," Pablo works several jobs around Santa Fe in addition to his employment at the ranch, and he has been receiving extra money from Susanna for surreptitiously completing her early-morning chicken-tending tasks.

In his work around Santa Fe, Pablo makes the acquaintance of many women, who invite him to walk them home from work. Pablo states: "I walk home with thees girl, and what happen? We go along the reever bank, and they's losta willow trees hangin' down, and bushes—and first theeng, you know, thees girl, she's gonna have a baby." The woman's father cautions Pablo that he must marry her, which prompts Pablo to describe his predicament to John: "My God, how I'm gonna marry seven, eight, nine girls!" Manuelita then enters the room to ask Pablo to walk her home (perfect timing!), and the departure of the two ranch laborers is immediately followed by Kay's entry to the chicken house, where she and John will also become a couple. Pablo's association with fertility is linked to the natural world in his remarks about the river, trees, and bushes, and like the cowboy Scoot, Pablo also has a penchant for folk singing. As Horace's assistant, Pablo has primary responsibility for the Kincaid apple orchard since, parallel to Susanna's failures at chicken rearing, Horace is a terrible gardener. Unsurprisingly, the apples contain usual associations with sexual temptation, but they also spur an early debate between Pablo and Horace about using chemical spray, with Horace likening pests to the weaknesses of the stock market, while Pablo shows sympathy for the "Poor leetle bugs!"[33] Though Horace, who is constantly lecturing Pablo, is not self-aware enough to notice, Pablo is the one who is secure in his financial situation and a father to many.

While Riggs subverts the economic domination of settlers in his rendering of Pablo's stability versus Horace's stock market losses, he also subtly asserts Native American presence in Santa Fe even though none of the main characters is Pueblo. Susanna, not exactly a model ally, nevertheless disabuses Effie of her incorrect assumption that all Indians are of the Great Plains, naming the unique towns, such as Santo Domingo and Tesuque, that form Pueblo communities: "Effie! There aren't any plains here. These are a different kind of Indian. They're Pueblos." When Susanna shows John his lodging in the chicken house, she assures him that there is no need to lock the doors, as "nobody'll come in." She corrects herself, however: "No one at all. Except maybe an Indian. We have many Indian friends in the nearby pueblos. Sometimes, if we're out, they just come and sit for hours—till we come back. It's all very friendly."[34] Susanna's naïveté is on display here; it's questionable whether any Pueblo people are truly her friends, even if she perceives them as "friendly." However, the presence of Pueblo people on the Kincaid Ranch is significant. Regardless of the ownership of the ranch or whether it is in a Pueblo town, it is still on Indigenous land, and the occupation of this space by Native people asserts this fundamental reality.

The final act of *Russet Mantle*, which contains the only appearance onstage of a Native character, returns to the set of act 1, with the new season and passage of time—and new life—marked by spring flowers and a dwindling string of chilies. Salvador's brief entry into the action of act 3 corresponds to the moment when Effie must finally confront the truth about her daughter and her lack of responsibility for her. As Effie waits for an update from Dr. Brown on a "cold" afflicting Kay, Salvador enters the scene, his appearance partially obscured as he sits in a chair outside the house. Effie, aware that someone is outside because of the cigarette he flicks at her feet, assumes this person is Horace, but when she discovers it is a Native American, she is shocked and frightened. When Susanna enters, she endeavors to make an introduction: "Did you meet Salvador, Effie? Salvador's from Ildefonso. . . . Salvador's one of our best friends, aren't you, Salvador? How's your family?" Salvador is uninterested in these pleasantries and simply asks, "Cigaret?" revealing his own motivation for interacting with the Kincaids—free cigarettes rather than friendship.

When Dr. Brown confirms the timeline of Kay's pregnancy, the family realizes that Scoot is not the father, and Effie instantly summons her privilege as a southern white woman to demand an act of racial terror. She calls for a lynching party against Salvador: "Someone came in the night, Somebody overpowered her! . . . Horace, lynchin' is too good for whoever's responsible. You got to organize a lynchin' party at once!" Salvador immediately exits, likely having been aware all along of the danger of trusting or befriending this family. Kay and her parents do not appease Effie, instead acknowledging and accepting the truth of John Galt's responsibility, with Kay, for the pregnancy. At the play's conclusion, Kay speaks directly to Effie about her relationship with John, disabusing her mother of her flawed assumption of Kay's victimization: "It isn't what you'd consider delicate and beautiful, it isn't a dream. It's real as hell—and I'm not ashamed." With John and Kay committing to a life together against the odds, John suggests to the older couple: "Imagine you're young again—and the world is beginning for you!" Susanna responds: "Horace. Sit down. Let's try."[35]

Kay's pregnancy represents Rigg's challenge to the "old world" values of Horace, Susanna, and Kay, including their views of Santa Fe as a dreamlike escape from reality. The play's critique of the materialism, classism, and racism that older white characters bring with them to Santa Fe from the North and South are amplified through characters such as Pablo and Salvador, who are rooted in the cultures that are Indigenous to this place, and John Galt, who, as a well-traveled Kansas City native, is less inhibited and more open to change. Riggs's resistance to the conventions of American captivity narratives, which so often play into European-American fears of white women's sexual violation, is striking. The young white man of the story is immediately trusted, never considered as the potential father of Kay's child. When he readily accepts responsibility, he has no fear for his safety. It is also notable that when *Russet Mantle* premiered in 1936, Riggs cast Pawnee actor Kuruks Pahitu in the role of Salvador. Darby, Mohler, and Stanlake call this casting, along with the content of the play and its staging, "courageous performances, inclusive spaces enriched by multiple narratives of the Americas, especially Native peoples."[36] With the casting of Pahitu, Riggs prevented a white actor from "playing Indian" just as he challenged the Kincaids' voyeuristic notions of Santa Fe—with all its associations with the Old World—as a "dream" that could redeem them.

Russet Mantle contains themes that are prominent across Riggs's body of writing and highlight the ways that Native American writers from Oklahoma shape as well as critique the urban culture of Santa Fe, linking it to shared histories of their homelands. In Pablo's and Scoot's songs, one can find a connection with the authentic folk speech that Riggs cultivated in his most well-known Oklahoma play, *Green Grow the Lilacs*. In the voice of John Galt, one can hear the debates and concerns about America that shaped Riggs's activist agenda, which grew stronger as his career progressed.

In the play's artful attention to set design and lighting, one can perceive Riggs's participation in avant-garde arts as a person with not only a deep knowledge and affection for the western environment and architecture but also a commitment to inclusiveness in those spaces. In his creation of the Kincaids and Rowleys, Riggs gives life to the settler patrons, tourists, and real estate speculators who formed the Santa Fe social scene he participated in, but rather than asserting a wholesale denunciation of their presence, he critiques their failures with empathy and a glimmer of hope for the future.

"There Is a Place for Us"

Like Riggs, Joy Harjo came to Santa Fe from Oklahoma as a young person seeking a change from her unsatisfying education and troubled home life, and identifying commonalities between the two writers links significant eras in Indigenous arts. As she describes in her memoir *Crazy Brave*, Harjo came to Santa Fe after requesting that her mother enroll her in boarding school there, the culmination of her increasingly desperate attempts to escape her abusive stepfather. Her admission was secure after she sent samples of her fashion sketches and cartoons. She writes of New Mexico: "I felt inspired about my life in a way that I hadn't been since early childhood when I used to go outside early in the morning to talk with the sun. . . . When I started Indian school in Santa Fe in 1967, I was fresh from escaping the emotional winter of my childhood. I had been set free."[37] In her writings about Santa Fe (and New Mexico in general), Harjo provides insight into the area's tremendous significance for Indigenous arts, especially in the contemporary era, and also the corresponding activism that propelled the Native American civil rights movement of the late twentieth century. Harjo has stated that she's lived in Santa Fe "more than anyplace else" and that the city is "a community that knows Native arts and artists. There's a place for us; we are recognizable as distinct cultures."[38] Like Riggs, Harjo experienced a creative awakening there that would shape the rest of her life, but in her case, her peers and mentors were mostly Native, which signals the way the city's relationship to its Indigenous residents and artists has evolved over time. Still, Harjo, like Riggs, pushes back against the enduring signs and symbols of settler history in Santa Fe and contemplates her own position as a Native writer in this urban environment.

In *Crazy Brave* Harjo describes Santa Fe as "the epicenter of hippiedom in the West," which influenced the community at the Institute for American Indian Arts (originally Santa Fe Indian School).[39] As the Santa Fe of Riggs's time was also a bohemian's alternative to the Left Bank of Paris or the Greenwich Village of New York City, the city retained its countercultural flavor as time passed. And just as the non-Indian enthusiasts of 1930s artistic primitivism dabbled in themes and images taken from American Indian cultures, the Anglo hippies of the 1960s and 1970s also were inspired by Natives whose continued struggles for sovereignty were receiving greater attention. As Sherry Smith recounts in *Hippies, Indians, and the Fight for Red Power*, "The particular confluence of contemporary issues made Indians especially interesting, appealing, and relevant to the nation's restless, reform-oriented, discontented, outraged, and alienated souls. Native Americans—or perhaps more accurately peoples' rather fuzzy 'understandings' of Native Americanness—suddenly had particular panache."[40] While hippie fashion incorporated headbands, beads, and feathers, similar to the southwestern influence on Anglo fashion in the earlier arts colonies, Harjo describes her Native American classmates' style of dress as also having been influenced by Anglo hippies who were trying to emulate Native Americans, a fascinating self-referential development that may be explained by the diverse, pan-Indian community that developed at IAIA. She writes: "At Indian school we were Inupiat from Alaska, Seminole from Florida, and people from tribes from Oklahoma to Washington State. And though we were allied as young artists of a generation, we still contended with our tribal and historical differences. . . . We were all 'skins' traveling together in an age of metamorphosis, facing the same traumas from colonization and dehumanization. We were direct evidence of the struggle of our ancestors. We heard them and they spoke through us, though like others of our generation, we wore bell-bottoms and Lennon eyeglasses."[41] The American Southwest, and New Mexico in particular, drew a counterculture movement fueled by opposition to the Vietnam War, and while many who participated were newcomers to the area seeking refuge (or a good time) in one of dozens of new communes in New Mexico—including one that Dennis Hopper founded as the Mud Palace in the former home of Mabel Dodge Luhan—others were joining diverse coalitions of activists committed to affecting lasting change.[42]

After attending IAIA, Harjo became a student at the University of New Mexico (UNM) in Albuquerque, which was an important if generally unacknowledged site for American Indian activism along with cities such as Chicago, Minneapolis, and San Francisco. But Harjo's transition to higher education was not seamless. In her last year at IAIA, she became immersed in the school's theater program and joined, as lead, a touring production of *Mowitch*, a play written by Klamath student Monica Charles. When the tour was over, as her peers moved on to new professional opportunities, Harjo returned to Tulsa. She writes, "I returned to the house of my stepfather, secretly pregnant by my Cherokee boyfriend and with no plans, no idea at all as to where I was going or how I was going to get there."[43] Harjo traveled to Tahlequah, Oklahoma, her boyfriend's hometown, and endured a desperate period of poverty while living with her resentful mother-in-law and newborn son. With the father of her child, she decided to return to Santa Fe. There the pair continued to struggle to find work, and when Harjo discovered her partner's affair with the babysitter, she left him. She had an opportunity to work as a nursing assistant at St. Vincent Hospital in Santa Fe, where she excelled: "This hospital work engaged me in a way nothing else had to that point. My innate impulse is healing, which is also standing up for justice, which can heal hearts and nations."[44]

Seeking a new beginning, and sponsored by the eight Northern Pueblos Talent Search as well as her own tribe, Harjo began college as a premed student at UNM in Albuquerque. There she found that "a revolution was going on. . . . We were waking up all over the country, at Alcatraz, in Pine Ridge, in Minneapolis, in Washington DC. As students active in the Kiva Club, the university's Indian student organization, we were on fire with the possibility of peace and justice for our peoples. . . . We aspired to be traditional-contemporary twentieth-century warriors, artists, and dreamers."[45] Harjo's experience documents the emergence of the contemporary Native American civil rights movement, which was deeply influenced by the leadership of Oklahomans. Organizations headquartered in New Mexico such as the National Indian Youth Council (NIYC) and Americans for Indian Opportunity (AIO) were shaped by Indigenous activists from Oklahoma, including LaDonna Harris (Comanche), Viola Hatch (Arapaho), Fred Warrior (Ponca), and Della Warrior (Otoe-Missouria). After a tumultuous relationship with Simon Ortiz and the birth of their daughter,

Rainy Dawn Ortiz, Harjo became determined to follow poetry as her avocation, a path out of a tormenting anxiety.

The communities in which Harjo participated in Santa Fe and Albuquerque combined activism with a flourishing artistic renaissance in Indian Country. Harjo writes: "The seed for my poetry writing was rooted in that circle of Old Ones in my tribal nation in Oklahoma, and it emerged and broke through to stand with young Indian artists in Santa Fe. I blossomed with that brave, brilliant, hilarious, and dedicated circle of friends and fellow students of the Kiva Club."[46] At IAIA especially, with the leadership of its inaugural art director, Lloyd Kiva New, a Cherokee from Fairland, Oklahoma, students collaborated under the mentorship of Native American instructors, progressing from the assimilationist aims of Santa Fe Indian School's early years. The Quapaw-Cherokee composer Louis Ballard, a native of Miami, Oklahoma, was especially important in planting the seeds of Harjo's musical prowess, and her first exposure to the New Orleans–based Preservation Hall Jazz Band occurred at the school.[47] Harjo also mentions several fine arts instructors, including Native artists with Oklahoma ties Allan Houser and Rolland Meinholtz, who nurtured students' creativity. Harjo writes, "As we made art, attended cultural events, and struggled with family and tribal legacies, we sensed that we were at the opening of an enormous indigenous cultural renaissance, poised at the edge of an explosion of ideas that would shape contemporary Indian art in the years to come." The enormity of this cultural moment was made clear to Harjo and her classmates in the spaces of schoolrooms that were constructed primarily for industrial and domestic education, where "previous generations of students were trained to be low-paid labor for white families in the towns and cities."[48] The academic side of the school curriculum, as Harjo reports, still retained traces of the uninspired teaching methods of the past. Still, as it had for others before her, Santa Fe served as a setting for Harjo's artistic awakening. She writes, "What I found there was a refuge, and more than that, a family made of her Native students from all over the country, and our arts teachers, all of us on the artist path together."[49]

As is the case with the other writers of my study, recognizing Harjo's relationship to urban spaces that hold important historical and cultural ties to Oklahoma is crucial for understanding her work and, more broadly, the diverse histories of Native American urbanity, activism, and creativity. In reimagining, singing, and writing about these spaces where Native Americans are supposed to be disappeared, Harjo is countering the abstraction of space that Lefebvre describes, which severs meaningful, everyday relationships with land and environment. Mishuana Goeman's analysis of Harjo's writing as a "(re)mapping" is helpful for articulating ways that urban Native writing counters masculinist framings of the West as empty/frontier and also intervenes in limiting ways that Indigenous studies scholars focus too strongly on relationships to land as reclaiming or recovering territories that are themselves spatialized through problematic mapping processes. One of the reasons Harjo is such an influential poet is that through her commitment to spatial justice, her reimagining of the limits of western geographies through poetry, she articulates an experience of being in place in lands across the globe, which in turn resonates with people of many national and cultural backgrounds. As other scholars such as Goeman and Craig Womack have noted, though Harjo's poetry can reasonably be contextualized within global and postcolonial frameworks, her relationship to specific homelands drives her conceptions of her place in the cosmos. In addition to centering Muscogee geographies in this spatial discourse, I argue for ways that Harjo's writing demonstrates a spatial practice that is significant for several Native writers from Oklahoma who exhibit connections across particular regional and urban geographies and community with mentors and peers along a similar path.

New Mexico, and specifically Santa Fe, has galvanized Harjo's career, and images of the area proliferate throughout Harjo's poetry, indicating its importance as an adopted homeland. In a piece she wrote for a 2004 special issue of *Studies in American Indian Literatures* honoring Simon Ortiz, Harjo credits Ortiz with inspiring her poetic gift during their life together in New Mexico: "What blew me open next was the realization that poetry lived within our native lands, our communities. And that poetry could be about the everyday of washing dishes, sunrise, crows carrying on, and that crickets in the corner of the room making a huge racket as well could be honoring songs for those we loved, for those who were working with us for justice. Poetry became a refuge in those times of gathering together, standing up, and reconfiguring. Poetry was Simon's gift to me, and it was here that my poetry began."[50] References to Santa Fe and Indian school in Harjo's poems complement her narrative attention to the area in *Crazy Brave*, providing a more impressionistic view of its influence on her life.

In the prose poem "Santa Fe," first published in *In Mad Love and War* (1990), Harjo confronts the city's colonial history in a way that is similar to her challenge to Hernando de Soto in "New Orleans." In effect, the two poems can be read as companion pieces. In "New Orleans" Harjo emphasizes the Mississippi River as an organizing spatial structure over man-made monuments; in "Santa Fe" a constant image of purple lilacs pervades, engulfing the poet as she walks the city in the shadow of St. Francis Cathedral. The cathedral, one of the city's most recognizable landmarks, was constructed in 1714 following the destruction of the previous church in the Pueblo Revolt. Harjo often walked by it as a high school student in Santa Fe.[51] Named for Saint Francis of Assisi, the patron saint of the city of Santa Fe, the cathedral carries the imprint of Spanish and French colonial influences and was elevated to the standing of basilica in 2005.[52] The lilacs signal the intersection of the East with the allure of the West and also prompts the poet to comment on the subversion of linear time that allows her to experience past and future at once. She writes: "The wind blows lilacs out of the east. And it isn't lilac season. . . . The lilacs have taken over everything: the sky, the narrow streets, my shoulders, my lips. I talk lilac."[53] As a gift-giving gesture, lilacs often symbolize first love, but at the same time, their eastern origin suggests the influence of Europe, where varieties of lilac are common in France and Spain. Like the conquerors of Santa Fe, lilacs have taken over.

As Riggs does in his city poems, Harjo renders nature as strongly intervening in the symbolism and architecture of the built environment as she experiences everyday life. And in another parallel with Riggs, this everyday experience in Santa Fe prompts the poet to consider the paradox of her presence as an Indigenous person in this space. As the poet is consumed by lilac, "a woman the size of a fox breaks through the bushes, breaks the purple web." Harjo describes the woman as "tall and black and gorgeous" and "on the arm of a white man who looks and tastes like cocaine." From the street the poet realizes she has moved to a room in the DeVargas Hotel. There the Black woman "has eaten her lover, white powder on her lips." Similar to LeAnne Howe's story "The Chaos of Angels," in which the narrator encounters a Black woman in a New Orleans hotel courtyard, this encoun-

14. Statue of Saint Francis of Assisi at St. Francis Cathedral, Santa Fe. Photo by iStock.com / Patrick Civello.

ter between the poet and a Black woman at a Santa Fe hotel intervenes into settler erasure, specifically a "tripartite" culture of erasure, of the shared histories of peoples of color. The Black woman's devouring a white man in a hotel named for DeVargas, governor of New Mexico who enacted an aggressive campaign against Indigenous residents, is telling. Harjo's time hop envisions an alternative to an all-consuming colonial conquest of the city.

Back on the sidewalk, Harjo is within close view of a statue of Saint Francis, and her gazing at the statue leads her to voice her position in this city. Harjo writes: "He has been bronzed, a perpetual tan, with birds on his hand, his shoulder, deer at his feet. I am Indian and in this town I will never be a saint. I am seventeen and shy and wild." Harjo's juxtaposition of the saint's appearance to her own is an effective snapshot of the ways that the settler city creates disorienting false ideologies. Saint Francis, so tied within Catholicism to messages of environmentalism, not only is friends with animals but also has been hitting the tanning bed, apparently. Was he Santa Fe's original hippie? Harjo, though not a member of one of the surrounding Native nations, is nevertheless "wild" because of her Indigenous identity, and in the settler logic here, she will never be at home.

Still, by the end of the poem, she asserts her own imagining of her place. She explains that "a man whose face I will never remember" drives up on a Harley-Davidson, lilacs in tow, inviting her to leave for "the flower kingdom of San Francisco," and while she considers it, she does not follow. San Francisco, namesake of Saint Francis (where he is also patron saint) and, like Santa Fe, a hippie culture hotbed, is ultimately not a persuasive alternative. In the face of a saint playing Indian, Harjo asserts an alternative "real time," marked by her own narrative. She concludes, "Maybe is vapor, has no anchor here in the sun beneath St. Francis Cathedral. And space is as solid as the bronze statue of St. Francis, the fox breaking through the lilacs, my invention of this story, the wind blowing." Though she will find no escape from what Saint Francis represents, she controls the narrative, her story as solid as his statue.

Both Riggs and Harjo represent a conflicted relationship with Oklahoma because of the trauma their peoples carried from eastern homelands and the impression that resettlement in Indian Territory left on their families, an experience that is so important for understanding the writing of Native peoples from Oklahoma. While these two writers are not often compared, they shared similar family struggles in their youth and a desire to find a more inspiring educational and creative community, which led them both to Santa Fe. Both writers also found communities that sustained their creative practices even while opening up spaces of critique for the settler ideologies of their adopted city. Finally, both writers share in their work reflection of their role in this paradox of a city, which is in many ways representative of America as a whole, and ultimately find a strong voice of Indigenous persistence informed by the experiences of the path they have followed from east to west.

"I Wanted to Make Something Bold and in Your Face"

Santa Fe endures as a center for Native arts, and yet, echoing concerns about urban development in Tulsa, the pressure of gentrification that newcomers following in the footsteps of the bohemians of the 1930s and the hippies of the 1960s have caused has led to dramatic change in the city's historic areas as well as in its art market. Policies to retain the historic character of central Santa Fe (and make it sufficiently attractive to tourists) have ironically led, in the eyes of some critics, to the creation of a *less* authentic, romanticized, faux Pueblo aesthetic. Joseph P. Sanchez, Robert L. Spude, and Art Gomez document the transformation of the Plaza: "Before the 1970s, it was the hub of daily community activity where local residents gathered . . . the plaza has been transformed into a menagerie of brand-name curio shops, jewelry stores, art vendors, and high-end restaurants that mainly beckon transient visitors. The result has been the gradual displacement of local merchants." Indigenous and Hispanic neighborhoods have been similarly impacted: "The Canyon Road neighborhood typifies what one critic calls the 'Anglo commercialization of Hispanic culture.' . . . the juniper-studded hillsides north of Santa Fe, heading in the direction of Tesuque Pueblo, have become favored sites of movie celebrities and other affluent homeowners."[54] Housing costs in Santa Fe have skyrocketed in recent years, buoyed by an influx of remote workers during the COVID pandemic.[55] While the injection of new wealth into the city may be promising for artists and entertainers seeking a market for their work, the increasing expense of living in the city relative to stagnant wages stymies the thriving young arts communities that Riggs, Harjo, and others enjoyed in earlier times. New Mexico's population is growing older, its percentage of residents over sixty-five years old outpacing national trends, and its rate of population loss due to out-migration has also accelerated within the last decade.[56] The expectations that wealthy and older arts consumers bring shape the market itself, leading to debate about signature events like Indian Market.

Dissatisfaction with what some Native artists, especially of a younger generation, feel are the restraints of Indian Market has led to the formation of alternative events for selling to collectors in Santa Fe. In 2014, frustrated with continuous non-Native control of Indian Market, Tailinh Agoyo and Paula Mirabal joined John Torres Nez, who had just resigned his directorship of the Southwestern Association for Indian Arts, to found the Indigenous Fine Arts Market, which they held in the Santa Fe Railyard District the same weekend as Indian Market. In an article in *Hyperallergic* about the new market, Matthew Irwin explains: "Many young Native artists in town whose parents were also artists will tell you that Indian Market paid the bills when they were growing up. And yet, they'll also likely tell you that the market has kept them in a 'Native box,' with its focus on traditional work such as pottery, rugs, and jewelry."[57] The very next year, SWAIA added the IM: Edge Contemporary show to showcase artists who don't fit into the traditional categories at Indian Market, complementing the growth of cinema and haute couture fashion events as well. Meanwhile, IFAM was short-lived; Mirabal and Agoyo parted ways with Torres Nez, who was indicted in 2016 for embezzlement stemming from his position at SWAIA. They began a nonprofit organization, We Are the Seeds, which began its own recurring market at the railyard district along with other events fostering outreach with Native artists across the country.[58]

Many older, more established artists have also recently been disenchanted with SWAIA. The elimination of the tenure policy in 2016 shut out families who had relied financially on the market since its beginning, and the acceptance of so many artists from outside the area was a particular point of concern.[59] To address the needs of these excluded artists, retired Native American studies professor Gregory Schaaf founded the Free Indian Art Market in 2018 (Edge). Though Indian Market will no doubt continue to be the premier venue for collectors of Native American art, the development of alternative markets and the changing demographics of Santa Fe are the results of realities that can be traced to the city's first market-

15. Paintings by Steven Paul Judd, Indian Market Edge exhibit, Santa Fe. Photo by the author.

ing campaigns as "the city different." With the SWAIA's appointment of executive director Kim Peone, the first Native American woman to lead the organization, the potential for it to be responsive to the concerns of its artists during changing times is promising.

For Oklahoma creatives, time in Santa Fe remains crucial for making a living, even as markets have developed elsewhere across the country. Back home, venues such as Cherokee Art Market and Greater Tulsa Indian Art Festival have grown, but the scale of Indian Market is unmatched. The importance of the market itself goes hand in hand with the opportunities it affords for networking with gallery owners, producers, and other professionals, and participating in the market is a way for many Oklahomans to connect with one another, even if they still live back home. Because of the expense of residing in Santa Fe, along with the growth of technologies that afford new ways for marketing and sharing one's work, making a permanent move to the city is a much different consideration than it was for earlier generations, however. IAIA now houses in the Plaza its Museum of Contemporary Native Arts (MoCNA), which focuses on artworks created after 1962, and in 2015 it began its low-residency Master of Fine Arts in Creative Writing program. These offerings foster greater opportunities for younger, more progressive artists and writers to develop and share their work among some of the most influential audiences and industry leaders even if they are only occasional residents of Santa Fe.

Writers of a new generation with Oklahoma ties, such as Erika T. Wurth, Jennifer Foerster, and Sterlin Harjo, have spent considerable time connecting with arts institutions in Santa Fe, and their experiences there surface in their work. Wurth writes, in her novel-in-stories *Buckskin Cocaine* (2016), with stark realism about film industry characters who participate in a Santa Fe film festival, feeling pressured to pay the bills with "buckskin gigs." Jennifer Foerster (Muscogee), a close friend of Joy Harjo and instructor at IAIA, features poems in her debut collection, *Leaving Tulsa* (2013), in which the Muscogee Nation of Oklahoma as well as the New Mexico landscape spark careful consideration of identity and history. The list of Oklahoma-affiliated writers who serve in the IAIA low-residency program continues to grow with the recent addition of Santee Frazier (Cherokee) as director and Kelli Jo Ford (Cherokee) and Brandon Hobson (Cherokee) to the list of mentors. As in its formative years, IAIA is deeply influenced by Oklahomans who help shape the creative community in Santa Fe while asserting agency over their work, a shift away from the restraints of non-Indian expectations of Indian art in the 1920s and 1930s.

Sterlin Harjo, in his growing visibility on the international film scene, remains committed to having a home in Oklahoma, though he is constantly traveling, and his relationships with other Native artists, writers, and filmmakers fuel his career. His documentary *Love and Fury* (2020) is a look into the lives of contemporary multimedia artists from across the country. Ranging from locations across the world, from Plymouth to Brussels to Tulsa, Harjo shows artists controlling their own narrative, commenting on their resistance to the pigeonholing of Native creativity. Harjo explains, "I wanted to make something bold and in your face, directly putting up a finger to the shackles of the art world and historic representation of our people."[60] Tulsan Yatika Fields (Osage/Muscogee/Cherokee) specifically discusses the differences between the paintings he creates and the work featured at Indian Market in Santa Fe, and while Santa Fe galleries have represented him, Fields ultimately concludes that the artwork Native artists are typically expected to make for that audience "doesn't do anything for me." Another of Harjo's friends, artist Cannupa Hanska Luger (Mandan/Hidatsa/Arikara/Lakota), is shown farting on the toilet in an English pub in Plymouth after visiting the site of the *Mayflower* departure. Luger's irreverent response to the colonial project the *Mayflower* launched is typical of the comedy that Harjo, together with Ryan Red Corn (Osage), Migizi Pensoneau (Ponca/Ojibwe), Bobby Wilson (Sisseton Wahpeton Dakota), and Dallas Goldtooth (Mdewakanton Dakota / Diné), have created as the comedy troupe the 1491s. The 1491s satirize aspects of contemporary Indigenous life through live performances and hundreds of YouTube videos, taking aim especially at pop culture. Predictably, Santa Fe, in all of its turquoise glory, was the subject of one of their first videos.

Though the whole group assembled for the first time in Minneapolis in 2009, Harjo names Santa Fe as birthplace of the 1491s, and "I'm an Indian Too" (2012), a nearly four-minute short filmed in the Plaza during Indian Market, perfectly captures the absurdity of many clichés about Indian life. Of the 1491s, Harjo explains, "The world needed Native humor, so the universe conspired to bring us together on the tough streets of Santa Fe." Of Indian Market, Harjo says: "Santa Fe Indian Market is the first place I ever saw an Indian man playing flute in full buckskin for a bunch of old white ladies. He had a basket out for tips. I thought to myself right then, 'I like this town.' . . . If I was based in Santa Fe, I'd probably wear more turquoise and I'd eat too much green chile."[61] Harjo's joking about the city indicates both its significance and its limitations in a changing world for Native artists. Whereas in the past Santa Fe beckoned as a place for rejuvenation and inspiration, today, with so many new outlets for making and marketing one's work, Santa Fe's association, at least in Harjo's estimation, with "old white ladies" is telling. Though Harjo and other Native artists continue to travel there to engage with colleagues and friends, in "I'm an Indian Too," the Plaza is not exactly as enchanting as this "Land of Enchantment" would suggest. The hints of humor, particularly the critique of primitivism, that were present in Riggs's representation of Santa Fe in *A Day in Santa Fe* are taken to a new level here.

The main "character" of "I'm an Indian Too" is a shirtless Ryan Red Corn. Dressed in boxer briefs with cloth secured on the front and back in order to approximate a breechcloth and with his head adorned with warbonnet and Ray-Bans, Red Corn gyrates across the screen in front of adobe structures of the Plaza with the word *Hipster* scrawled on his naked chest. Racist images of Native peoples, especially sexualized depictions of Native women, from movies, books, and advertising, are interspersed with footage of Red Corn dancing among the tents and booths being erected for Indian Market. A disco cover of the Irving Berlin song "I'm an Indian Too," from the 1946 musical *Annie Get Your Gun*, plays in the background. As the short film progresses, several young Native Americans, including Harjo and Wilson, look straight into the camera, knowingly bobbing their heads in time to the soundtrack, obviously appearing much different than the stereotypical cigar store Indians that guard the entrance to a curio shop where Red Corn dances. Red Corn and Wilson are then seen dancing in front of confused tourists in some cases and enthusiastic collectors wearing turquoise, cowboy hats, and leather bolos in others. The white participants in the Market eventually recede into the background as the focus turns to the Indigenous people who are there: patrons of the Market, artists in booths, and even a large flash mob, all grooving to the beat and playfully dancing in downtown Santa Fe. The conclusion of the video is a dance party in a black box theater, apparently occurring at the end of a 1491s performance, and the dancers are a mix of Native and non-Native audience members of various ages, enthusiastically raising their hands and moving their bodies along with the 1491s to an electronic beat with no lyrics.

The contrast between staid, racist images of Indians and the spontaneous and free-form dancing of Native people in the streets of Santa Fe is key to its visual impact as well as its humor. In her article on "I'm an Indian Too," Mary Stuckey states, "Rather than arguing against . . . stereotypes, an exercise we know to be unproductive, the 1491s instead attack them sideways by satirically embodying them. . . . the 1491s also point to a different reality, shared and experienced by contemporary native people."[62] This subversive humor is nothing new to Native communities, following an established trickster tradition. I also want to emphasize the importance of the space in which this happens, in a city that has continually promoted itself in the modern era as a place where non-Indians can try on Indigenous cultures, primarily by buying stuff. Natives have thrived financially in this marketplace while also bristling at its oversight by non-Indians, and in more recent years, with some growing pains within the organizations that produce Santa Fe's art markets, Natives have attained hard-fought leadership positions that will determine the future of the arts scene here. For Oklahomans like Sterlin Harjo, Yatika Fields, and others, Santa Fe will no doubt continue to be a destination for learning, networking, and growing an audience, but as the city—and the arts industries that support it—change, the question of how the city will adapt to meet the needs of a new generation remains unanswered.

Santa Fe has long been a magnet for those seeking a uniquely creative community amid the beauty of the Sangre de Cristo Mountains and the leisure of Canyon Road. A closer look at Santa Fe's history and arts cultures uncovers ways that this city different has been formed of conflicts and conquests that link it to New Orleans, a sister city of trade and European colonial incursion, and in turn to Oklahoma, from which many have come to make a living. While settlers from Oklahoma brought with them ideologies about race and nation that contributed to New Mexico's formation into a U.S. state, Natives from Oklahoma have also greatly impacted the development of arts and activism in Santa Fe in particular, bringing with them their experiences of place and placelessness and their practice of forming social relations across divisions of nation, race, and region. For writers such as Lynn Riggs, Joy Harjo, Sterlin Harjo, and others, Santa Fe has brought the possibilities and problems of marketplaces and institutions built on urban tourism—an economic engine that has lagged back home in Oklahoma—into stark relief. Alongside Indigenous urbanization in the United States spurred by the Urban Relocation Program, this story of self-driven travel, cultural exchange, and artistic production between urban Indians in Oklahoma and New Mexico, particularly writers with roots in the Southeast, draws more attention to long-standing patterns of migration and modernity that are not dictated simply by programs of the Bureau of Indian Affairs. In these writings are responses to—and reclamations of—urban spaces that disappear Indigenous peoples, responses that also sharpen critiques of settler colonialism that extend back to Oklahoma.

AFTERWORD

In this book I have uncovered ways that Native writers from Oklahoma expose and critique settler histories that weaponize spatial ideologies. These ideologies disappear Native rights to cities—New Orleans, Tulsa, and Santa Fe—that are key to the histories, laws, cultures, and arts of the writers in my project. Here in Tulsa, the *McGirt v. Oklahoma* decision and its aftermath are revealing for their encapsulation of ongoing conflicts in this space of Indian Territory. The *McGirt* decision determined that Muscogee lands, which include a large swath of the city of Tulsa, have never been disestablished as a reservation in Oklahoma, and as a result, jurisdiction over Muscogee lands were never transferred to the state of Oklahoma from the federal government. The prosecution of crime will now follow practices that are more closely aligned with the collaboration of tribal law enforcement and the FBI in other parts of Indian Country where there are reservations. In some cases that concern tribal citizens who commit or are victims of violent crimes, the state of Oklahoma now must defer to tribal and federal law, rather than simply following state protocols. It would seem that the symbols of Indigeneity that appear everywhere here—such as the Osage shield on our state flag—have new meaning.

When the *McGirt* decision was handed down in the summer of 2020, it was hailed across Indian Country as a victory for tribal sovereignty and here in Oklahoma as validation of what some already believed: that tribal governments are in some ways more equipped than our state to govern here. For the tribes in eastern Oklahoma that were operating under the precedent that their reservations had been disestablished, namely the "Five Civilized Tribes" (Cherokee, Chickasaw, Muscogee, Seminole, and Choctaw), *McGirt* was a shot in the arm; Governor Kevin Stitt (a Tulsan and himself a Cherokee citizen) has been in a drawn-out and expensive fight with Oklahoma tribes over gaming compacts. Specifically, he has maintained (in conflict with numerous court decisions) that tribes' gaming compacts with the state do not automatically renew and must be annually renegotiated. Renegotiated, he hopes, in the state's favor. *McGirt* is one more loss in the state's recent record of conflict with tribes and emboldens the tribes as they continue to assert their rights. The law affirms that Tulsa, now the highest population Indian reservation in the country, is a Native city.

Conservative politicians immediately spread alarmist predictions about the effects of the *McGirt* ruling predicated on tired assumptions of the tribes' inability to effectively govern, especially in areas with large white populations. On the day of the decision, 9 July, Texas senator Ted Cruz, pointing toward the ruling's implications for urban areas, tweeted: "Neil Gorsuch & the four liberal Justices just gave away half of Oklahoma, literally. Manhattan is next." Stitt, who coincidentally announced that he, like past presidential nominee Herman Cain, had come down with the COVID-19 virus not long after participating unmasked in a Trump rally in Tulsa in June 2020, on 20 July announced the formation of the Oklahoma Commission on Cooperative Sovereignty. He filled the commission with several political, energy, and economic personalities, not one of them Native American.[1] Senator Jim Inhofe promised a working group with members of the Oklahoma congressional delegation, presumably to advocate for a legislative "fix" to *McGirt*, a move that the tribes strongly resist.[2] Front and center in Stitt's agenda ever since has been vociferous opposition to the decision. Driving the narrative are questions about the rule of law and who the state will allow people of color to police.

A fear of lawlessness at the hands of Native American authority voiced by these politicians is ironic considering the horrific violence that settlers enacted here, particularly on the streets of downtown Tulsa. In a story for the *Atlantic* filed in response to Trump's visit, Rebecca Nagle explained why the presence of the president in the particular space in which the rally would occur was such a flashpoint for this community and significant for the country overall. Along with the documentaries, speaker series, art exhibits, and tourist opportunities planned for Greenwood to commemorate the centennial of the Tulsa Race Massacre, the city is also undertaking a search for mass graves of victims, which has long been discussed among survivors and their descendants. Downtown contains buildings that sit atop burial sites—confirmed and suspected—and questions have arisen about whether those sites afford the proper respect to these earlier Tulsans. Not far west of the BOK Center, for example, a Tullahassee Creek Indian cemetery sits in the middle of a strip mall parking lot. A new Minor League Baseball field is adjacent to Greenwood, and many North Tulsa leaders feel that due diligence was not conducted to determine whether Race Massacre victims are buried there. As Nagle reports, the BOK Center, the site of Trump's rally, is itself built upon a cemetery, where bones, likely of some Native Americans, were unearthed during its construction. Nagle describes downtown Tulsa as being soaked in racial violence. "The history is buried underneath the skyline itself," she writes.[3]

In his rhetoric against *McGirt*, Stitt has relied on an ideology of the city as being devoid of Indigenous authority or rights, suggesting that despite histories of settler violence against Native Americans here, it is tribal sovereignty that will usher in violence and lawlessness. For shock value, Stitt, like Cruz, compared Tulsa to New York City to assert the incommensurability of urban, cosmopolitan life and Native Americans. A story with Tulsa's Fox News affiliate reports:

> Stitt—a fourth-generation Oklahoman and Native American by heritage—compared the ruling as "coming into Manhattan, New York City, and people claiming that [it] is now [an] Indian reservation." . . . "So, literally, we have two million people living in eastern Oklahoma—a million people in the MSA of Tulsa have grown up—and now it's called an Indian reservation," said Stitt. "So, nowhere else is it like this in the United States." Stitt said a "true reservation" is land that is commonly held by a tribe and that there are people from all walks of life in eastern Oklahoma on land the governor says "has been sold 100 times."[4]

The story attempts to establish Stitt's authority not only as governor but also as a longtime Oklahoman and Native American, never mind the authority or the specifics of the law. The undermining of *McGirt* in these comments relies on feelings about which spaces are available to Native Americans to exert power—only reservations that are isolated and segregated.

Stitt builds his case for feelings over facts concerning the laws of Indian Country partially on his own heritage. But some Cherokees have not been comfortable with Stitt's relationship to the tribe. The Cherokee Nation in the early 1900s sought to remove Stitt's ancestor Francis M. Dawson from the tribal rolls because of an allegedly fraudulent identity claim. According to Cherokee genealogist David Cornsilk, the move was overruled by the federal government by a law that allowed enrollment to anyone on the 1880 Cherokee census. Stitt's turbulent relationship to the state's tribes has been disappointing to many, including Cherokee citizen Collin Walke, a Democrat and former member of the Oklahoma House of Representatives: "It's one thing to be able to claim a heritage, and it's a whole other thing to respect what that heritage means. . . . Gov. Stitt's affiliation with the tribe, I think he used that as a talking point, not so much as a substantive appreciation of what his actual heritage is."[5] Cornsilk notes that tribal citizens have varying connections to community, and many, like Stitt, decline to participate in tribal elections or events. Yet Stitt's continual and confrontational approach to tribal relations as a tribal citizen in the Governor's Office is unprecedented in recent memory.

As the COVID-19 pandemic held its grip on Oklahoma, Stitt declined to encourage public health policy that would restrict business activity or in-person schooling. In his 1 February 2021 State of the State address, Stitt touted his pro-business approach, including fully reopening the state by 1 June 2020 and deciding against a statewide mask mandate in favor of "personal responsibility."[6] He called these actions the "smart approach," though in January, a month before he gave the speech, Oklahoma saw its worst month of the pandemic thus far, with almost 100,000 people testing positive and more than 1,000 dying in that month alone. Oklahoma's COVID death rate has remained one of the highest in the country, with one study from Johns Hopkins naming Oklahoma as the state with the highest death rate in 2021.[7] Despite these circumstances, Stitt called changes to the *McGirt* decision the most pressing issue for Oklahoma's future.

Since the *McGirt* ruling, tribes have also made responding to the decision a priority. On the anniversary of the ruling, the Cherokee Nation reported filing new major crimes cases in tribal court at an unprecedented pace and adding six new prosecutors, two new district court judges, and thirteen more marshals. Said Chief Chuck Hoskin Jr.: "Despite attempts at fearmongering, the past year has proven wrong those who unfortunately continue to spout anti-Indian rhetoric and who mislead the public on McGirt to undermine our rights. Criminals did not suddenly all run free, local police officers still have the resources they need, and our justice system did not descend into chaos."[8] In a similar statement, Muscogee chief David Hill announced on the anniversary of *McGirt* that the Indian nation had doubled its cross-deputization agreements with law enforcement agencies; more than doubled the number of police officers on the ground; increased its law enforcement budget by seven million dollars in tribal funds; increased funding for its Attorney General's Office by one million dollars, adding five prosecutors, a criminal investigator, and other staff; and added judges, among other actions.[9] The Osage Nation, the third tribe whose jurisdiction lies within the city of Tulsa, also asserted its sovereignty during the *McGirt* anniversary, with Chief Geoffrey Standing Bear announcing, "The Osage Reservation remains intact."[10]

With tribes recognizing the anniversary of *McGirt* as an occasion to reaffirm tribal sovereignty, the Governor's Office used it as an opportunity to reiterate its sense that the decision would imperil Oklahomans and cause confusion for crime victims. On 13 July 2021 the governor, along with Tulsa County district attorney Steve Kunzweiler, hosted a panel in downtown Tulsa, "*McGirt v. Oklahoma* Community Impact Forum," which featured several area district attorneys as well as Tulsa County sheriff Vic Regalado. No tribal officials were on the panel, which set the event up for a contentious response from Native Americans. Though both the Governor's Office and Kunzweiler insisted that tribal leaders had been invited, the tribal leaders maintained that they did not receive an invitation to participate and would not be present. Apparently, Stitt's office had sent an email ten days earlier to the attorneys general of Cherokee, Muscogee, and Chickasaw Nations notifying them of the event, informally inviting them "and your chiefs," but according to the leaders of the tribes, a formal invitation never followed.[11] Many Native Americans attended the forum, speaking out against the lack of tribal representation on the panel and loudly disagreeing with the comments and questions from panelists. Because the speakers could not be heard and he was becoming frustrated with the crowd, Stitt ended the event an hour early, attributing the disruption to "people in here from other states right now."[12] After the event, a Stitt spokeswoman declared that it had been "hijacked by fringe activists."[13]

These assignations of blame to outsiders suggest that the city is somehow without Native Americans who would be empowered enough to take exception to the settler logic of this panel, and Stitt remains undeterred in his campaign against *McGirt*. After Attorney General Mike Hunter resigned abruptly in May 2021, an extramarital affair with a state employee having been made public, on 23 July, Stitt appointed John O'Connor as Hunter's replacement. O'Connor is a Tulsa attorney whom the American Bar Association had determined to be unqualified to serve as a federal judge upon his nomination by President Trump in 2018. Fourteen days after O'Connor's appointment, on 6 August, the new attorney general filed a petition with the U.S. Supreme Court to overturn *McGirt*, kicking off a series of moves to prompt the nation's highest court to reconsider or limit *McGirt*. In September, Justice Ruth Bader Ginsburg died, and a month later Amy Coney Barrett was confirmed as her replacement. The next year, on 29 June, with Barrett joining the majority (Kavanaugh, Roberts, and Thomas), the court handed down its decision in *Oklahoma v. Castro-Huerta*. The decision, undermining the reach of *McGirt*, determined that the state of Oklahoma holds joint jurisdiction with the federal government to prosecute non–Native Americans for crimes on Native lands. Justice Neil Gorsuch, who had drafted the majority opinion in *McGirt*, wrote the dissent for the minority (Breyer, Kagan, and Sotomayor) in *Castro-Huerta*. He argued that Congress is the proper venue for determining the application of laws in Indian Country and that the court should still defer to the precedent established in the 1832 *Worcester v. Georgia* decision, which determined that Indigenous Nations (specifically the Cherokee) are nations holding distinct sovereign powers not subject to state jurisdiction.[14]

While the rancor between the governor and the tribes reached a fever pitch, the COVID-19 pandemic also exposed their widely divergent approaches to governance in health policy, which has had a measurable impact in Tulsa. According to the CDC, Native Americans are at higher risk of severe COVID-19 outcomes, and as a result, the agency has allocated over $200 million to tribes for pandemic support.[15] As vaccines became available to the public, in early 2021, Oklahoma regularly ranked among the top ten states for the speed of vaccine distribution. By late March it was ahead of many other areas of the country in making the vaccine available to everyone who was eligible in the state. The efficient distribution was directly the result of having multiple tribal health authorities working with state and local health authorities.

National news outlets reported on tribes being the "surprising source" of widespread access to vaccines in the state.[16] But to Indigenous Tulsans who regularly receive health care from tribal clinics, this access to the vaccine was perhaps not as surprising. Notable, however, was that while tribal clinics typically do not serve non-Natives, once the vaccination targets were reached within tribal communities, tribes began vaccinating non-Natives, especially prioritizing teachers when the state was still weeks away from allowing teachers to get the shot. The move was said to be evidence of Indigenous values; as Cherokee Nation deputy principal chief Bryan Warner stated, for example, "Protecting everyone living within the boundaries of our reservation. . . . That's the Cherokee way to help each other."[17] These comments are quite a contrast to Stitt's doctrine of personal responsibility. Other major tribal health initiatives recently announced include a partnership between Oklahoma State University and the Cherokee Nation to open the United States' first tribally affiliated college of medicine and the Muscogee Nation's purchase of the site of the former Cancer Treatment Center of America campus to open a tribal hospital in southern Tulsa. Health care is just one way of many that tribes contribute to urban life in Tulsa, with "care for one another" an inspiring way to enact what Indigenous cosmopolitanism can mean.

The violence of settler colonialism—and strategies for surviving it—are experienced immediately and viscerally in cities. As is the case with the *McGirt* decision, other landmark cases and laws have sought to "settle" questions about the parameters of tribal sovereignty within a framework that classifies tribes as "domestic dependent nations." These cases and laws have prompted continual challenge, negotiation, and opportunity. *Worcester v. Georgia* remains a reference point for tribal sovereignty, a rebuke to Andrew Jackson's campaign for Indian removal instigated through the

Indian Removal Act of 1830. Yet Jackson would get his way, though not without protest, accelerating the rise of New Orleans as a hub of westward expansion (and Indigenous entrepreneurship) and Tulsa as a burgeoning Muscogee city in a new territory. The Bursum Bill was intended to be an iteration in the West of laws that diminished Natives' land rights (especially land held communally), but with Pueblo governors leading a coalition of resistors, especially those committed to a particular urban aesthetic in Santa Fe, a new era for Native rights followed in the 1930s, which resonated nationally. The national implications of *McGirt* are likewise clear despite its political challenges. Coupled with growing representation of Native Americans in the courts and Congress, the decision creates an opening for "land back" claims beyond Tulsa.[18] Urban Indigenous histories are thus expansive and inclusive, particularly shaping the histories and futures of Native peoples that would come to call Oklahoma home.

There is a sense of grief that comes with living in Oklahoma. The diasporic histories of Native Americans now rooted in Oklahoma are coupled with violence, in experiences of forced removal, conflict between existing and settler tribes, and the disenfranchisement of Freedmen, among other realities. Unfortunately, in our politics, even as U.S. law affirms the sovereignty of nations that are critical to the economy and infrastructure of this state, it is standard practice to obscure and disappear those nations from settler talking points on safety, progress, and community in cities like Tulsa. And yet, perhaps more than ever before and for all the world to see, the Indigenous creative realm is dispelling notions of Oklahoma as a space, or "no-place," incommensurate with cosmopolitan life. Perhaps the world is finally ready for Indigenous storytelling on its own terms, and in keeping with a long tradition, Native Oklahomans are critical to this movement from this city: Native land.

NOTES

Introduction

1. Askew, *Most American*, 3.
2. Appiah, *Cosmopolitanism*, xiv.
3. Appiah, "Cosmopolitan Patriots," 618.
4. Appadurai, *Modernity at Large*, 1, 4, 64.
5. Fixico, *Urban Indian Experience in America*, 162, 180.
6. Lobo, "Is Urban a Person or Place," 77.
7. Ramirez, *Native Hubs*, 1.
8. Peters and Anderson, *Indigenous in the City*, 652–80.
9. Blomley, *Unsettling the City*, 114.
10. Wilson and Peters, "'You Can Make a Place for It,'" 399.
11. Tomiak, "Unsettling Ottawa," 9.
12. Rosaldo, "Imperialist Nostalgia," 107–8; Thrush, *Native Seattle*, 9.
13. Rosenthal, *Reimagining Indian Country*, 3.
14. Peters and Anderson, *Indigenous in the City*, 7–8.
15. Lefebvre, *Urban Revolution*, 3-4.
16. Lefebvre, *Urban Revolution*, 27, 20.
17. Stefan Kipfer and Kanishka Goonewardena provide an overview of the potential for Lefebvre's work to speak to postcolonial situations but ultimately conclude that his work is unable to overcome its "Eurocentric roadblocks." See "Urban Marxism and the Post-Colonial Question," 76–116.

18. Soja, *Postmodern Geographies*, 78, 105, 153, 210, 238, 225.
19. Soja, *Seeking Spatial Justice*; Soja, *My Los Angeles*.
20. Soja, *Postmetropolis*, 18.
21. Soja, "Beyond Postmetropolis," 461.
22. Lefebvre, *Writings on Cities*, 101, 158.
23. Rader, *Engaged Resistance*, 1.
24. Goeman, *Mark My Words*, 1, 32, 7.
25. Furlan, *Indigenous Cities*, 8–9.

1. Beyond Monuments

1. Usner, *American Indians in the Lower Mississippi Valley*, 46, 47.
2. Ethridge, *Mapping the Mississippian Shatter Zone*, 38, 40.
3. Ethridge, *From Chicaza to Chickasaw*, 174, 216.
4. Usner, *American Indians in the Lower Mississippi Valley*, 68–69.
5. Sublette, *World That Made New Orleans*, 41.
6. Sublette, *World That Made New Orleans*, 115.
7. Usner, *American Indians in the Lower Mississippi Valley*, 112.
8. Sublette, in *World That Made New Orleans*, draws a distinction between nineteenth-century voodoo practiced in the city, the Bayou St. John, and the outlying areas and the vodou of Haiti. He explains that the Afro-Louisianan spiritual practice had African roots "as well as influences from the Choctaws, the Natchez, the Houmas, and other Indian groups" (283). Sublette also notes that the practice was heavily female dominated and by the 1870s had become a tourist attraction (284–85).
9. O'Brien, *Choctaws in a Revolutionary Age*, 9–10.
10. Debo, *Rise and Fall of the Choctaw Republic*, 41, 49.
11. Choctaw Nation, "About the Choctaw Nation of Oklahoma," accessed 15 August 2021, https://www.choctawnation.com/about.
12. Carson, *Searching for the Bright Path*, 71, 72.
13. J. Johnson, "Colonial New Orleans," 39.
14. Ethridge, *Mapping the Mississippian Shatter Zone*, 359.
15. Usner, *American Indians in the Lower Mississippi Valley*, 124.
16. Hudson, *Creek Paths and Federal Roads*, 14, 15, 16, 24, 57.
17. Braund, *Deerskins and Duffels*, 7, 12.
18. Ethridge, *Creek Country*, 10, 17, 148.
19. Kokomoor, *Of One Mind and of One Government*, 331, 342–43.
20. Lamar, "Preface," xv.
21. Brand, "Introduction," 3.
22. Waselkov, "Fort Jackson and the Aftermath," 163.
23. Thrower, "Causalities and Consequences of the Creek War," 25.

24. Hudson, *Creek Paths and Federal Roads*, 113.
25. Saunt, *New Order of Things*, 281.
26. Kokomoor, *Of One Mind and of One Government*, 376.
27. Green, *Politics of Indian Removal*, 74–75.
28. Hudson, *Creek Paths and Federal Roads*, 149.
29. Ellisor, *Second Creek War*, 158.
30. Haveman, "Removal of the Creek Indians from the Southeast," 268.
31. Paul Louis LeBlanc de Villeneufve's play *The Festival of the Young Corn, or The Heroism of Poucha-Houmma* (1809), the first play written in Louisiana, dramatizes this feasting among Houma characters near New Orleans. The play is an unfortunately typical tragic Indian hero plot.
32. Evans, *Congo Square*, 19; J. Johnson, "Colonial New Orleans," 35.
33. Breunlin, "Bridge Work," 50, 53.
34. Becker, "New Orleans Mardi Gras Indians," 42.
35. King, "George Bush May Not Like Black People," 35–36.
36. Thrush, *Native Seattle*, 9, 10.
37. Kelman, *River and Its City*, 10–11.
38. Evans, *Congo Square*, 9.
39. Fixico, *Urban Indian Experience in America*, 12, 16.
40. Denison, *Ute Land Religion in the American West*, 9.
41. Barr, *Peace Came in the Form of a Woman*, 7.
42. O'Dell, *La Harpe's Post*, 1.
43. DuVal, *Native Ground*, 6.
44. Hämäläinen, *Comanche Empire*, 2, 11.
45. Hämäläinen, *Comanche Empire*, 45.
46. Barr, *Peace Came in the Form of a Woman*, 71.
47. Hämäläinen, *Comanche Empire*, 150.
48. Bernstein, *How the West Was Drawn*, 124, 160.
49. DeLay, *War of a Thousand Deserts*, 4.
50. DuVal, *Native Ground*, 196.
51. Hämäläinen, *Comanche Empire*, 153.
52. DeLay, *War of a Thousand Deserts*, 106.
53. Hämäläinen, *Comanche Empire*, 150.
54. Debo, *Tulsa*, 3–4.
55. Saunt, *Black, White, and Indian*, 35.
56. Haveman, "Removal of the Creek Indians from the Southeast," 60.
57. Haveman, "Removal of the Creek Indians from the Southeast," 267.
58. Goble, *Tulsa*, 16; Debo, *Tulsa*, 13.
59. Trepp and Trepp, "Perryman Family."
60. Debo, *Tulsa*, 37.

61. Haveman, "Removal of the Creek Indians from the Southeast," 280.
62. Clampitt, *Civil War and Reconstruction in Indian Territory*, 3.
63. Debo, *Road to Disappearance*, 131.
64. Trepp and Trepp, "Perryman Family."
65. Zellar, *African Creeks*, 194–200.
66. Debo, *Tulsa*, 79.
67. Baird, *Story of Oklahoma*, 280–337.
68. Debo, *Tulsa*, 80–85.
69. Debo, *Tulsa*, 90.
70. Herrera and Cobb, "Tracing Tulsa's Creek Roots," kosu.org/post/tracing-tulsas-creek-roots; Thrush, *Native Seattle*, 10; Rader, *Engaged Resistance*, 190.
71. Jackson and Pittman, "Throwback Tulsa" (Woodward Park); Jackson, "Throwback Tulsa" (Utica Square).
72. *An Appeal to the Great Spirit*, sculpture, Smithsonian American Art Museum.
73. H. Johnson, *Black Wall Street*, 5.
74. H. Johnson, *Black Wall Street*, 67.
75. H. Johnson, *Black Wall Street*, 46–47.
76. Nate Morris, "Tulsa's Black History Being Erased? Concern Grows over the Rapid Gentrification of Greenwood," *Black Wall Street Times*, 26 February 2019, https://theblackwallsttimes.com/2019/02/26/tulsas-black-history-being-erased-concern-grows-over-the-rapid-gentrification-of-greenwood.
77. Carpio, *Indigenous Albuquerque*, xviii, xxi.
78. Sanchez, Spude, and Gomez, *New Mexico*, 97.
79. Sanchez, Spude, and Gomez, *New Mexico*, 51.
80. Simmons, *New Mexico*, 68–69.
81. Noble, *Santa Fe*, 40.
82. Sanchez, Spude, and Gomez, *New Mexico*, 57.
83. Hodge, *Ecology and Ethnogenesis*, 144.
84. Brooks, *Captives and Cousins*, 71.
85. Simmons, *New Mexico*, 110.
86. Sanchez, Spude, and Gomez, *New Mexico*, 104–5; Simmons, *New Mexico*, 127.
87. Gonzales, *Politica*, 3.
88. Simmons, *New Mexico*, 153.
89. Sanchez, Spude, and Gomez, *New Mexico*, 187.
90. Carpio, *Indigenous Albuquerque*, 34.
91. Sanchez, Spude, and Gomez, *New Mexico*, 217.
92. Hyer, *One House, One Voice, One Heart*, 69.
93. Gritton, *Institute of American Indian Arts*, 2.
94. Rader, *Engaged Resistance*, 184.
95. Dilworth, *Imagining Indians in the Southwest*, 2.

96. Rodriguez, "Art, Tourism, and Race Relations in Taos," 94.
97. Wilson, *Myth of Santa Fe*, 8.
98. Mullin, *Culture in the Marketplace*, 26.
99. Evans-Pritchard, "How 'They' See 'Us,'" 95.
100. Hoerig, *Under the Palace Portal*, 16, 96.
101. Sweet, "Burlesquing 'The Other' in Pueblo Performance," 64.

2. Where It All Started

1. LeFebvre, *Introduction to Modernity*, 1–2.
2. Howe, "Prologue," *Choctalking on Other Realities*, 3, 8.
3. Howe, "The Story of America," *Choctalking on Other Realities*, 13–14, 22, 36.
4. Rader, foreword, *Choctalking on Other Realities*, vii.
5. Bauerkemper, "Introduction," 7.
6. Byrd, "Tribal 2.0," 55.
7. Allen, *Earthworks Rising*, 2.
8. Howe, *Shell Shaker*, 100.
9. Howe, *Shell Shaker*, 1, 3.
10. Howe, *Shell Shaker*, 14.
11. Howe, *Shell Shaker*, 39, 40.
12. Howe, *Shell Shaker*, 42.
13. Howe, *Shell Shaker*, 41.
14. Howe, *Shell Shaker*, 41, 42.
15. Howe, *Shell Shaker*, 42–43.
16. Howe, *Shell Shaker*, 59, 93.
17. Howe, *Shell Shaker*, 169.
18. Appiah, *Cosmopolitanism*, xiv.
19. Ethridge, *From Chicaza to Chickasaw*, 190.
20. Howe, *Shell Shaker*, 159.
21. Allen, *Earthworks Rising*, 305.
22. Howe, *Shell Shaker*, 193, 194.
23. Allen, *Earthworks Rising*, 314.
24. Hollrah, "Decolonizing the Choctaws," 74.
25. Squint, "Choctaw Homescapes," 2.
26. Howe, "Chaos of Angels," xxvii, 23.
27. Howe, "Chaos of Angels," 23, 24.
28. Squint, "Choctaw Homescapes," 4.
29. Howe, "Chaos of Angels," 27, 30.
30. Howe, "Chaos of Angels," 32–33.
31. Howe, "Embodied Tribalography," 173, 174, 177–78.
32. Howe, "Embodied Tribalography," 189.

33. Evans, *Congo Square*, 19; J. Johnson, *Congo Square in New Orleans*, 35; Kaplan-Levenson, "In New Orleans."
34. Howe, *Miko Kings*, 90.
35. Howe, *Miko Kings*, 112.
36. Howe, *Miko Kings*, 116, 127.
37. Davis, "Unspoken Intimacies," 90, 84.
38. Howe, *Miko Kings*, 70, 71, 79.
39. Howe, *Miko Kings*, 204, 80.
40. Howe, *Miko Kings*, 81.
41. Davis, "Unspoken Intimacies," 86.
42. Hollrah, "Decolonizing the Choctaws," 41.
43. Howe, *Miko Kings*, 24.
44. Howe, *Miko Kings*, 44, 221.
45. Doerfler, "Making It Work," 72.
46. Kallet, "In Love and War and Music," 58.
47. Harjo, *Catching the Light*, 43.
48. Joy Harjo, "We Were There When Jazz Was Invented," blog, 2 November 2006, http://joyharjo.blogspot.com/2006/11/we-were-there-when-jazz-was-invented.html.
49. Harjo, "New Orleans," 42–44.
50. Watts, "Haunted Memories," 121.
51. Womack, *Red on Red*, 249.
52. Harjo, "We Were There When Jazz Was Invented," *Conflict Resolution for Holy Beings*, 20.
53. Womack, *Red on Red*, 250–51.
54. Lewis and Jordan, *Creek Indian Medicine Ways*, 6–7; Harjo, "We Were There When Jazz Was Invented," 21–23.
55. Harjo, *Soul Talk*, 5.
56. Warrior, "Your Skin Is the Map," 340.
57. Goeman, *Mark My Words*, 1, 15, 123.
58. Goeman, "Introduction to Indigenous Performances," 8.
59. "Joy Harjo," "The Art of Change," Ford Foundation, accessed 20 February 2019, https://www.fordfoundation.org/campaigns/the-art-of-change-meet-our-fellows/joy-harjo.
60. Harjo, *Catching the Light*, 45.
61. Jefferson, "Ripping Off Black Music," 41.

3. Finding Tallasi

1. Howe, "Prologue," 3.
2. Harjo, "Oklahoma," 125–26, 127–28.

3. Harjo, "Sleepwalkers," 43, 44.
4. Harjo, "Flood," 14.
5. Hudson, *Creek Paths and Federal Roads*, 15.
6. Harjo, "Flood," 16–17.
7. Harjo, "Last Song," 9.
8. Harjo, "Washing My Mother's Body," 30, 31.
9. Harjo, "Washing My Mother's Body," 30–34.
10. Townsend, *San Antonio Rose*, 44–45, 46.
11. Boyd, *Jazz of the Southwest*, i.
12. Harjo, *Crazy Brave*, 17–18.
13. Harjo, *Crazy Brave*, 20.
14. Harjo, *Crazy Brave*, 18, 19.
15. Harjo, *Crazy Brave*, 62.
16. Harjo, *Crazy Brave*, 73, 84.
17. Harjo, "American Sunrise," 105.
18. Zongker, "Joy Harjo Appointed to Third Term as U.S. Poet Laureate."
19. Harjo, "Living Nations, Living Words."
20. Harjo, *Poet Warrior*, 215.
21. Thorne, "Meet Sterlin Harjo."
22. Raheja, *Reservation Reelism*, 18–19.
23. Dowell, *Sovereign Screens*, xii.
24. Joanna Hearne notes that like Sherman Alexie's groundbreaking film *Smoke Signals*, Harjo's representation of funeral rituals revises media stereotypes of vanishing Indians. See Hearne, *Smoke Signals*, 124.
25. Bevis, "Native American Novels," 582.
26. Hearne, *Smoke Signals*, 6.
27. Schweninger, *Imagic Moments*, 202.
28. Littlefield, *Seminole Burning*, 4.
29. See *The Creek Runs Red*, a documentary directed by Julianna Brannum, Bradley Beesley, and James Payne, for a moving representation of the impact of the EPA superfund designation on the Quapaw tribe.
30. Dan Shepherd, "Last Residents of Picher, Oklahoma Won't Give Up the Ghost (Town)," *NBCNews.com*, 28 April 2014, www.nbcnews.com/news/investigations/last-residents-picher-oklahoma-wont-give-ghost-town-n89611.
31. Allison Herrera, "FX Series 'Reservation Dogs' Showcases Oklahoma, Breaks New Ground with Native Cast and Crew," *KOSU Radio*, 6 August 2021.
32. Ken Miller, "Choctaw, Cherokee Man Paralyzed in Fall from Bridge during Oklahoma Protest," *Indian Country Today*, 11 June 2020, https://indiancountrytoday.com/news/choctaw-cherokee-man-paralyzed-in-fall-from-bridge-during-oklahoma-protest.

33. Ruth Etiesit Samuel, "Black Natives Want to See Themselves in 'Reservation Dogs,' Too," *HuffPost*, 23 November 2021, https://www.huffpost.com/entry/black-natives-want-to-see-themselves-in-reservation-dogs-too_n_615b7d6fe4b0487c856285f7.
34. Dominic Patten, "'Reservation Dogs' Star Devery Jacobs Joins Expanded All Indigenous Writers Room for Season 2," *Deadline*, 21 September 2021, https://deadline.com/2021/09/reservation-dogs-devery-jacobs-season-2-writers-sterlin-harjo-erica-tremblay-blackhorse-lowe-chad-charlie-ryan-redcorn-dallas-goldtooth-1234841604.
35. Mays, "Representation and Black and Hip Hop Culture in 'Reservation Dogs.'"
36. Rena Detrixhe, "Open, Awake, and Alive—Exhibition at the Tulsa Garden Center," Facebook, 13 January 2018.

4. "The City Different"

1. Dilworth, *Imagining Indians in the Southwest*, 8.
2. Weigle, *Santa Fe and Taos*, 11.
3. Cline, *Literary Pilgrims*, 127–28.
4. Cline, *Literary Pilgrims*, 25.
5. Dorman, *Revolt of the Provinces*, 97.
6. Qtd. in Dorman, *Revolt of the Provinces*, 98.
7. Cline, *Literary Pilgrims*, 16.
8. Brown, *Stoking the Fire*, 13.
9. Dorman, *Revolt of the Provinces*, xiii, 2, 1, 33, 65.
10. Foster, "Of One Blood," 270.
11. Womack, *Art as Performance*, 117, 121.
12. Worden, "*Laughing Horse* Magazine," 196.
13. Parker, *Changing Is Not Vanishing*, 342.
14. Qtd. in Braunlich, *Haunted by Home*, 17.
15. Cox, *Political Arrays of American Indian Literary History*, 120.
16. For further reading on Whitman's representations of Native Americans, see Bruchac, "To Love the Earth"; Folsom, *Walt Whitman's Native Representations*; and Kenny, "Whitman's Indifference to Indians."
17. Horak, "First American Film Avant-Garde," 30–31.
18. Riggs, "Day in Santa Fe," 5.
19. Ruoff, "Home Movies of the Avant Garde," 295.
20. Cox, *Political Arrays of American Indian Literary History*, 120.
21. Riggs, "Day in Santa Fe," 5.
22. Cox, *Political Arrays of American Indian Literary History*, 124–26.
23. Braunlich, *Haunted by Home*, 11.
24. Tobias and Woodhouse, *Santa Fe*, 92.

25. Cox, *Political Arrays of American Indian Literary History*, 125.
26. Horak, "First American Film Avant-Garde," 27, 31.
27. Brown, *Stoking the Fire*, 128.
28. Darby, Mohler, and Stanlake, *Critical Companion to Native American and First Nations Theatre and Performance*, 68.
29. Riggs, *Russet Mantle*, 6.
30. Riggs, *Russet Mantle*, 6, 8, 12, 13.
31. Riggs, *Russet Mantle*, 17, 26, 22, 83.
32. Riggs, *Russet Mantle*, 41, 9, 48.
33. Riggs, *Russet Mantle*, 61, 62, 64–65, 7.
34. Riggs, *Russet Mantle*, 13, 80.
35. Riggs, *Russet Mantle*, 99, 109, 119, 121.
36. Darby, Mohler, and Stanlake, *Critical Companion to Native American and First Nations Theatre and Performance*, 78, 85.
37. Harjo, *Crazy Brave*, 83–84.
38. Jennifer Levin, "Speaking Poetry to Power: Joy Harjo," *Santa Fe New Mexican*, 17 August 2018, https://www.santafenewmexican.com/pasatiempo/books/speaking-poetry-to-power-joy-harjo/article_1b5c9f12-cabd-57fa-b869-201e8b6dcb2e.html.
39. Harjo, *Crazy Brave*, 86.
40. Smith, *Hippies, Indians, and the Fight for Red Power*, 6.
41. Harjo, *Crazy Brave*, 86.
42. For more on the countercultural movement in New Mexico, see Loeffler and Davidson, *Voices of Counterculture in the Southwest*.
43. Harjo, *Crazy Brave*, 115.
44. Harjo, *Poet Warrior*, 101.
45. Harjo, *Crazy Brave*, 138–39.
46. Harjo, *Poet Warrior*, 108.
47. Harjo, *Catching the Light*, 14.
48. Harjo, *Crazy Brave*, 87.
49. Harjo, *Catching the Light*, 12–13.
50. Harjo, "Poetry Can Be All This," 48.
51. Harjo, *Catching the Light*, 87.
52. "Our Parish History," Cathedral Basilica of St. Francis of Assisi website, accessed 17 July 2020, https://www.cbsfa.org/parish-life/about.
53. Harjo, "Santa Fe," 42.
54. Sanchez, Spude, and Gomez, *New Mexico*, 319, 320.
55. Marquez, "Nowhere Left to Go."
56. Barry Massey, "New Mexico's Population Growing Older," *Santa Fe Mexican*, 15 July 2014, https://www.santafenewmexican.com/news/local_news

/new-mexicos-population-growing-older/article_60addfe3-5a2d-5e9d-a61f-b275ddc79175.html.

57. Irwin, "Native American Artists Take Control of Their Market."
58. Michael Abatemarco, "Creators of Indigenous Fine Art Market Break from Group to Launch Newer Event," *TCA Regional News*, 17 September 2016, ProQuest, http://argo.library.okstate.edu/login?url=https://search-proquest-com.argo.library.okstate.edu/docview/1820111485?accountid=4117.
59. Iris McLister, "Market Values," *Santa Fe Reporter*, 29 May 2018, https://www.sfreporter.com/news/2018/05/30/market-values.
60. "Director's Note," *Love and Fury*.
61. Spivey, "Sterlin Harjo," 38, 39.
62. Stuckey, "Arguing Sideways," 76.

Afterword

1. Acee Agoyo and Todd York, "Oklahoma Governor Stumbles into Treaty Rights Debate," *Indianz.com*, 21 July 2020, https://www.indianz.com/News/2020/07/21/oklahoma-governor-stumbles-into-treaty-r.asp.
2. Associated Press, "Tribal Groups Warn Inhofe Bill Could Undermine Sovereignty," *Oklahoma City Journal Record*, 17 August 2020, https://journalrecord.com/2020/08/17/tribal-groups-warn-inhofe-bill-could-undermine-sovereignty.
3. Nagle, "Trump Will Stand Atop a Land of Tragedies."
4. Houston Keene, "Oklahoma Gov. Stitt Says Dangerous Criminals Walking Free Thanks to 'Horribly Wrong' Supreme Court Ruling," Foxnews.com, 7 April 2021, https://www.foxnews.com/politics/oklahoma-governor-supreme-court-mcgirt-criminals-released.
5. Sean Murphy, "Oklahoma Governor's Tribal Fight Raises Ancestry Questions," *ABC News*, 29 February 2020, https://abcnews.go.com/Politics/wireStory/oklahoma-governors-tribal-fight-raises-ancestry-questions-69306593.
6. Carmen Forman, "Governor Kevin Stitt Praises His COVID-19 Response, Outlines Priorities in State of the State," *Oklahoman*, 1 February 2021, https://www.oklahoman.com/story/news/politics/2021/02/02/gov-kevin-stitt-praises-his-covid-19-response-outlines-priorities-in-state-of-the-state-speech/324731007.
7. Chris Polansky, "Report Finds Oklahoma Has the Highest COVID Death Rate in the Country in 2021," Public Radio Tulsa, 28 December 2021, https://www.publicradiotulsa.org/local-regional/2021-12-28/report-finds-oklahoma-has-the-highest-covid-death-rate-in-the-country-in-2021.
8. Samantha Vicent, "Cherokee Nation Highlights Expansion of Legal System on Anniversary of *McGirt* Ruling," *Tulsa World*, 10 July 2021.

9. Muscogee Nation, "Muscogee Nation Proclaims Sovereignty Day on Anniversary of *McGirt* Decision," *Musokogee Phoenix*, 9 July 2021.
10. Lenzy Kriehbel-Burton, "Osage Nation Seeks Court Affirmation That Its Reservation Also Was Never Disestablished," *Tulsa World*, 20 July 2021.
11. Randy Kriehbel, "'*McGirt v. Oklahoma* Community Impact Forum' Set for Tuesday; Tribal Leaders Irked," *Tulsa World*, 9 July 2021.
12. Samantha Vicent, "Watch Now: Contentious *McGirt* Forum Ends Early after Shout-Down from Audience," *Tulsa World*, 14 July 2021.
13. Chris Polansky, "Stitt Leaves Tribal Sovereignty Forum Early as Crowd Jeers Lack of Native Representation on Panel," *Public Radio Tulsa*, 14 July 2021.
14. John Marshall and Supreme Court of the United States, *U.S. Reports: Worcester v. the State of Georgia, 31 U.S. 6 Pet. 515.*
15. "CDC Data Show Disproportionate COVID-19 Impact in American Indian / Alaska Native Populations," Center for Disease Control and Prevention, press release, 19 August 2020, https://www.cdc.gov/media/releases/2020/p0819-covid-19-impact-american-indian-alaska-native.html.
16. Erin Schumaker, "Native Tribes Have Expanded Vaccines to Everyone in Oklahoma," *ABC News*, 17 March 2021.
17. Allison Herrera, "Tribes in Oklahoma Begin Opening Vaccine Eligibility to Non-Natives," KOSU, 11 March 2021.
18. Blumenthal, "'We Hold the Government to Its Word.'"

BIBLIOGRAPHY

1491s. *I'm an Indian Too*. Video. YouTube, 21 September 2021. https://www.youtube.com/watch?v=9bhvpwp2v9y.

Adamson, Joni. *American Indian Literature, Environmental Justice, and Ecocriticism: The Middle Place*. Tucson: University of Arizona Press, 2001.

Allen, Chadwick. *Earthworks Rising: Mound Building in Native Literature and Arts*. Minneapolis: University of Minnesota Press, 2022.

Appadurai, Arjun. *Modernity at Large: Cultural Dimensions of Globalization*. Minneapolis: University of Minnesota Press, 1996.

Appiah, Kwame Anthony. *Cosmopolitanism: Ethics in a World of Strangers*. New York: Norton, 2006.

———. "Cosmopolitan Patriots." *Critical Inquiry* 23, no. 3 (1997): 617–39.

Askew, Rilla. *Most American: Notes from a Wounded Place*. Norman: University of Oklahoma Press, 2017.

Baird, W. David, and Danney Goble. *The Story of Oklahoma*. Norman: University of Oklahoma Press, 1994.

Barking Water. Directed and written by Sterlin Harjo. Film. Tulsa: Indion Entertainment, 2009.

Barr, Julianna. *Peace Came in the Form of a Woman: Indians and Spaniards in the Texas Borderlands*. Chapel Hill: University of North Carolina Press, 2007.

Bauerkemper, Joseph. "Introduction: Assessing and Advancing Tribalography." *Studies in American Indian Literatures* 26, no. 2 (2014): 3–12.

Becker, Cynthia. "New Orleans Mardi Gras Indians: Mediating Racial Politics from the Backstreets to Main Street." *African Arts* 46, no. 2 (2013): 36–49.

Bernstein, David. *How the West Was Drawn: Mapping, Indians, and the Construction of the Trans-Mississippi West*. Lincoln: University of Nebraska Press, 2018.

Bevis, William. "Native American Novels: Homing In." In *Recovering the Word: Essays on Native American Literature*, edited by Brian Swann and Arnold Krupat, 580–620. Berkeley: University of California Press, 1987.

Blackhawk, Ned. *Violence over the Land: Indians and Empires in the Early American West*. Cambridge: Harvard University Press, 2008.

Blakeslee, Donald J. "The Miguel Map Revisited." *Plains Anthropologist* 63, no. 245 (2018): 67–84.

Blomley, Nicholas. *Unsettling the City: Urban Land and the Politics of Property*. New York: Routledge, 2004.

Blumenthal, Claire. "'We Hold the Government to Its Word': How *McGirt v. Oklahoma* Revives Aboriginal Title." *Yale Law Journal* 131, no. 7 (2021): 2326.

Botkin, B. A. *The American Play-Party Song: With a Collection of Oklahoma Texts and Tunes*. Lincoln: University of Nebraska Press, 1937.

Boyd, Jean A. *The Jazz of the Southwest: An Oral History of Western Swing*. Austin: University of Texas Press, 1998.

Braund, Kathryn E. Holland. *Deerskins and Duffels: The Creek Indian Trade with Anglo-America, 1685–1815*. Lincoln: University of Nebraska Press, 2008.

———. "Introduction." In *Tohopeka: Rethinking the Creek War and the War of 1812*, edited by Kathryn E. Holland Braund, 1–9. Tuscaloosa: University of Alabama Press, 2012.

Braunlich, Phyllis Cole. *Haunted by Home: The Life and Letters of Lynn Riggs*. Norman: University of Oklahoma Press, 2002.

Breunlin, Rachel. "Bridge Work: Repatriating Mardi Gras Indian Photography with the House of Dance and Feathers." *African Arts* 46, no. 2 (2013): 50–61.

Breunlin, Rachel, Jeffrey David Ehrenreich, Victor Harris, Collins "Coach" Lewis, Wesley Phillips, and Jack Robertson. "How We Do It: A Collaborative Interview and Photo Essay." *African Arts* 46, no. 2 (2013): 62–69.

Brody, J. J. *Pueblo Indian Painting: Tradition and Modernism in New Mexico, 1900–1930*. Santa Fe: School for American Research, 1997.

Brooks, James F. *Captives and Cousins: Slavery, Kinship, and Community in the Southwest Borderlands*. Chapel Hill: Published for the Omohundro Institute of Early American History and Culture (Williamsburg VA), University of North Carolina Press, 2002.

Brown, Kirby. *Stoking the Fire: Nationhood in Cherokee Writing, 1907–1970*. Norman: University of Oklahoma Press, 2018.

Bruchac, Joseph. "To Love the Earth: Some Thoughts on Walt Whitman." In *Walt Whitman: The Measure of His Song*, edited by Jim Perlman, Ed Folsom, and Dan Campion, 274–78. Minneapolis: Holy Cow! 1981.

Byrd, Jodi. *The Transit of Empire*. Minneapolis: University of Minnesota Press, 2011.

———. "Tribal 2.0: Digital Natives, Political Players, and the Power of Stories." *Studies in American Indian Literatures* 26, no. 2 (2014): 55–64.

Byrd, Jodi, and Michael Rothberg. "Introduction." *Between Subalternity and Indigeneity: Critical Categories for Postcolonial Studies. Interventions* 13, no. 1 (2011): 1–12.

Carpio, Myla Vicenti. *Indigenous Albuquerque*. Lubbock: Texas Tech University Press, 2011.

Carson, James. *Searching for the Bright Path: The Mississippi Choctaws from Prehistory to Removal*. Lincoln: University of Nebraska Press, 1999.

Clampitt, Bradley R. *The Civil War and Reconstruction in Indian Territory*. Lincoln: University of Nebraska Press, 2015.

Cline, Lynn. *Literary Pilgrims: The Santa Fe and Taos Writers' Colonies, 1917–1950*. Albuquerque: University of New Mexico Press, 2007.

"Congo Square." Louisiana Historical Markers, New Orleans. Waymarking.com. Accessed 1 August 2016. https://www.waymarking.com/waymarks/wmPHYT_Congo_Square__New_Orleans_LA.

Cox, James. *The Political Arrays of American Indian Literary History*. Minneapolis: University of Minnesota Press, 2019.

The Creek Runs Red. Directed and written by Julianna Brannum, Bradley Beesley, and James Payne. Film. Dallas TX: Independent Lens (PBS), 2007.

Darby, Jaye, Courtney Ellen Mohler, and Christy Stanlake. *Critical Companion to Native American and First Nations Theatre and Performance: Indigenous Spaces*. London: Methuen Drama, 2020.

Davis, LaRose. "Unspoken Intimacies, *The Miko Kings*, HIU, and Red-Black Convergences: A Conversation with LeAnne Howe." *Wicazo Sa Review* 26, no. 2 (Fall 2011): 83–91.

A Day in Santa Fe. Directed by Lynn Riggs and James Hughes. Film. *Unseen Cinema: Early American Avant-Garde Film, 1893–1941*. Disc 6: *The Amateur as Auteur: Discovering Paradise in Pictures*. Filmmakers Showcase, 1931.

Debo, Angie. *The Rise and Fall of the Choctaw Republic*. Norman: University of Oklahoma Press, 1961.

———. *The Road to Disappearance: A History of the Creek Indians*. Norman: University of Oklahoma Press, 1979.

———. *Tulsa: From Creek Town to Oil Capitol*. Norman: University of Oklahoma Press, 1943.

DeLay, Brian. *War of a Thousand Deserts: Indian Raids and the U.S. Mexican War.* New Haven CT: Yale University Press, 2008. ProQuest Ebook Central, https://ebookcentral.proquest.com/lib/oks-ebooks/detail.action?docid=3420505.

Denison, Brandi. *Ute Land Religion in the American West, 1879–2009*. Lincoln: University of Nebraska Press, 2017. JSTOR. Accessed 11 May 2021. www.jstor.org/stable/j.ctt1q8jhvw.

Dilworth, Leah. *Imagining Indians in the Southwest: Persistent Visions of a Primitive Past*. Washington DC: Smithsonian Institution Press, 1996.

Doerfler, Jill. "Making It Work: A Model of Tribalography as Methodology." *Studies in American Indian Literatures* 26, no. 2 (2014): 65–74.

Dorman, Robert L. *Hell of a Vision: Regionalism and the Modern American West*. Tucson: University of Arizona Press, 2012.

———. *Revolt of the Provinces: The Regionalist Movement in America, 1920–1945*. Chapel Hill: University of North Carolina Press, 1993.

Dowell, Kristin. *Sovereign Screens*. Lincoln: University of Nebraska Press, 2013.

DuVal, Kathleen. *The Native Ground: Indians and Colonists in the Heart of the Continent*. Philadelphia: University of Pennsylvania Press, 2006.

Edge, Sami. "An Alternative Indian Market in Santa Fe." *Santa Fe New Mexican*, 18 August 2018. https://www.santafenewmexican.com/news/local_news/an-alternative-indian-market-in-santa-fe/article_732421b3-f3c5-5aa0-bac0-6f72a4b61802.html.

Ellisor, John T. *The Second Creek War: Interethnic Conflict and Collusion on a Collapsing Frontier*. Lincoln: University of Nebraska Press, 2010.

Ethridge, Robbie Franklyn. *Creek Country: The Creek Indians and Their World*. Chapel Hill: University of North Carolina Press, 2003.

———. *From Chicaza to Chickasaw: The European Invasion and the Transformation of the Mississippian World, 1540–1715*. Chapel Hill: University of North Carolina Press, 2010.

———. *Mapping the Mississippian Shatter Zone: The Colonial Indian Slave Trade and Regional Instability in the American South*. Lincoln: University of Nebraska Press, 2009.

"Etzanoa—The Great Settlement." Etzanoa Conservancy. Accessed 13 August 2020. Etzanoa.com.

Evans, Freddi Williams. *Congo Square: African Roots in New Orleans*. Lafayette: University of Louisiana Press, 2011.

Evans-Pritchard, Deirdre. "How 'They' See 'Us': Native American Images of Tourists." *Annals of Tourism Research* 16 (1989): 89–105.

Fixico, Donald. *The Urban Indian Experience in America*. Albuquerque: University of New Mexico Press, 2000.

Folsom, Ed. *Walt Whitman's Native Representations*. Cambridge: Cambridge University Press, 1994.

Foster, Tol. "Of One Blood: An Argument for Relations and Regionality in Native

American Literary Studies." *Reasoning Together: The Native Critics Collective*, 265–302. Norman: University of Oklahoma Press, 2008.
Four Sheets to the Wind. Directed by Sterlin Harjo. Film. Los Angeles: Alchemy, 2007.
Furlan, Laura. *Indigenous Cities: Urban Indian Fiction and the Histories of Relocation.* Lincoln: University of Nebraska Press, 2017.
Goble, Danney. *Tulsa! Biography of the American City.* Tulsa: Council Oak Books, 1997.
Goeman, Mishuana. "Introduction to Indigenous Performances: Upsetting the Terrains of Settler Colonialism." *American Indian Culture and Research Journal* 35, no. 4 (2011): 1–18.
———. *Mark My Words: Native Women Mapping Our Nations.* Minneapolis: University of Minnesota Press, 2013.
Gonzales, Phillip B. *Politica: Nuevomexicanos and American Political Incorporation, 1821–1910.* Lincoln: University of Nebraska Press, 2016.
Goodnight, Irene. Written and directed by Sterlin Harjo. Film. Tulsa: Indion, 2005.
Grayson, Eli. "Black Lives Matter for Freedmen Descendants of the Five Civilized Tribes." *Oklahoma Eagle*, 7 July 2020.
Green, Michael. *The Politics of Indian Removal: Creek Government and Society in Crisis.* Lincoln: University of Nebraska Press, 1982.
Gritton, Joy. *The Institute of American Indian Arts.* Albuquerque: University of New Mexico Press, 2000.
Hämäläinen, Pekka. *The Comanche Empire.* New Haven CT: Yale University Press, 2008.
Harjo, Joy. "An American Sunrise." *An American Sunrise: Poems.* New York: Norton, 2019.
———. *Catching the Light.* New Haven CT: Yale University Press, 2022.
———. *Crazy Brave.* New York: Norton, 2012.
———. "The Flood." *The Woman Who Fell from the Sky.* New York: Norton, 1994.
———. "The Last Song." *How We Became Human: New and Selected Poems.* New York: Norton, 2002.
———. "Living Nations, Living Words." Poet Laureate Project. Library of Congress. Accessed 15 August 2021. https://www.loc.gov/programs/poetry-and-literature/poet-laureate/poet-laureate-projects/living-nations-living-words.
———. "New Orleans." *She Had Some Horses.* New York: Thunder's Mouth Press, 1983.
———. "Oklahoma: The Prairie of Words." *Western American Literature* 35, no. 2 (2000): 125–28.
———. "Poetry Can Be All This: All of You, All of Me, All of Us." *Studies in American Indian Literatures* 16, no. 4 (2004): 47–50.
———. *Poet Warrior: A Memoir.* New York: Norton, 2021.
———. "Santa Fe." *A Map to the Next World.* Middletown CT: Wesleyan University Press, 1990.

——. "Sleepwalkers." *A Map to the Next World*. New York: Norton, 2000.

——. "Washing My Mother's Body." *An American Sunrise: Poems*. New York: Norton, 2019.

——. "We Were There When Jazz Was Invented." *Conflict Resolution for Holy Beings*. New York: Norton, 2015.

——. "We Were There When Jazz Was Invented." *Joy Harjo's Adventures in the Last World Blog*, 2 November 2006.

Harjo, Joy, and Tanaya Winder. *Soul Talk, Song Language: Conversations with Joy Harjo*. Middletown CT: Wesleyan University Press, 2011.

Harjo, Sterlin. "Director's Note." *Love and Fury*. Film. Netflix, 2020. https://www.loveandfuryfilm.com.

Harkins, Elisa, dir. *For Hellen Woodward: Performed by Two Female Indigenous Artists*. Video. Vimeo.com. Accessed 26 January 2018. vimeo.com/251403043.

Haveman, Christopher. "The Removal of the Creek Indians from the Southeast, 1825–1838." PhD diss., Auburn University, 2009.

Hearne, Joanna. *Smoke Signals: Native Cinema Rising*. Lincoln: University of Nebraska Press, 2012.

Herrera, Allison. "Glory in All Things Creek." KOSU, 12 December 2016. https://www.kosu.org/post/watch-glory-all-things-creek.

——. "Indigenous and Black Leaders Express Solidarity against Racial Injustice, Police Brutality." KOSU, 19 June 2020. https://www.kosu.org/post/indigenous-and-black-leaders-express-solidarity-against-racial-injustice-police-brutality.

Herrera, Allison, and Russell Cobb. "Tracing Tulsa's Creek Roots." Audio and print stories. KOSU, 22 June 2016.

Hodge, Adam. *Ecology and Ethnogenesis: An Environmental History of the Wind River Shoshones, 1000–1868*. Lincoln: University of Nebraska Press, 2019.

Hoerig, Karl A. *Under the Palace Portal: Native American Artists in Santa Fe*. 1st ed. Santa Fe: University of New Mexico Press, 2003.

Hollrah, Patrice. "Decolonizing the Choctaws: Teaching LeAnne Howe's 'Shell Shaker.'" *American Indian Quarterly* 28, no. 1–2 (2004): 73–85.

——. "'The Lord and the Center of the Farthest': Ezol's Journal as Tribalography in LeAnne Howe's *Miko Kings: An Indian Baseball Story*." *Studies in American Indian Literatures* 26, no. 2 (2014): 40–54.

Horak, Jan-Christopher. "The First American Film Avant-Garde." *Experimental Cinema: The Film Reader*. London: Psychology Press, 2002.

Howe, LeAnne. "The Chaos of Angels." *Evidence of Red: Poems and Prose*, 23–33. Cambridge: Salt, 2005.

———. "Embodied Tribalography." *Choctalking on Other Realities*, 173–93. San Francisco: Aunt Lute Books, 2013.

———. "Prologue." *Choctalking on Other Realities*, 1–12. San Francisco: Aunt Lute Books, 2013.

———. *Shell Shaker.* San Francisco: Aunt Lute Books, 2001.

———. "The Story of America." *Choctalking on Other Realities*, 13–40. San Francisco: Aunt Lute Books, 2013.

Hudson, Angela Pulley. *Creek Paths and Federal Roads: Indians, Settlers, and Slaves and the Making of the American South.* Chapel Hill: University of North Carolina Press, 2010.

Hyer, Sally. *One House, One Voice, One Heart: Native American Education at the Santa Fe Indian School.* Albuquerque: Museum of New Mexico Press, 1990.

Invisible Nations. Localore.com. Accessed 21 February 2017. www.localore.org/15-communities/invisible-nations.

Irwin, Matthew. "Native American Artists Take Control of Their Market." *Hyperallergic*, 21 August 2014. https://hyperallergic.com/144781/native-american-artists-take-control-of-their-market.

Jackson, Debbie. "Throwback Tulsa: Utica Square Wasn't Always So Fashionable." *Tulsa World*, 17 April 2016. https://tulsaworld.com/news/local/history/throwback-tulsa-utica-square-wasnt-always-so-fashionable/article_8f287080-1c4b-591b-8b6d-f50e5206d3d4.html.

Jackson, Debbie, and Hilary Pittman. "Throwback Tulsa: Woodward Park and the Creek Woman Who Once Owned It." *Tulsa World*, 1 April 2014. https://tulsaworld.com/news/local/history/throwback-tulsa-woodward-park-and-the-creek-woman-who-once-owned-it/article_0d30d9aa-b9cc-11e3-8b4f-001a4bcf6878.html.

Jefferson, Margo. "Ripping Off Black Music from Thomas 'Daddy' Rice to Jimi Hendrix." *Harper's Magazine* 246 (1973): 40–45.

Johnson, Hannibal. *Black Wall Street: From Riot to Renaissance in Tulsa's Historic Greenwood District.* Austin TX: Eakin Press, 1998.

Johnson, Jerah. "Colonial New Orleans: A Fragment of the Eighteenth-Century French Ethos." *Creole New Orleans: Race and Americanization*, 12–57. Baton Rouge: Louisiana State University Press, 1992.

———. *Congo Square in New Orleans.* New Orleans: Louisiana Landmarks Society, 1995.

"Joy Harjo." *Collections from the IWP Experience.* International Writing Program. Accessed 27 January 2018. www.iwpcollections.org/hw2-joy-harjo.

Kallet, Marilyn. "In Love and War and Music: An Interview with Joy Harjo." *Kenyon Review* 15 (1993): 57–66.

Kaplan-Levenson, Laine. "In New Orleans, before Baseball, Football or Soccer, There Was Raquette." *TriPod: New Orleans at 300*. WWNO, 10 March 2016. https://beta.prx.org/stories/173744.

Kelman, Ari. *A River and Its City: The Nature of Landscape in New Orleans*. Berkeley: University of California Press, 2003.

Kenny, Maurice. "Whitman's Indifference to Indians." In *The Continuing Presence of Walt Whitman*, edited by Robert K. Martin, 28–38. Iowa City: University of Iowa Press, 1992.

King, C. Richard. "George Bush May Not Like Black People, but No One Gives a Dam about Indigenous Peoples: Visibility and Indianness after the Hurricanes." *American Indian Culture and Research Journal* 32, no. 2 (2008): 35–42.

Kipfer, Stefan, and Kanishka Goonewardena. "Urban Marxism and the Post-Colonial Question: Henri Lefebvre and 'Colonisation.'" *Historical Materialism* 21, no. 2 (2013): 76–116.

Kokomoor, Kevin. *Of One Mind and of One Government: The Rise and Fall of the Creek Nation in the Early Republic*. Lincoln: University of Nebraska Press, 2018.

Lamar, Jay. "Preface." *Tohopeka: Rethinking the Creek War and the War of 1812*, xv–xvi. Tuscaloosa: University of Alabama Press, 2012.

Lanner, Ronald M. *The Piñon Pine: A Natural and Cultural History*. Reno: University of Nevada Press, 1981.

Lefebvre, Henri. *Critique of Everyday Life*. Translated by John Moore. London: Verso, 2014.

———. *Introduction to Modernity: Twelve Preludes*. Translated by John Moore. London: Verso, 1995.

———. *The Urban Revolution*. Translated by Robert Bononno. Minneapolis: University of Minnesota Press, 2003.

———. *Writings on Cities*. Translated and edited by Eleonore Kofman and Elizabeth Lebas. Oxford: Blackwell, 1996.

Lewis, David, and Ann Jordan. *Creek Indian Medicine Ways: The Enduring Power of Mvskoke Religion*. Albuquerque: University of New Mexico Press, 2002.

Lindsey, Donal F. *Indians at Hampton Institute: 1877–1923*. Urbana: University of Illinois Press, 1994.

Littlefield, Daniel. *Seminole Burning: A Story of Racial Vengeance*. Oxford: University Press of Mississippi, 1996.

Lobo, Susan. "Introduction." In *American Indians and the Urban Experience*, edited by Susan Lobo and Kurt Peters, xi–xvi. Walnut Creek CA: Alta Mira Press, 2001.

———. "Is Urban a Person or Place? Characteristics of Urban Indian Country." In *American Indians and the Urban Experience*, edited by Susan Lobo and Kurt Peters, 73–84. Walnut Creek CA: Alta Mira Press, 2001.

Loeffler, Jack, and Meredith Davidson, eds. *Voices of Counterculture in the Southwest*. Santa Fe: Museum of New Mexico Press, 2017.

Love and Fury. Directed by Sterlin Harjo. Film. Tulsa: FireThief Productions, 2020.

Manhatta. Directed by Charles Sheeler and Paul Strand. Film. MoMA Learning. Accessed 9 August 2020. www.moma.org/learn/moma_learning/paul-strand-charles-sheeler-manhatta-1921.

Marquez, Christian. "Nowhere Left to Go." *Searchlight New Mexico*, 1 October 2019. https://searchlightnm.org/nowhere-left-to-go.

Marshall, John, and Supreme Court of the United States. *U.S. Reports: Worcester v. the State of Georgia, 31 U.S. 6 Pet. 515*. 1832. Periodical. Retrieved from the Library of Congress. www.loc.gov/item/usrep031515.

Mays, Kyle T. *Hip Hop Beats, Indigenous Rhymes: Modernity and Hip Hop in Indigenous North America*. Albany: State University of New York Press, 2018.

———. "Representation and Black and Hip Hop Culture in 'Reservation Dogs.'" *Ethnomusicology Review*, 1 November 2021. https://ethnomusicologyreview.ucla.edu/content/representation-and-black-hip-hop-culture-reservation-dogs.

McFarland, Melanie. "'Reservation Dogs' Creator on Evolving the Show's Representation and Storytelling: 'It's Not Finished.'" *Salon*, 20 September 2021. https://www.salon.com/2021/09/20/reservation-dogs-sterlin-harjo-fx-on-hulu.

Mecoy, Don. "Tribal Activities Make $10.8b Impact on Oklahoma's Economic Output, Study Suggests." *Newsok.com*, 26 October 2012. newsok.com/article/3719667.

Mekko. Directed by Sterlin Harjo. Tulsa: Indion Entertainment, 2015.

Momaday, N. Scott. *House Made of Dawn*. London: Harper and Row, 1968.

Mullin, Molly. *Culture in the Marketplace: Gender, Art, and Value in the American Southwest*. Durham: Duke University Press, 2001.

Nagle, Rebecca. "Cherokee Nation Adopted Racism from Europeans. It's Time to Reject It." *High Country News*, 10 July 2020, www.hcn.org.

Nardone, Kathryn. "Tulsa, Oklahoma: Some Aspects of Its Urban Settlement." *Proceedings for the Oklahoma Academy of Sciences* 46 (1966): 378–81.

Noble, David Grant. *Santa Fe: History of an Ancient City*. 1st ed. Santa Fe: School of American Research Press; distributed by University of Washington Press, 1989.

O'Brien, Greg. *Choctaws in a Revolutionary Age, 1750–1830*. Lincoln: University of Nebraska Press, 2002.

O'Dell, George. *La Harpe's Post: A Tale of French-Wichita Contact on the Eastern Plains*. Tuscaloosa: University of Alabama Press, 2002.

Osiyo: Voices of the Cherokee People. OsiyoTV, https://osiyo.tv/episodes.

Owsley, Frank. *Struggle for the Gulf Borderlands: The Creek War and the Battle of New Orleans, 1812–1815*. Gainesville: University Presses of Florida, 1981.

Parker, Robert Dale. *Changing Is Not Vanishing: A Collection of Early American Indian Poetry to 1930*. Philadelphia: University of Pennsylvania Press, 2011.

Peters, Evelyn, and Chris Andersen. *Indigenous in the City: Contemporary Identities and Cultural Innovation*. Vancouver: UBC Press, 2013.

Peters, Evelyn, and Vince Robillard. "'Everything You Want Is There': The Place of the Reserve in First Nations' Homeless Mobility." *Urban Geography* 30, no. 6 (2009): 652–80.

Piña, Apollonia [@hokte.cimarron]. Photo of *Reservation Dogs* premiere. Instagram, 1 August 2021. https://www.instagram.com/p/csdtsbijkkxxbmqe_m51gyvsqag4zelntrtog0/?utm_medium=copy_link.

Polansky, Chris. "Stitt Leaves Tribal Sovereignty Forum Early as Crowd Jeers Lack of Native Representation on Panel." *Public Radio Tulsa*, 14 July 2021.

Rader, Dean. *Engaged Resistance: American Indian Art, Literature, and Film from Alcatraz to the NMAI*. Austin: University of Texas Press, 2011.

———. "Foreword." *Choctalking on Other Realities*, by LeAnne Howe, i–vii. San Francisco: Aunt Lute Books, 2013.

Raheja, Michelle. *Reservation Reelism: Redfacing, Visual Sovereignty, and Representations of Native Americans in Film*. Lincoln: University of Nebraska Press, 2011.

Ramirez, Renya K. *Native Hubs: Culture, Community, and Belonging in Silicon Valley and Beyond*. Durham: Duke University Press, 2007.

Riggs, Lynn. "Acequia Madre." *The Iron Dish*. New York: Doubleday, Doran, and Company, 1930.

———. "The Arid Land." *Laughing Horse* 14 (Fall 1927): 7.

———. "Bootheels." *Laughing Horse* 11 (September 1924).

———. "The Choice." *Laughing Horse* 10 (May 1924).

———. "A Day in Santa Fe." *Cine-Kodak News*, January–February 1932, 5.

———. *The Iron Dish*. New York: Doubleday, Doran, and Company, 1930.

———. "Morning Walk: Santa Fe." *The Iron Dish*. Doubleday, Doran, and Company, 1930.

———. "Russet Mantle." Russet Mantle *and* The Cherokee Night*: Two Plays by Lynn Riggs*, 1–121. New York: Samuel French, 1936.

———. "Sanitarium." *Laughing Horse* 9 (December 1923).

———. "Santa Domingo Corn Dance." In *Native American Writing in the Southeast: An Anthology, 1875–1935*, edited by Daniel F. Littlefield Jr. and James W. Parins, 198–200. Oxford: University Press of Mississippi, 1995.

———. "Santa Fe Sonnets." *Laughing Horse* 12 (August 1925): 18.

———. "The Shaped Room." *This Book, This Hill, These People: Poems by Lynn Riggs*. Edited by Phyllis Braunlich. Tulsa: Lynn Chase, 1982.

———. "Spring Morning: Santa Fe." In *Native American Writing in the Southeast: An*

Anthology, 1875–1935, edited by Daniel F. Littlefield Jr. and James W. Parins, 198. Oxford: University Press of Mississippi, 1995.
Rodriguez, Sylvia. "Art, Tourism, and Race Relations in Taos: Toward a Sociology of the Art Colony." *Journal of Anthropological Research* 45, no. 1 (1989): 77–99.
Rosaldo, Renato. "Imperialist Nostalgia." *Representations* 26 (1989): 107–22.
Rosenthal, Nicholas. *Reimagining Indian Country: Native American Migration and Identity in Twentieth-Century Los Angeles.* Chapel Hill: University of North Carolina Press, 2012.
Rumble: The Indians Who Rocked the World. Directed by Catherine Bainbridge and Alfonso Maiorana. Film. Montreal: Rezolution Pictures, 2017.
Rumble Fish. Directed by Francis Ford Coppola. Film. San Francisco: Zoetrope Studios, 1983.
Ruoff, Jeffrey. "Home Movies of the Avant Garde: Jonas Mekas and the New York Art World." In *To Free the Cinema: Jonas Mekas and the New York Underground*, edited by David James, 294–312. Princeton: Princeton University Press, 1992.
Rutland, Amanda. "'Mekko' Film Event Held in Okmulgee." MVSKOKE Media, 20 April 2016. mvskokemedia.com/mekko-film-event-held-in-okmulgee.
Sanchez, Joseph P., Robert L. Spude, and Art Gomez. *New Mexico: A History.* Norman: University of Oklahoma Press, 2013.
Saunt, Claudio. *Black, White, and Indian: Race and the Unmaking of an American Family.* New York: Oxford University Press, 2005.
———. *A New Order of Things: Property, Power, and the Transformation of the Creek Indians, 1733–1816.* Cambridge: Cambridge University Press, 1999.
Schweninger, Lee. *Imagic Moments: Indigenous North American Film.* Athens: University of Georgia Press, 2013.
Silko, Leslie Marmon. *Ceremony*. London: Penguin, 1977.
Simmons, Marc. *New Mexico: An Interpretive History*. Albuquerque: University of New Mexico Press, 1988.
Smith, Sherry. *Hippies, Indians, and the Fight for Red Power*. Oxford: Oxford University Press, 2012.
Soja, Edward. "Beyond *Postmetropolis*." *Urban Geography* 32, no. 4 (2011): 451–69.
———. *Postmetropolis: Critical Studies of Cities and Regions.* Hoboken NJ: Wiley-Blackwell, 2000.
———. *Postmodern Geographies: The Assertion of Space in Critical Social Theory.* Verso: London, 1989.
Spivey, Whitney. "Sterlin Harjo: Filmmaker Spotlights Native American Culture." *Santa Fean*, August–September 2016, 38–39.
Squint, Kirstin. "Choctaw Homescapes: LeAnne Howe's Gulf Coast." *Mississippi Quarterly* 66, no. 1 (2013): 115–37.

Stanek, Lukasz. *Henri Lefebvre on Space*. Minneapolis: University of Minnesota Press, 2011.

Stuckey, Mary. "Arguing Sideways: The 1491s' *I'm an Indian Too*." *Disturbing Argument*, 75–80. London: Routledge, 2015.

Sublette, Ned. *The World That Made New Orleans: From Spanish Silver to Congo Square*. Chicago: Lawrence Hill Books, 2008.

Sweet, Jill D. "Burlesquing 'The Other' in Pueblo Performance." *Annals of Tourism Research* 16 (1989): 62–75.

"This Land." Crooked Media. Accessed 3 August 2021. crooked.com/podcast-series/this-land.

This May Be the Last Time. Directed by Sterlin Harjo. Produced by Sterlin Harjo. Tulsa. 2014.

Thorne, Vicki May. "Meet: Sterlin Harjo." *This Land Press*, 21 January 2012. thislandpress.com/2012/01/21/meet-sterlin-harjo.

Thrower, Robert G. "Causalities and Consequences of the Creek War: A Modern Creek Perspective." *Tohopeka: Rethinking the Creek War and the War of 1812*, 10–29. Tuscaloosa: University of Alabama Press, 2012.

Thrush, Coll. *Native Seattle: Histories from the Crossing-Over Place*. Seattle: University of Washington Press, 2007.

Tobias, Henry, and Charles Woodhouse. *Santa Fe: A Modern History*. Albuquerque: University of New Mexico Press, 2001.

Tomiak, Julie. "Unsettling Ottawa: Settler Colonialism, Indigenous Resistance, and Politics of Scale." *Canadian Journal of Urban Research* 25, no. 1 (2016): 8–21.

Townsend, Charles. *San Antonio Rose: The Life and Music of Bob Wills*. Urbana: University of Illinois Press, 1976.

Trepp, Monetta, and Robert Trepp. "The Perryman Family: Ranchers from the Creek Nation," by Jon Erling. *Voices of Oklahoma*, 9 September 2010.

"Tulsa, Oklahoma: Reconciliation Way." *State of the Reunion*. Accessed 27 January 2018. stateofthereunion.com/tulsa-ok-reconciliation-way/#prettyPhoto.

United States Supreme Court. McGirt v. Oklahoma. https://www.supremecourt.gov/opinions/19pdf/18-9526_9okb.pdf.

———. Oklahoma v. Castro-Huerta. https://www.supremecourt.gov/opinions/21pdf/21-429_8o6a.pdf.

Usner, Daniel. *American Indians in the Lower Mississippi Valley*. Lincoln: University of Nebraska Press, 1998.

Warrior, Robert. "Your Skin Is the Map: The Theoretical Challenge of Joy Harjo's Erotic Poetics." In *Reasoning Together: The Native Critics Collective*, edited by Janet Acoose et al., 340–52. Norman: University of Oklahoma Press, 2008.

Waselkov, Gregory A. "Fort Jackson and the Aftermath." In *Tohopeka: Rethinking the Creek War and the War of 1812*, edited by Kathryn E. Holland Braund, 158–69. Tuscaloosa: University of Alabama Press, 2012.

Watts, Tracey. "Haunted Memories: Disruptive Ghosts in the Poems of Brenda Marie Osbey and Joy Harjo." *Southern Literary Journal* 46, no. 2 (2014): 108–27.

Weigle, Marta. *Santa Fe and Taos: The Writer's Era, 1916–1941*. Santa Fe: Ancient City Press, 1994.

Wenzl, Roy. "Lost City Found: Etzanoa of the Great Wichita Nation." *Wichita Eagle*, 17 April 2017. https://www.kansas.com/news/state/article144968264.html.

Whitman, Walt. "Mannahatta." Walt Whitman Archive. https://whitmanarchive.org/published/LG/1881/poems/271.

Wilson, Chris. *The Myth of Santa Fe: Creating a Modern Regional Tradition*. Albuquerque: University of New Mexico Press, 1997.

Wilson, Kathi, and Evelyn Peters. "'You Can Make a Place for It': Remapping Urban First Nations Spaces of Identity." *Environment and Planning D: Society and Space* 23 (2005): 395–413.

Womack, Craig. *Art as Performance, Story as Criticism: Reflections on Native Literary Aesthetics*. Norman: University of Oklahoma Press, 2009.

———. *Red on Red: Native American Literary Separatism*. Minneapolis: University of Minnesota Press, 1999.

Worden, Daniel. "*Laughing Horse* Magazine and Regional Modernism in New Mexico." *Journal of Modern Periodical Studies* 5, no. 2 (2015): 195–221.

Zellar, Gary. *African Creeks: Estelvste and the Creek Nation*. Norman: University of Oklahoma Press, 2007.

Zongker, Brett. "Joy Harjo Appointed to Third Term as U.S. Poet Laureate." *News from the Library of Congress*, 19 November 2020, https://loc.gov/item/prn-20-075.

INDEX

Italicized page numbers refer to figures.

www.ingramcontent.com/pod-product-compliance
Lightning Source LLC
Chambersburg PA
CBHW060806310726
48980CB00002B/249

* 9 7 8 1 4 9 6 2 1 5 5 3 6 *